London's Riverside

London's Riverside

From Hampton Court in the west to
Greenwich Palace in the east

Suzanne Ebel and Doreen Impey

with drawings by Cetra Hearne

William Luscombe Publisher Limited

First published in Great Britain by
WILLIAM LUSCOMBE PUBLISHER LTD
The Mitchell Beazley Group
Artists House
14 Manette Street
London W1V 5LB
1975

ISBN 0 86002 064 9 (cased)
ISBN 0 86002 137 8 (limp)

Set and printed by Cox & Wyman Ltd,
London, Fakenham and Reading

Contents

INTRODUCTION 11

1 LEFT BANK 13
Hampton Court The Mitre Hampton Court Bridge
Thames Ditton Bushey Deer Park Hampton Wick
Teddington Teddington Lock

2 LEFT BANK 35
Strawberry Hill Eel Pie Island Barmy Arms
St. Mary's Twickenham York House Ham Ferry
White Swan Orleans House Marble Hill

3 RIGHT BANK 49
Clattern Bridge Kingston Ham House and Ham Walks
Petersham, St. Peter's Church Sudbrook House
Richmond Bridge White Cross Inn Asgill House
The White Swan Old Richmond Palace Trumpeter's House
Richmond Green Maids of Honour Row

4 LEFT BANK 62
Twickenham Bridge The London Apprentice, Isleworth
All Saints Church Syon House and Gardens
Ferry Lane, Brentford ford Kew Bridge Strand-on-the-Green
Steam Packet Zoffany House City Barge
RIGHT BANK 69
Kew Church and Green Kew Gardens
Kew Palace

5 *RIGHT BANK* 80

St. Paul's School Barnes Terrace White Hart
St. Mary's, Mortlake Burton's Tomb at Mortlake
St. Mary Magdalene's Ship Inn, Mortlake
Chiswick Bridge

LEFT BANK 82

Chiswick House and gardens Hogarth's House
St. Nicholas's Church Chiswick Mall Hammersmith Terrace
Upper Mall The Dove Inn Furnivall Gardens Lower Mall
Rutland, and Blue Anchor pubs Hammersmith Bridge

6 *RIGHT (SOUTH) BANK* 97

Barn Elms Duke's Head and Star & Garter Boat race
Putney Bridge St. Mary the Virgin Wandsworth Park
Wandsworth Bridge Old Swan, Battersea St. Mary's, Battersea
Battersea Bridge Battersea Park

7 *LEFT BANK* 105

Fulham Church of All Saints Sir William Powell's Almhouses
Fulham Palace and Bishop's Park Hurlingham House
Battersea Bridge Chelsea Embankment Cheyne Walk
King's Arms Crosby Hall Chelsea Old Church
King's Head and 8 Bells Cheyne Row, Carlyle's House
Albert Bridge Physic Garden Royal Hospital, Chelsea
Ranelagh Gardens Chelsea Bridge Vauxhall Bridge
Tate Gallery Millbank Tower Lambeth Bridge ICI Building

8 *RIGHT (SOUTH) BANK* 127

Vauxhall Bridge Albert Embankment Old Father Thames
Lambeth Bridge Lambeth Palace St. Thomas's Hospital
The South Bank Lion County Hall South Bank Gardens
Shell Centre Hungerford Bridge Royal Festival Hall,
other halls and National Film Theatre National Theatre

9 *LEFT BANK* 137

Victoria Tower Gardens Jewel Tower Houses of Parliament
and Westminster Hall Parliament Square The Abbey
St. Margaret's, Westminster

10 *LEFT BANK* 161

Westminster Bridge Boadicea's Statue Westminster Pier
Victoria Embankment Queen Mary II's Steps
Banqueting House by Inigo Jones
Plaque to Sir Joseph Bazalgette
Victoria Embankment Gardens York House Watergate

10 LEFT BANK—continued
The Adelphi Cleopatra's Needle The Hospital of the Savoy
The Chapel of the Savoy The Old Caledonia Waterloo Bridge
Waterloo Pier Somerset House Roman Bath, Strand Lane
H.M.S. Discovery City Gryphons Submariners' Memorial
Wellington, Chrysanthemum, President The Temple
Blackfriars Bridge

11 LEFT BANK 181
Mermaid Theatre St. Benet's St. Paul's Cathedral
The Samuel Pepys Southwark Bridge The Old Wine Shades
Fishmongers' Hall London Bridge The Monument
St. Magnus Martyr

12 RIGHT (SOUTH) BANK 199
Bankside Wren's House, Cardinal's Wharf
Bear Gardens Museum Anchor Tavern Winchester Palace
Southwark Cathedral George in Borough High Street
H.M.S. Belfast Rotherhithe: Angel Inn Mayflower Inn
and St. Mary's Church Rotherhithe Tunnel

13 LEFT BANK 211
Billingsgate Custom House St. Mary At Hill
St. Dunstan's-in-the-East St. Olave's, Hart Street
All Hallows by the Tower Tower Pier Tower of London
Tower Wharf Port of London Authority Tower Bridge
St. Katharine's Dock: World Trade Centre
St. Katharine-by-the-Tower Wapping: Thames Tunnel,
Town of Ramsgate, Wapping Old Stairs, Execution Dock,
Prospect of Whitby, King Edward Memorial Park, Rotherhithe
Tunnel Bunch of Grapes, Limehouse Royal Naval
Victualling Yard, Deptford Milwall

14 RIGHT (SOUTH) BANK 233
Greenwich Cutty Sark Gypsy Moth IV
Footway Tunnel to the Isle of Dogs Trafalgar Tavern
The Yacht Trinity Hospital almshouses
Old Palace of Greenwich Queen's House Greenwich Park
Royal Naval College National Maritime Museum

Bibliography 248

Index 249

Illustrations

Photographs

1. Hampton Court—the Great Gatehouse, with the King's Beasts in the foreground   *facing page 64*

2. View of Ham ferry and Twickenham riverside from the towpath in front of Ham House   *facing page 65*

3. View of Eel Pie Island, from the Barmy Arms, Twickenham   *facing page 80*

4. Richmond Bridge, built in 1777, is the oldest of the bridges over London river   *facing page 81*

5. Willows, river walk and old houses at Strand-on-the Green   *facing page 81*

6. Hammersmith Bridge, designed by Sir Joseph Bazalgette in 1887 – fancifully decorated, much loved by Londoners   *facing page 128*

7. One of the few London churches which stands right on the river's edge—St. Mary's, Battersea (1777) where Turner often painted the Thames   *facing page 129*

8. The Royal Hospital, Chelsea, designed by Christopher Wren for Charles II's army veterans   *facing page 144*

9. The National Theatre designed by Derys Lasdun, seen from Waterloo Bridge   *facing page 145*

10. The Houses of Parliament, with police launch from the Thames Division on patrol *facing page 145*

11. *H.M.S. Discovery*, the ship which took Captain Scott to the Antarctic in 1901–4. In the foreground, one of the dolphin-wreathed Embankment lamps *facing page 176*

12. Launches of Thames division patrolling the river *facing page 177*

13. William the Conqueror's White Tower, of Caen stone from Normandy, was built to guard the river approach to the city *facing page 177*

14. Dolphin and Girl fountain outside the new hotel at St. Katharine's dock, built beside Tower Bridge *facing page 192*

15. Greenwich's *Cutty Sark*, the tea clipper launched in 1869 and now in dry dock near the Royal Naval College *facing page 193*

Both Author and Publisher wish to thank the British Cycling Bureau for permission to use pictures No 2, 3; The Central Office of Information, No. 10, 12. All other pictures were specially taken for this book by Mr Gordon Le Masurier.

Drawings by Cetra Hearne

Hampton Court—Anne Boleyn's gateway 13
Strawberry Hill, Twickenham 35
Kingston 49
Gates of Syon House 61
Barnes Terrace in 1823 79
Detail from Battersea shield 97
Albert Bridge 105
Houses of Parliament 127
Lambeth Palace, 1708 130
Tomb of Mary, Queen of Scots 137
Middle Temple Hall 161
St Benet's Church 181
St Paul's Cathedral 184
Globe Theatre, Bankside 199
Tower Bridge 211
Greenwich 233
The endpaper design is reproduced by permission of The Mansell Collection.

INTRODUCTION

London's river is always changing.

In the twenty-eight snaking miles from Hampton Court to Greenwich it changes character constantly, flowing beside suburban gardens, Georgian mansions, gasworks, breweries, the palaces of Parliament and miles of deserted docks. It used to be a highway so crowded with traffic that Walpole described it as a floating town; these days, with much of the commercial traffic gone, part of London's Thames is sometimes empty of craft for hours together. And the river changes haven't stopped. For a century and a half a solid wall of docks cut the people off from the river; and the Thames which was used to bring riches and prosperity into Victorian London was itself filthy, stinking and dead. Nothing could live in it.

At the time we write the dock walls are coming down, and there are going to be new walks, riverside houses, water buses to take people to work. Downriver beyond Greenwich there's a school on a barge.

By 1980 the Thames Barrier will be finished, the tide will fall only half as much as it does today and the river, which grows cleaner every year, will be wider too. The fish and the birds are coming back; so is the life on and near the London Thames.

S. E.
D. I.

Hampton Court—Anne Boleyn's Gateway

1 LEFT BANK
Hampton Court
The Mitre
Hampton Court Bridge
Thames Ditton
Bushey Deer Park
Hampton Wick
Teddington
Teddington Lock

Wolsey built it in 1514 at the height of his career. His enemies said he was the son of a butcher; he rose to be the richest man in England next to the king, and 'the proudest prelate that ever breathed'. His arrogant ostentations were an insult to Henry VIII. The Venetian ambassador wrote: 'This cardinal is the person who rules both the king and the entire kingdom; he used to say "His Majesty will do so and so"; subsequently he said "We shall do so and so"; now he has reached the pitch of saying "I shall do so and so".'

In 1526 Wolsey, sensing his danger, and in a desperate attempt to avoid his downfall, gave the palace to Henry VIII. The king complacently accepted the stately buildings, gold and silver, tapestries, furniture and paintings, but had no intention of taking the Cardinal back into favour. Wolsey was later arrested for treason and died on a long, doomed journey towards London and the Tower.

Henry set out to enjoy his new palace. He spent a great deal of time there. So did the English kings and queens who came after him. Until the end of George II's reign, Hampton Court was much used by royalty who travelled from London in wonderful gilded barges, often taking musicians to play on the journey. The nobility lived in a courtly village beside the palace or built houses within river-reach, such as Ham and York House. And Hampton Court was always a favourite retreat for the Royal family in the recurring times of London plague: the air, they said, was purer.

It is still delightful to travel to Hampton Court by river, particularly midweek on a fine day to avoid the crowds at week-ends. The Thames passenger boats run a modified service from early May; the full service begins at the Spring bank holiday and continues until late September. Boats run every hour, and at the height of the season as often as every twenty minutes: the river journey takes between two and four hours each way from Westminster Pier, depending on the tide. From the launch deck one watches other boats going by and can play the game of collecting their names. Yachts seem to choose romance: *Fleur de Lys, Zephyrine*. Motor-boats may be suitably named *Hasty Fred* or *Cart Horse*, but the dirtiest of tugs can be *Duchess* or *Cleopatra*, while tankers are simply *Toots* or *Bouncer*. The launches elevate themselves to royalty—*Princess Freda* and *Princess Rose*.

From George II's Trophy Gates, Wolsey's marvellous Tudor

buildings look their best; low, handsome, of rosy brick latticed with black, and set off by chimneys of many patterns, all twisted like barley sugar.

Henry VIII lived at Hampton Court with his succession of queens; some traces, some sad echoes, remain.

Anne Boleyn's Gateway

Under the tower on the arched ceiling is a pattern of Tudor roses and the initials 'A' and 'H' twined in a lovers' knot. Henry decorated the palace with the initials and badges of this maid-in-waiting whom he adored, calling her 'My Mistress and My Friend', 'My Own Sweet Heart'. Anne Boleyn was a sprightly, beautiful girl with a sweet singing voice; somebody called her 'this noble imp'. One ambassador remarked that she wasn't the handsomest woman in the world, had a swarthy skin and a long neck, adding: 'she has nothing but the King's great appetite and her eyes, which are black and beautiful and take great effect.' The little finger of her left hand was malformed with something like the indication of a sixth finger.

Of Henry's six queens, Anne was the one who most thirsted for admiration and pleasure. She wanted power and grandeur, and chose for her family badge a crowned white falcon with the vain-glorious words: 'Me and Mine'. Henry was utterly under her spell when he married her; at the Royal wedding she wore tissue of silver and a circlet of rubies. But after her daughter Elizabeth was born, the King grew tired of her. Anne's glory lasted three short years before she was condemned to death, probably on false evidence. Knowing the king, she disdained to beg for mercy. Witnesses said she was wonderfully courageous on the scaffold and had never looked so beautiful.

The day after she was beheaded the king married Jane Seymour. He commanded that Anne's badges should be obliterated from Hampton Court. But there are still a few of the crowned falcons including this one above the gateway, and some high on the carved ceiling of the Great Hall.

The magnificent astronomical clock made for Henry in 1540 was designed before the discoveries of Galileo and Copernicus. On this clock the sun revolves round the earth; the clock shows the hour, month, day, numbers of days since the beginning of the year, phases of the moon and signs of the zodiac and the time of high tide at London Bridge. The face has recently been restored to its original golds and blues.

Clock Court

When Elizabeth was queen, there was a splendid fountain in this courtyard, topped with a statue of Justice. It was also a practical joke designed to spray water over anybody standing near. The Elizabethans lived with vigorous zest, hunting, hawking, playing games that needed great physical stamina, and—high or low—they enjoyed practical jokes. At Nonsuch palace, the queen had an even huger fountain which played more tricks still.

On the right of the court a small door with the initials 'C.W.' above it is where Christopher Wren lived when working on the Renaissance part of Hampton Court. Wren began work two months after William III came to the throne, work on the palace took him eleven years, and he also used to travel downriver to continue work on St. Paul's. Wren lived much at Hampton Court in the last years of his life.

The State Apartments

Only a visitor of rare stamina can enjoy the whole of Hampton Court in one visit. To make a shorter tour, a choice of interesting things from ten of the thirty-one Renaissance rooms have been picked out.

The King's Staircase

Through the colonnade in Fountain Court is the entrance to the Renaissance wings. The great staircase is not unlike a stair in a palace of Louis XIV and made for the same reason—glory. The walls and ceilings were painted by the Italian painter Verrio.

Horace Walpole thought these paintings hideous; and declared that Verrio had painted them badly on purpose as a kind of revenge on the new king, after James II was deposed.

Today, Verrio's theatricality, his muses, gods, Roman emperors and cherubs, are rather enjoyed and admired. But art experts still think the work, in spite of its vigour, is coarsely done.

Verrio was an Italian who had worked for two previous kings before William III employed him to do the Royal staircase—he had been painter to Charles II and James II. His work in the style of the architecture of the time (the palatial buildings of Wren and Vanbrugh) was very baroque, very Italian. To paint the huge surfaces of ceilings and walls in the palaces and mansions he decorated, Verrio had a whole army of specialists

—more than twenty-four people to grind the colours, to gild, to paint the flowers in the pictures. When James II lost the Crown, Verrio remained loyal to his old Royal master and refused to work for William, but eventually his friends among the nobility —many of their houses contained his work—persuaded the painter back to Royal service. He worked for William, and later for Anne; he died at Hampton Court.

At the top of the staircase is the *King's Guard Room*; when William III was in residence the Yeoman of the Guard were on duty here. The walls are covered with enough arms for a thousand soldiers—halberds and swords, daggers and bayonets all made into close-fitting complicated designs including a huge Garter star. They were arranged on the walls by William's gunsmith.

The rooms beyond open one on to another in a vista as in a French palace, giving a seemingly endless effect of space. Wren designed the Renaissance wing to be larger and more commodious for the new king and queen, who had decided to live mainly at Hampton Court. But William's affection for the palace (it reminded him of his Dutch palaces at home) and the time and money he spent on it annoyed Londoners, and his Ministers made a great fuss. So the King made Kensington Palace his other Residence: he continued to ride out to Hampton Court as often as possible to supervise the new building of what he called his country house.

William, Mary and Wren between them might have destroyed the whole of Wolsey's Tudor palace. They did demolish two of his courts: but Wren's classic building has its own spacious charm.

The King's First Presence Chamber

Kneller's noble painting of William III was designed for this room and shows the king as Peacemaker. He wears armour and the collar of the Garter, and rides by the sea, watched by the goddesses of peace and plenty, Ceres and Flora.

William didn't look much like this Courtly picture; he was thin and suffered from asthma, had a white face pitted with the smallpox. His temper was morose, his nature cold and dry. He was a long way from the English people's idea of a Protestant hero arriving to save the country from the Catholics. But he was a brilliant soldier and a brave man, and so careless of personal danger that his ministers had to implore him to keep out of the centre of a battle.

17

His chair of state faces his portrait. Its canopy is embroidered with tarnished silver, its cover once royal red is now a split and dying pink.

The Hampton Court Beauties, like a bunch of silken roses, are collected together in this room. Queen Mary II commissioned Kneller to paint her ladies, hoping to eclipse Sir Peter Lely's Windsor beauties painted in Charles II's reign. The voluptuous Restoration group can be seen in the Communications gallery.

The ladies painted by Kneller were the Queen's ladies-in-waiting. She chose full-length portraits of them. She was delighted with the pictures and hung them in her Water Gallery, remarking they were the more beautiful because the originals were there to be compared with the paintings. Mary's girls are demure and thoughtful, a long way from the rakish Restoration women. Diana de Vere, Duchess of St. Albans is a starry-eyed innocent, holding that Royal symbol, an orange. Mary Scrope, later Mrs. Pitt, considered the greatest Hampton Court beauty, is plump and sweetly innocent.

William III's State Bedroom

The vast state bed made for William has blackened feathers that seem more suitable for a royal funeral. On the ceiling is Endymion asleep in the arms of Morpheus—more of Verrio. Decorations for royal bedrooms are often very amusing; in the Queen's bedroom, further on, Night and Sleep float on the ceiling. Royalty preferred elegant allegories to counting sheep.

King's Dressing Room

All the paintings here, which include a Holbein, are early sixteenth century and have been in the Royal collection for hundreds of years. A painting of Henry VIII shows the king when he was young and handsome, when his powerful voice echoed through Hampton Court, singing songs he himself composed on a theme of constancy:

As the holly groweth green and never changeth hue
So I am—ever have been—unto my lady true.

When he played tennis, people said it was beautiful to see his fair skin glow through a fine-textured shirt. He was a strong

18

young man, over 6 foot tall, a prince who wrote poetry and hunted, wrestled, jousted, danced and sang.

Writing Closet
The mirror over the corner fireplace is set at an angle so that it is possible to watch the whole length of the corridor of rooms. The story is that William used it to see who was approaching without their seeing him. If he didn't want to receive the visitor, he slipped through the little door which leads straight down to the Fountain Garden.

Queen's Gallery
The great Gobelin tapestries hanging in this gallery were embroidered in Brussels in the seventeenth century. But more humanly interesting, perhaps, is a pair of curious tall blue and white Delft vases made to hold tulips and hyacinths which William brought over from Holland; cut flowers had never been used in houses until that time.

William and Mary completely re-designed the gardens at Hampton Court with topiary and many orange groves as a symbol of the House of Orange. Mary was an impassioned gardener. Her dour husband did not pay much attention to her, and the queen gossiped with her ladies under the intertwined trees in Queen Mary's Bower. Her one extravagance was the garden; she sent gardeners as far as Virginia and the Canary Islands to bring back rare and exotic plants.

Queen's Bedroom and Drawing Room
Both rooms have wonderful views of the gardens, set with umbrella-shaped yews, fountains and paths between the green lawns.

Mary's sister Anne followed the Royal couple to the throne. She did not particularly like Hampton Court (preferring Kensington Palace) but she came here to hunt sometimes and to see her ministers. Pope's poem about Great Anna taking Counsel and Tea (pronounced Tay) was set in Hampton Court. So was the *Rape of the Lock*, based on a true incident which happened here.

Verrio towards the end of his long life decorated the walls and the ceiling of the Drawing Room for Queen Anne.

Poor Anne. She married dull, goodhearted George of Denmark and they loved each other dearly. But they had a lifetime of sorrow, losing every one of their children except a beloved son,

19

the Duke of Gloucester, who died at the age of 11. Anne was pregnant seventeen times and became a semi-cripple as a result. By the time she came to the throne, on William III's death, she was 37, fat, middle-aged, without hope of another child.

At first sight England's last Stuart monarch seems a limited small-minded woman, saddened by life, tortured by gout. She liked to gamble and was fond of hunting—Swift gallantly called her 'a mighty hunter, like Nimrod'. With no children except her delicate doomed little son, she was much too fond of the fascinating, intolerable Sarah Churchill; the bizarre friendship lasted twenty years, finishing with the women as enemies.

Yet Anne unified England in so many ways. G. M. Trevelyan writes that 'The story of the reign of Queen Anne is no parochial theme. It involves great issues, moves among brilliant societies, and reveals distant landscapes.' At this time the English genius flowered to an almost unprecedented extent—in architecture, design, literature, poetry, and even in war, great men abounded: Pope, Swift, Addison and Steele, Grinling Gibbons, and the towering figures of Wren and Marlborough.

In the Drawing Room, an odd place to be, are Anne's state bed, chairs and benches upholstered in crimson damask. On the walls and ceiling she gazes down, serene, youthful, in her role as Justice, or receiving homage from the four quarters of the world. On the north wall is kindly George, the husband she nursed devotedly through many illnesses. He is looking glorious as Lord High Admiral, and gestures towards the British fleet.

Audience Chamber

Two pictures in this room are of Jeffrey Hudson, a dwarf in the court of Charles I and Henrietta Maria. It was said that until he was 30, Jeffrey was only 18 inches high. The queen first saw him at the Duchess of Buckingham's when for a joke he was brought to the table in a pie. She was enchanted by the little creature and he became a kind of court jester, with the nickname 'Strenuous Jeffrey'. During the Civil War he fought for the Royalists, and he also killed a man in a duel. He left England when the king was defeated, was captured at sea and sold into slavery. Jeffrey maintained that misery made him grow: he shot up to 3 foot 6 or so. Somehow he got back to England at the Restoration and spent the rest of his life quietly in the country. In the paintings he has a boyish haggard face, and wears, as suits a Court personage, modish clothes of costly style.

The Drawing Room

Outside the window is a little private garden where the Duke of Wellington used to sit with his mother Lady Mornington, who had apartments at Hampton Court; the garden is named after her. Wellington was amused by a certain seat facing the Fountain Garden which was a favourite place for gossiping old ladies; he nicknamed it Purr Corner.

Cartoon Gallery

Wren designed this gallery to display the Cartoons painted by Raphael for a set of Vatican tapestries. Charles I bought the Cartoons which are among the greatest Royal treasures; these are now in the Victoria and Albert Museum. The seven seventeenth century tapestries of the cartoons are magnificent. There is also The Family of Henry VIII, by an unknown artist. Painted about 1545, it shows five full-length royal figures under a colonnade; the king sits on his throne, his arm round Prince Edward. His daughter Mary is on his right, young Elizabeth on his left. The queen is almost certainly Jane Seymour. People have sometimes thought it must be Catherine Parr but the figure of Jane is based on Holbein's celebrated painting. The picture is Henry's dynastic record; he sits with the future king and two princesses. The only queen to give him a living son is in the painting, though she died when that son was 12 days old.

Communications Gallery

Peter Lely was commissioned by Anne Hyde, Duchess of York, to paint the handsomest people in Court, and the result was this sexy group, the Windsor Beauties. Pope describes the sitters:

> 'The sleepy eye that spoke the melting soul,
> The nightgown fastened by a single pin.'

There is amorous Mary Bagot, whose silk gown seems about to fall off. And Barbara Villiers dressed suitably for the hunt; she bore the king six children.

In the nineteenth century Hazlitt considered the Windsor Beauties a tawdry collection, a set of kept mistresses 'showing off their meritricious airs and graces'.

Peter Lely, Dutch born, became the Restoration's most fabulously successful painter; 'Lely' was a sort of nickname: there was a lily painted on the door of his house at the Hague.

He was a close friend of Charles II's and everybody at Court—the Royal family, dukes, duchesses and ministers wanted their portraits by Lely and queued for the honour. So did every girl who occupied the King's bed. Lely became stately and rich, a man of high fashion who spent money lavishly. Pepys thought him 'mighty proud'.

The Haunted Gallery

The gallery, which leads to the Royal chapel, is light and well-decorated, and seems an unlikely place for ghosts; yet Catherine Howard's phantom is said to rush down the gallery in a wild attempt to reach the Royal closet where the king was hearing Mass, to beg for her life.

Catherine was 19 or 20 when she became queen, a plump blooming girl with a lively, happy face and auburn hair, more a romping teenager than a courtly beauty. The ageing Henry was passionately attached to her; she was his last love. He called her Rose Without a Thorn, and had this struck on the gold coin commemorating their marriage. A year and a half after she became queen she was indicted for treason, accused of infidelity for a love affair she'd had with the man she was engaged to, Francis Dereham, before she knew the king. Other men were said to have confessed to being Catherine's lovers, but under torture. Catherine and the men accused were all beheaded. People have seen her figure in white rushing towards the closet, then returning with terror, screaming as she vanishes through the door at the end of the gallery. The screams have been distinctly heard in the autumn (Catherine was indicted in November).

A man working in the gallery some years ago also said that in broad daylight on several occasions a hand came between him and his work. The hand wore a remarkable ring which he later sketched; it was identified as being a ring given to Catherine by the king.

Ghost stories persist in Hampton Court. Jane Seymour is also said to haunt the Tudor part of the palace. When her baby son was born, Jane was wrapped in crimson and ermine and carried to the chapel for the Royal christening by torchlight. The ceremony lasted 2 or 3 hours. Twelve days later the queen was dead. The Corporation of London ordered 12,000 masses for the repose of her soul, but Jane is still believed to walk on the anniversary of Prince Edward's birth; many people have seen her carrying a lighted taper, going up the stairs to the queen's apartments.

Hampton Court has other ghosts; the gaunt grey figure of Edward VI's nurse, Mrs. Penn. And a doorkeeper saw six people wearing Tudor clothes walking in the Broad Walk, talking and gesticulating without making a sound. They vanished.

The residents don't encourage talk and if you ask about ghosts, nobody admits to having seen or heard anything.

On the right of the gallery is the beautiful Tudor *Chapel Royal*, where the king heard mass and the baby prince was baptised. It has the most elaborate hammerbeam roof in the palace, with wonderful pendants carved with angels holding trumpets or sceptres. The gilding and paintwork has recently been restored, and the colours at present are rather too brilliant. The Royal Pew upstairs overlooks the chapel and there is a little place with an altar next to it called the Holyday Closet, for the king's private devotions. Over the door are Henry's and Jane's initials.

The Royal Pew was given a painted ceiling by Sir James Thornhill in the eighteenth century, decorated with fat flying cherubs; in one corner of the ceiling the artist's rough sketches for the design can still be seen.

The windows in the Haunted Gallery look down on to the Round Kitchen Court. The passage leads to the *Great Watching Chamber*. This is the room where Henry VIII's guards were on duty next to his state rooms, now alas demolished. The Great Watching Chamber is enhanced by some marvellous tapestries believed to have been bought by Wolsey for the palace in 1522. Embroidered in dull blues, pinks and faded terra-cottas, the tapestries show a mysterious cavalcade of figures, men and girls on horses, dragons and camels with human faces in a deep forest of trees and flowers. On the elaborate ceiling are the badges of the King and Jane Seymour.

Jane chose as her motto 'Bound to obey and serve' with a unicorn, emblem of chastity, as supporter. There are mixed opinions about Henry's third queen; the king called her his dear friend and Mistress and signed himself 'your loving servant and Sovereign', and in her short reign she proved submissive and discreet. Little is known of her doings as queen except that on one occasion she rode across the frozen Thames at Greenwich with Henry and the courtiers; and that on another she commanded that her maids in waiting wore heavily jewelled belts. Jane had regular features, a good figure and rather starry, starey eyes. She remains enigmatic. The king who detested black and any reminder of death actually wore mourning for her for four months—an unheard-of Royal gesture. In his will he commanded the bones of his 'loving queen Jane' should be placed in his tomb. and ordered a great monument to be erected to them both in Windsor Chapel, showing Jane not dead but 'sweetly sleeping'. The monument was never finished and the materials were stolen or sold during the Civil War.

The Great Hall

The king was so anxious to see this hall completed that his workmen worked all through the night by candles as well as through the day. The hammer-beam roof is one of the most beautiful things in the palace. Little Tudor heads peer down from among carved foliage, the pendants are carved and gilded into exquisitely decorated lanterns. Anne Boleyn's badges and initials are on the roof among the carvings but she was dead before the hall was finished. There is a gallery across one end of the hall for the minstrels and a dais where the king and a few chosen courtiers sat at the high table.

The hall epitomises the elaborately-decorated gilded fantasy of Tudor taste; it matches their ruffs and lace, pearl-sewn clothes, jewels shaped like fishes and flowers, cloaks embroidered with butterflies and lined with cloth of silver. It is thought that James I saw the latest plays of Shakespeare performed here.

Henry VIII's and Wolsey's Kitchens

The King's Great Kitchen lives up to its name, being 37 feet long and 27 feet wide, with a row of outsized brick ovens. There is a fireplace where boys sat turning the spit which roasted a whole sheep or oxen. The kitchens in their heyday were crammed with palace cooks preparing huge Tudor meals for as many as 400 guests in the Great Hall upstairs. Troops of servants waited at the serving hatches to hurry upstairs with the food, other servants had to wash the solid gold and silver cutlery between courses. There was a fish kitchen, a spicery, a place for pastry-making, for confectionery, a 'scalding house' and a 'boiling house'. Tudor appetites and Tudor hospitality were on a massive scale.

On the table in the King's Kitchen is a pewter still. George I brought this with him when he left Hanover for England, so that the Royal schnapps could be distilled on the premises.

Much of the *Tudor section* of the palace is being repaired at the time this book is being written. But it may be possible to visit *Wolsey's Closet*. This is a tiny, richly-coloured room which is strongly evocative of Tudor times—a small, secret place with marvellous linenfold panelling and with walls painted with glowing figures. Recently a whole new series of paintings has been discovered under those already on the walls, and there are some of these older figures now, appearing like bright ghosts.

Tennis Court

Facing the canal and formal gardens are the galleries of the Royal tennis court built by Henry VIII. This is the oldest court in the world where this game is still played. Tudor tennis, different from the modern game, needs an enclosed court. Henry played here; Elizabeth watched her favourite, Leicester, in a match against the Duke of Norfolk. Charles I played tennis here on the day he escaped from Hampton Court. In the present century Edward VII learned the game and there is a locker with his name still painted on it.

The Gardens

It's refreshing to leave the state rooms, the paintings and the Royal bedchambers and wander in the gardens which are beautiful and varied. The flower-beds change with the seasons, and in summer there are still red and white roses like those Henry VIII grew to symbolize the union of York and Lancaster. There is a modern *knot garden* reproducing the close-clipped herbs in geometric designs which were fashionable when Wolsey lived here. There are secluded nooks enclosed by old brick walls against which espaliered pears flower and ripen.

In the grounds there is every kind of flowering shrub and tree. In spring the *wilderness* is wild with daffodils and blue-bells, the shrubberies thick with camellias; in early summer the *laburnam walk* is a long tunnel of yellow flowers. There is the *Great Vine* to see: a Black Hamburg planted in 1769 and still flourishing. It has become so enormous, its main branch over a 100 feet long, that it has a whole vinery to itself and bears over 750 bunches of grapes a year. These are sold to the public at the end of August or early September. Most people enjoy, at least once, getting lost in the *Maze*, that living puzzle of greenery planted when Queen Anne was on the throne. It still confuses visitors, whose shrieks of laughter can be heard from over the high hedges.

Hampton Court has wild life too; house martins nest under the eaves of the palace, there is a herd of fallow deer, and many glossy water birds live in the park and swim on the ponds. One is allowed to fish in the ponds—but it is necessary to apply to the Superintendent.

There are kestrels and jackdaws and little owls living in the park, which is large and still wild enough for them to nest there in safety.

In the gardens facing the river is the little *Banqueting House* built in William's reign. It was never large enough for more than a dozen guests, and was used as a place for the Royal family to escape from the formal grandness of the palace. The Tudor palace was, in actual fact, very much larger than just a series of buildings round courtyards. In the old engravings there are long galleries, courts and buildings going right down to the edge of the river.

River Bank

The palace gardens stretch almost to the river, bounded by *Jean Tijou's Screen*; this is a marvellous set of wrought-iron gates originally meant for the Great Fountain Garden, and exquisite as lace. Ducks swim by the bridge among the willows, seagulls land on the roofs of old grace-and-favour apartments. The Barge Walk is a long pleasant vista of the curving Thames towards the village of Thames Ditton.

THE KINGS AND QUEENS AT HAMPTON COURT

From Wolsey's day to the accession of George III, Hampton Court saw a great cavalcade of royalty. Here, in brief, are its bright figures of the past.

Wolsey [1475?–1530]. He built it. Lived here in splendour. Was forced to give it away to the King to try and avert his own fall from power.

Henry VIII [1491–1547]. He was 38 when he acquired the palace. He enjoyed it and spent lavishly on beautifying and enlarging it. He hunted and jousted, gave pageants and practised archery. He covered the palace with the badges of his various queens.

Prince Edward [1537–1553]. He was born at Hampton Court. No one was allowed to approach his nursery, or touch his cradle or anything belonging to him without a special permit.

There was an etiquette for brushing and airing his baby clothes.

Henry's Queens all lived here except Katharine of Aragon. Anne Boleyn and Henry spent their honeymoon here; Jane Seymour gave birth to Edward here and died here too. Anne of Cleves waited here for her Royal divorce. Poor pretty Catherine Howard, Henry's rose without a thorn, lived here briefly as queen and still haunts the palace. The last queen, Catherine Parr, spent much time here with Henry, mothering the three royal children.

Mary Tudor [1516–1558]. 'Plain, pious and ill-dressed', she came here with her husband Philip of Spain. Her sober reign at Hampton Court was very different from the brilliant days of her father.

Elizabeth [1533–1603]. She was 26 when she came here as queen. She made Hampton Court as splendid as her father had done, coursing with greyhounds, hunting, flirting with Robert Dudley or with foreign ambassadors, dancing galliards, dressed in her favourite colours, black and white looped with pearls.

James I [1566–1625]. Son of Elizabeth's rival, the fated Mary Queen of Scots, James came here with his young queen Anne of Denmark. They celebrated their first Christmas at Hampton Court with a masque (probably arranged by Inigo Jones who'd just returned from Denmark). The cupboards at the palace were found to be full of the late queen's magnificent dresses, over 500 of them, which were adapted for the classic costumes of the masque.

Charles I [1600–1649]. When he came to the palace with his bride, 15 year-old Henrietta Maria, she brought thirty priests with her from France; the royal couple spent their honeymoon quarrelling. At the end of the Civil War, Charles was kept a prisoner here; he escaped by the river and fled to the Isle of Wight, but surrendered a second time.

Cromwell [1599–1658]. It is not unsuitable to include him though he would feel uncomfortable among royalty. But he was Lord Protector and lived here with his family in a quiet domesticity, loving music, and sometimes listening to Milton playing to him on the Hampton Court organ. Cromwell's daughter died at Hampton Court when he himself was growing old and frail. Her funeral cortège, with much splendour, travelled downriver to the Abbey.

Charles II [1630–1685]. He and his queen, Catherine of Braganza, spent their honeymoon here. They played tennis, had excursions on the river in a gondola which the State of Venice had presented to them. Hampton Court became the height of fashion again, with plays, balls, music and beautiful women.

William and Mary: William [1650–1702] and Mary [1662–1694]. The first monarchs after Henry VIII to make dramatic changes to the palace. Christopher Wren built a whole series of State Apartments, very different in style and size from the Tudor palace. William died as a result of his horse throwing him when riding in Hampton Court grounds.

Anne [1665–1714]. The last Stuart monarch, Anne didn't live much at Hampton Court, preferring Kensington. But she came here for her favourite pastime, hunting; when not well enough to ride, she drove herself to the hunt 'furiously' in a chaise with one horse.

George I [1660–1727]. Hampton Court pleased him; he lived here quietly with his two German mistresses, one tall and thin, the other fat, christened by his English subjects the Maypole and the Elephant and Castle. He was not popular with his subjects—they thought him unattractive, and he spoke no English. George was intensely musical, and travelled to London and back by river, with a group of musicians. Handel's water music was written for one of these journeys; some historians have the lovely theory that Handel's music was commissioned so that it would drown the boatmen's appalling language. The Thames boatmen's language, called 'water language' was notorious.

George II [1683–1760]. The last king to live at the palace, he spent two months every summer here, and enjoyed stag-hunting. His astute Queen Caroline, Robert Walpole and the clever effeminate Hervey came to the palace; as in Elizabeth's day, English policy was planned here.

Post-Script. It is said that when George II was walking in Hampton Court gardens with a new mistress, Lady Yarmouth, he sharply reprimanded his grandson, the future George III, and boxed the boy's ears. Perhaps George III remembered that. He never lived here.

In 1837, the year she came to the throne, the youthful
Queen Victoria threw open the palace and its gardens to
the public. No sovereign has lived at Hampton Court
since.

The Mitre, Hampton Court

On the site of a Tudor inn which later housed the Roundheads,
the Mitre was built in 1665 by order of Charles II to make
extra accommodation for courtiers who had no rooms at the
palace. Paintings, tapestries and low ceilings give the Mitre a
style and charm; it has three restaurants and seven bars,
including one in the old wine cellars with vaulted stone ceilings
very similar to those at Hampton Court. In the reception hall is
the old bow window from the original Toye Inn, glazed with
handmade panes of glass.

The *Toll Bar* opens on to a garden with willows overhanging
the river. The bar is both a summer and a winter place; doors
open on to the garden on sunny days, and there is always a
bright fire in cold weather. Food, drink and ambiance are all
delightful.

Hampton Court Bridge

It was designed as recently as the 'thirties, by Edward Lutyens,
but blends pleasantly with the palace for it is partly built of red
brick.

Fishing is free from this bridge to Kingston bridge.

From the palace walls of Hampton Court which edge the
towpath, it is half a mile to the pleasant riverside part of
Thames Ditton. Thames Ditton Island, shaped like the segment
of an orange, is in mid-stream; the whole place is villagey, and
busy with boats. In the 1820's the gentry gave a 'Dandies' Fete'
here on the waterside.

Of all the walks by the Thames, for its entire length from
Hampton Court to Greenwich, the longest with the unin-
terrupted company of the river is the *Barge Walk*. This is on the
north bank from Hampton Court bridge to Kingston; it is
country all the way beginning with Hampton Court park on the
left and continuously lined with wonderful trees, cedars, elms,
willows and in the spring with bushes smothered in flowering
may.

Moored in the river or journeying up and down are countless
craft, skiffs, houseboats, punts, sailing dinghies; the little
island of *Raven's Ait* is particularly crowded with boats.

Bushey Deer Park

This stretch of land, named after the thorn bushes which once thickly covered it, was originally enclosed by Wolsey with high brick walls in which crucifixes were set at intervals. The Cardinal turned the land into a royal park stocked with deer, partridges and pheasants.

When Henry VIII owned Hampton Court, he hunted and practised archery in Bushey Deer Park. There was a special rabbit warren made here; roasted rabbit with parsley sauce was a favourite palace dish.

In the 1700's Christopher Wren, busy redesigning Hampton Court, had grand ideas for Bushey Deer Park. He planned to make the Lion Gate and the long avenue into a new entrance to the palace and to put the Great Diana fountain in the centre of the avenue. This fountain had played in the Privy Garden of the palace in Charles I's day; it was an elaborate work of Francesco Fanelli, the one-eyed Italian sculptor who had called himself with pride, 'Sculptor to the King of Great Britain'. Wren had the fountain repaired and regilded, and re-erected it in the centre of the long avenue of Bushey Park. It is an elaborate creation, with nymphs and sea monsters and boys holding dolphins; the graceful bronze at the top, which people call Diana, may be Venus, the goddess of love.

The fountain is still where Wren placed it but his grand design was never accomplished: Bushey Park remains unconnected with Hampton Court. It is a beautiful place in summertime. When the chestnuts and the lime trees are in flower and a herd of deer in the distance, it is green and fresh as deep country.

Hampton Wick still has the atmosphere of a riverside village, with old cottages and old gardens. Shops sell fishing tackle, coils of tarry rope and sailing clothes, and even when the river is not in sight, it seems close. Facing *The Swan*, a Tudor building much renovated inside, is a house called *Wolsey's Cottage*. Old rumours say the Cardinal kept a mistress in secret here when he lived in glory in Hampton Court (the cottage is an easy boat journey from his palace). Wolsey's Cottage is stone-faced and miniscule with an oddly shaped entrance below pavement level. Through low windows there's a glimpse of a walled garden which once stretched to the river's edge before the present boatyard intervened. The house isn't open to the public, which is a pity as it has a Tudor fireplace patterned with twined initials, swans and leaves. One of the initials is a 'T' . . . Wolsey's name was Thomas.

A minute's walk past the cottage is a footpath which leads under Kingston Bridge and emerges as the towpath, edged with chestnuts and elms. On the opposite bank is the town of Kingston, flags flying. Boats are moored at the jetty, some shiny with chromium, others homely with pots of flowers. The river is wide, with boats swinging away from the pier on their way to Hampton Court, and the views upstream of trees and meadows are spacious and satisfying.

Teddington is mainly known as the place where the tidal reaches of the Thames end. People still think it was named 'Tide End Town'. Napoleon III mentioned this (surprisingly) in a life of Julius Caesar, and Kipling tells the same story in an enchanting poem about the Thames. The experts maintain that the old name of the village was merely Tudington; in ancient times it is certainly true that the Thames tide went much higher upriver than Teddington.

At the top of Ferry Road which leads to the lock is a low ivy-covered building in a churchyard of mossy gravestones: the old Parish church of *St. Mary's, Teddington*. There are services on Sundays and Wednesdays but the church is locked during the week. Visitors may telephone the Vicar (01:977–4104) who will arrange to have the church opened and some kindly, interested person to tell the church's history.

Doctor Stephen Hales was vicar here from 1709 to 1761; he had the odd title of 'Clerk to the Closet of the Princess of Wales' but was known all over the world as a physicist, botanist and biologist. He was the first physicist to show that plants take nourishment from the air; he worked on the circulation of the blood and—a curious combination—pioneered ventilation and sanitation, introducing ventilation into eighteenth century hospitals, naval vessels and Newgate Prison. His work on sanitation gave Teddington village a clean, plentiful water supply; in the church's records around the time he did this, the local people who'd been dying at the age of 40 began to live until 70 or 80.

Hales, Pope's friend, is buried under the tower which he had built but one can only make out a faint 'H' and an 'a' on the worn stone. There is a tablet on the wall above his grave. Outside the church, as near as possible to Hales, is the tomb of Isabella, Countess of Denbigh who expressed the romantic wish to be buried close to him. Her inscription, recently re-pointed, describes her 'lively talents and open heart', and adds:

'Like Hales, the gen'rous friend of humankind
With love of philosophie learning fraught
She wisely practis'd what his virtues taught
Then seal'd his praises with her dying breath
And grateful courts his last remains in death.'

On the left of the chancel is a plaque to Margaret Woffington, the celebrated Peg who lived at Twickenham. In her will she left money to build the charming almshouses in a row by the church: one is named after her. Peg, daughter of a bricklayer, was a vivacious Irish actress adored by audiences. She played spirited ladies of rank and the taxing roles of high tragedy; she was specially enchanting in male roles, wearing breeches. She acted in Garrick's company and for a time they lived together. Peg was known for her many love affairs and her generous nature. She used to lend her dresses to the Gunning sisters, two penniless Irish beauties, to help them with their many conquests. Her plaque is decorated with palms, cherubs, shells and a Hamlet-like skull.

Another Teddington name is that of Sir Orlando Bridgeman whose tomb is in the crypt. A plaque with his coat of arms is opposite Peg Woffington's. Bridgeman was a man of high reputation who held the Great Seal in Charles II's reign. He was rather an obstacle for the devious Charles, resisting the king's plans with Louis XIV of France and also the grants Charles wanted for his mistresses. Finally Bridgeman, shocked by the king's extravagance, retired to Teddington where he was much loved for his goodness to the poor. In 1833 when work was being done in the crypt, it was discovered that his coffin was open and his embalmed body was perfect. There he lay with red hair and pointed beard, just as he'd been in life. His descendant, Lord Bradford, came hurrying across England to have a look at him.

Near the river at the bottom of Ferry Road is *The Anglers*, a handsome eighteenth century pub in an untidy attractive garden with a huge bay tree: a pleasant place to drink a glass of wine in summertime. Across the road is a boatyard where the beautiful shapes of unfinished racing yachts may sometimes be seen.

At *Teddington Lock* the Thames is 250 feet wide. There are three locks: the Long Lock is large enough to take a tug and its string of barges. The weir prevents the salt sea-water from mixing with the river water which provides London with most of her water supply. The weir roars steadily in the distance, a long dirty white line of falling water; high water here is 1½ hours after it has reached London Bridge, 20 miles away. A footway suspension bridge from the Lock island crosses the backwater to Teddington.

Facing the weir is a glass and concrete building, Thames Television Studios, built beside their namesake. The windows of an upstairs restaurant overlook the river and crowds of people can often be seen lunching there. At first glance one might imagine that here is a new hotel with one of the best views on the Thames. Unfortunately, not so.

The wide backwater jostles with craft: punts, cruisers, motor boats, gilded Thames barges transformed into luxurious houseboats. Across the footbridge a grassy path on the right leads upriver to the outskirts of Kingston or downriver through Petersham to Richmond, past the Deer Park, Kew Gardens and under Kew bridge to Chiswick. The river here at Teddington is as willowy and countrified as Wargrave.

Strawberry Hill, Twickenham

2 LEFT BANK
Strawberry Hill
Eel Pie Island
Barmy Arms
St. Mary's Twickenham
York House
Ham Ferry
White Swan
Orleans House
Marble Hill

Strawberry Hill, Waldegrave Road, Twickenham

The most famous of all riverside houses in Twickenham is paradoxically no longer in sight of the Thames. When Horace Walpole built Strawberry Hill he could sit and watch the barges from his window. Now there is a barrier of high trees and rows of houses between the mansion and the river. To get there means a short bus journey from Twickenham High Street to Waldegrave Road.

Strawberry Hill now belongs to the Catholic Education Council and can be visited by appointment. One of the College students takes people round the house. Everybody at Strawberry has affectionate knowledge of the place and the tour is a pleasure.

If Walpole walked into his 'little plaything house' today he wouldn't find it much changed. There have been some well-matched additions and of course his great collections are gone. But the miniature Gothic castle remains with its arched windows and fretwork screens, stained glass, and the gold antelopes on the stairs. This is where he entertained his friends and, day in and day out, wrote the letters which made him the chronicler of his age.

In the classical eighteenth century, Walpole had the quirky idea of building a castle out of the Middle Ages, but on a tiny scale. He thought that his 'romance in lath and plaster' would alter people's taste, and it did. Strawberry Hill helped to begin the Gothic revival which in the next century influenced Byron and Victor Hugo and the Victorian taste of the later period, good and bad.

Walpole bought a coachman's cottage in 1747 on the fringe of fashionable Twickenham. He discovered in the old deeds that the name of the ground was Strawberry Hill Shot (shot is a Saxon measurement of land) and revived the name. He enjoyed altering names. He changed his own from Horatio—which he disliked—to Horace. He altered the name of a little neo-gothic house he bought along the road from Strawberry Hill, first calling it Little Strawberry and later, when Kitty Clive lived there, altering the name again to Cliveden.

After he'd moved into the coachman's cottage he wrote delightedly that 'the house is so small I can send it you in a letter to look at ... the prospect is as delightful as possible, commanding the river, the town, and Richmond Park'. His little house was the prettiest bauble 'set in enamelled meadows, Barons of the Exchequer move under my window ... and

Pope's ghost is just now skimming under my window by a most poetical moonlight'.

Determined to share his new interest and to be sure the house he'd decided to create was 'True Gothic', he set up a Committee of Taste of three—himself, John Chute, his 'oracle in taste' (whom he'd met on the Grand Tour) and Richard Bentley, artist and designer. With Bentley, Walpole visited cathedrals and abbeys, castles and manors. They made copies of whatever interested them . . . windows, cloisters, tombs, borrowing from Westminster, Durham, Oxford, Salisbury and Cambridge. He asked a friend in Italy, Sir Horace Mann, to 'pick me up any fragments of old painted glass, arms, anything' to be found in ancient châteaux. By degrees, Walpole transformed the cottage into a castle. It took him many years and became one of his most serious occupations.

The house can be seen from the road, it is only a short distance from the gate to the entrance. Looking at the turrets and battlements, one imagines a true Gothic interior: dark halls of smoke-blackened oak, ghostly stairs, rusty armour and dim stained glass glimmering in gloomy passages. But Strawberry is an eighteenth century vision of the Gothic. For all its fan-vaulting and fireplaces copied from tombs, it is light and sparkling, its paint creamy-white and gold, the fan-vaulting gold-patterned. Even the inserted lunettes of fifteenth and sixteenth century stained-glass masterpieces are set above clear glass windows through which Walpole could still see the garden and the river.

Walpole was fascinated with the idea of reviving Gothic things; he was also an aristocrat, the fourth son of Sir Robert, Prime Minister and power in the land. The idea of building a Walpole family castle (even a small one), and discovering a few romantic ancestors appealed to him. He ferreted out a certain Sir Terry Robsart from the mists . . . Sir Terry had been in the Crusades. On the ceiling in the library, together with a painted decorative 'W' for Walpole, and a Saracen's head for good measure, Walpole had an 'R' for Robsart inscribed. Writing to Sir Horace Mann six years after the castle was begun, he described the house: 'Stone-coloured Gothic paper, Gothic fretwork . . . lean windows fattened with rich saints in painted glass . . . broadswords, quivers, longbows, arrows and spears, all *supposed* to be taken by Sir Terry Robsart in the holy wars.'

Walpole wanted to show that Gothic design could work in a house even when taken from unlikely sources. The fretwork fronts to bookcases are copied from the screens in Old St. Paul's, the exquisite fan-vaulted ceiling in the Long Gallery (made of papier maché), copied from Henry VII's chapel in Westminster. In the Round Room is a fireplace from designs used in Edward the Confessor's tomb, 'improved by Mr. Robert Adam'. The design of the ceiling in the Holbein bedchamber, where Walpole hung a collection of Holbein portraits, came from the Queen's Dressing Room at Windsor which no longer exists. This is now its only record.

He was a passionate collector, a magpie, filling his castle with beautiful and curious things . . . pictures and vases, manuscripts and arms, jewels and coins, tapestries and rare books . . . he owned Holbein's portrait of Katherine of Aragon, Wolsey's red Cardinal's hat, a missal illustrated by Raphael, a set of Hillyard miniatures. His Strawberry Hill treasures are scattered all over the world. Some are in Buckingham Palace, others in the British Museum or Yale University. Many of the richest private collectors own things which were once in this house. There are only two of the treasures still here: a pair of Limoges enamels of saints was discovered a few years ago attached to the back of an old chair.

Walpole led an extremely busy social life; he often began a morning at Strawberry feeding the birds and squirrels in the garden, then set off for an auction, took a carriage to London to lunch with friends, attended the House of Commons where he must have been an engaging M.P., dined and talked until two in the morning. But he always hurried back as soon as possible. He loved his river view, 'exactly like a sea-port in miniature', the 'serengas' which filled his garden with scent, the view of the road below his terrace, enlivened 'with coaches, post-chaises, waggons and horsemen constantly in motion and with the fields speckled with cows, horses and sheep'.

Walpole was tall and thin, with lively dark eyes and a quiet voice. He had a way of coming into a room with 'affected delicacy', holding his hat and walking on tiptoe; he dressed in lavender suits, waistcoats embroidered with silver, and liked ruffles, frills and lace.

His Gothic house soon became high fashion; everybody wanted to see it. George III and Charlotte visited it, so did dukes and ministers and famous visitors from abroad. Walpole pretended to be annoyed but was secretly gratified. When there were too many visitors he issued cards of admission, four people on a set day between 12 and 3 p.m., and no children. He wrote an illustrated guide printed in the press he had set up in the garden. His friend Thomas Gray's poems were printed there, and Walpole also used the press for a courtly form of compliment. When expecting a distinguished visitor, Walpole would prepare a poem in his praise. After the visitor had been shown round the house he would be taken to the printing press which would start busily printing. The poem would appear from the machine and be presented to the visitor with a flourish.

As well as the thousands of enchanting letters, Walpole also wrote a romance, a skilful blend of modern and ancient, called The Castle of Otranto; this work had a strong influence on the novels of Sir Walter Scott.

Parties at Strawberry Hill were famous:

'Strawberry has been in great glory: I have given a festino there that will almost mortgage it. Last Tuesday all France dined there . . . we were four-and-twenty. They arrived at two. At the gates of the castle I received them, dressed in the cravat of Gibbons' carving, and a pair of gloves embroidered up to the elbows that belonged to James I. The French servants stared, and firmly believed this was the dress of English country gentlemen. . . . We . . . went to see Pope's grotto and garden, and returned to a magnificent dinner in the refectory. In the evening we walked, had tea, coffee and lemonade in the Gallery, which was illuminated with a thousand, or thirty candles, I forget which . . . at one the company returned to town, saluted by fifty nightingales, who, as tenants of the manor, came to do honour to their lord.'

Scores of friends stayed at his castle and many friends lived nearby. Pope at Twickenham, John Gay, Lady Suffolk at Marble Hill to whom he was a constant friend until her old age. He was particularly fond of his neighbour Kitty Clive, the comic actress. 'My chief employ,' he wrote, 'is planting at Mrs. Clive's . . . I have lately planted the green lane that leads from her garden to the common.' 'Well,' said she, 'when it's done, what shall we call it?' 'Why,' said I, 'What would you call it but Drury Lane?'

Walpole lived to the age of 80; his last years glowed in an Indian summer of friendship with Agnes and Mary Berry. After Kitty Clive died, Walpole let Little Strawberry to the Berrys and their father. Walpole thought the girls the best informed and most perfect of creatures. They visited him every Sunday and when they were away he wrote them playful, affectionate letters, calling them his strawberries, beloved spouses, amours. 'Being in love with both, I glory in my passion, and think it proof of my good sense.' It suited Walpole perfectly to have these attractive girls to visit and admire him and listen to his amusing talk.

He was 30 when he bought the cottage. He spent fifty years here, creating and improving his castle, adding to his collections, and enjoying 'my two passions, lilacs and nightingales . . . in full bloom'.

Twickenham is a pretty place. The riverside is willowy, the water meadows full of flowers in late spring and summer. There is a Regatta at the end of May. A short lane, sloping from Twickenham High Street to the river, leads to the pretty hoop-shaped bridge over to *Eel Pie Island*, which is only two acres in size. It used to be a favourite spot for anglers and boating parties and was named after one of the dishes served at Eel Pie House in the eighteenth century. It is no longer a landing-place for picnics or riverside meals, and has become a kind of miniature bungalow town, with cottages and bungalows, each in its patch of garden or remnant of some old apple orchard among the boatyards and rowing clubs. Some of the houses are very odd, as if Londoners had landed and built their own sketchy ideas of country cottages. There are some new houses being built by the water. The fishing at Eel Pie isn't bad and from a boat it is possible to get a goodish catch of roach, bream or perch.

Back across the bridge to the mainland on the right is an inn-sign on the towpath, for the *Barmy Arms*; the sign has the ugly Duchess from *Alice in Wonderland* painted upside down. The inn was a boys' school from the sixteenth century until 1727 when it became a riverside tavern. Victorian fishermen used to weigh their fish in the bar parlour and it is still a port of call for the Swan Uppers when they make their yearly trip to put identifying marks on Thames swans.

At the pub they say that the word 'Barmy' could be the medieval name for the froth on top of beer: it could also mean crazy, of course. The Barmy Arms is pleasant and friendly; people arrive by boat and almost everybody wears jeans. A sycamore tree in the paved courtyard facing the river is shady in sunny weather and there are open fires in the bar in wintertime. Hot and cold snacks are inexpensive and wine is served by the glass.

Beyond the pub is a high wall curving round the churchyard of *St. Mary the Virgin*. A 7½ feet high mark shows the level to which the Thames flooded in March 1774.

The battlemented church tower is very old but the body of the church collapsed in 1713 and a new church was built, joined to the tower. The effect is not incongruous. Many famous eighteenth century people who lived in Twickenham attended services here: Alexander Pope and the painter Kneller (who was Church Warden), Kitty Clive the actress, and Lady Mary Wortley Montagu, the spirited beauty whom Pope loved so passionately.

Pope is buried in a vault under the middle aisle: a plain brass tablet marks the spot. Once when the church was repaired, the poet's coffin was opened and a cast of his skull taken before 'being reverently restored to its place'.

Outside on the east church wall, is the plaque which Pope put up to his nurse. 'Mary Beach . . . Alex Pope, whom she nursed in his infancy, and constantly attended for thirty-eight years, in gratitude to a faithful old servant erected this stone.' There is also a tablet to Horace Walpole's actress friend Kitty Clive:

'her
moral virtues and her well earn'd fame . . .
In comic scenes the stage she early trod
Nor sought the critic's praise, nor fear'd
his rod . . .
And nobly bounteous from her slender store
She bade two dear relations not be poor.'

Kitty was one of the cleverest of eighteenth century comediennes. Doctor Johnson considered her a 'better romp than any I ever saw in nature'. She was famous for her acting, notorious for her bad language, bad spelling and quarrels waged with rival actresses. Tate Wilkinson, a comic actor in Garrick's company remarked that Kitty was 'a mixture of combustibles: she was passionate, cross, vulgar yet sensible, a very sensible woman and as a comic actress of genuine worth—indeed, indeed, she was a diamond of the first water'. She was also particularly kind to her family. Among the tombs in the well-kept churchyard is that of William Tryon, once Governor of the Province of New York, who died in 1788.

The church has a tradition of bellringing and inside the tower are esoteric details. 'In 1749 the Society of Twickenham scholars rang a complete peal of 6,000 changes.' 'In 1812, the Oxford Treble Bob of 5,088 changes was run in 3 hours 8 minutes.' The bells ring every Sunday at 10.30 and 6 p.m. before morning and evening service for around half an hour. St Mary's is sometimes visited by the Middlesex Association of Bellringers for special performances.

The road in front of St. Mary's runs parallel to the river between high brick walls which in summer spill with flowering syringas. High on the right above the wall is what seems a private garden where a naked marble girl can be seen, with flowing hair, driving some winged sea-horses with sea-serpent tails. The girl and a number of her sisters are part of a fountain in the grounds of *York House*.

This historic house, now Municipal offices, is occasionally open for amateur theatre and concerts and it is possible to see some of its rooms, and learn a little of his history, by writing to the Town Clerk at Richmond. The gardens are open to the public and are extremely beautiful.

York House was the home of Edward Hyde, Lord Clarendon, the seventeenth-century lawyer, architect of the Restoration and Lord Chancellor of England. During the Commonwealth he stayed loyal to the exiled Stuarts and they largely owed their return to the throne to him. At one time, under Charles II, Clarendon held the greatest political power in England.

He describes himself in his autobiography, in the third person, 'He had originally in his nature so great a tenderness and love towards mankind . . . did really believe that all men were such as they seemed . . . had the same justice and candour and goodness in their nature as they professed to have.' The Civil War utterly disillusioned him; '. . . a barbarous and bloody fierceness and savageness [which] hardened the hearts and bowels of all men; and an Universal malice and animosity covered the most innocent and best-natured people and nation upon the earth.'

This moderate, serious man abhorred scandal and found himself in the middle of one, and a Royal scandal at that. His favourite daughter Anne became pregnant by the King's brother James, Duke of York and they were secretly married. Clarendon, who'd known nothing of the match, thought he was ruined as the King's indignation would rightly fall on him. It was un-thinkable for a commoner's daughter to become Duchess of York. Charles II 'seeing his swollen eyes from whence floods of tears had fallen', consoled poor Clarendon. And York House, which Charles had given to his brother, was James's gift to Clarendon when the wedding was announced.

The scandal didn't die at once. Anne Hyde was said to be a whore and her baby son fathered by somebody else. Henrietta Maria, arriving back in England from France, refused to see James. But Anne Hyde was strong, clever and discreet. The old Queen was persuaded that Anne had been slandered, and consented to receive her as Royal Duchess; Clarendon was pardoned for something he hadn't done.

Clarendon lived at York House when he was Charles II's Chancellor, travelling by river to Hampton Court daily and returning to Twickenham at night. He was an eloquent talker and marvellous writer—no man fitter, said a contemporary, to guide a wavering master. Clarendon later lost his power with the king and was dismissed.

James and Anne also lived at York House. James was consistently unfaithful but the pair were happy just the same. Pepys said Anne led James by the nose. It suited her to be a duchess: she wore her strawberry leaves with a majestic air. She had a good figure, a witty tongue; people said her court was more select than Charles II's raffish collection. Two of Anne's daughters were destined to be English queens; the future Queen Anne was born at York House in 1665.

In the early nineteenth century a famous duellist, Lieutenant Colonel Webber, lived at York House. He was a crack shot and determined to stay that way; every morning he ordered a boatman to row out into the middle of the Thames, taking a number of empty bottles. The Colonel aimed at these one by one, and wouldn't go in for breakfast until he'd shot the lot.

In mid-Victorian times the house was altered to be a royal residence for the Orleans prince the Comte de Paris. Later it was owned by an Indian merchant prince, Sir Ratan J. Tata, who built the fountain.

The entrance to the gardens is in Sion Row, past some eighteenth century balustraded houses. In the gardens there are pools, beds of different coloured heathers, miniature azaleas, and in summer masses of heavy-scented syringa. Tall copper beeches grow near the river and there's a ginko tree with fan-shaped leaves.

A footbridge spans the walled road below, leading to more gardens, seats, and to Sir Ratan's fountain. Newspapers of the time say this was intended as a marble swimming pool, but it took thirty hours to fill and the water in any case was bitterly cold. Perhaps its owner transformed it into a fountain because only girls made of marble were hardy enough to swim in it. Magnificent naked beauties sport in the water and on the rocks. One nymph climbs from the pool, another leans over to help her. A tall beauty commands the fountain and the sea-horses. Another lies apparently sunbathing—pigeons land occasionally on her marble buttocks.

Towards Richmond, with York House garden walls on either side, the road passes the ancient Twickenham ferry, now called *Ham Ferry*. Pedestrians can be ferried across the river to Ham House on most fine days in the morning and afternoon.

Up a flight of wood steps, out of reach of the sometimes-flooding Thames, is an old inn, built in 1640, *The White Swan*, a favourite place for Thames bargemen in the past. It is modest and sociable, with a good view of the river and the willows.

Down the road beyond the Swan is the entrance to the grounds of *Orleans House*. There are some fine trees, daffodils in springtime, and squirrels in the garden; but all that is left of the mansion is the Octagan Room. This, an addition to the main house, was designed by James Gibbs (who designed Sudbrook House in Petersham) in 1720. When Orleans House was being pulled down in 1927, Mrs. Nellie Ionides managed to save the Octagan Room in the nick of time—by buying it. This bene-factress left the room, and a collection of eighteenth and nineteenth century pictures to Twickenham in her will. There is a recently-built picture gallery where the stately brick mansion once stood.

The house was part Tudor and part seventeenth century, and Queen Anne stayed there as a princess. There were 16 acres of cherry orchards, pleasure gardens and wildernesses. In the eighteenth century James Johnstone, Secretary of State for Scotland, lived here; Defoe said he had the 'best collection of fruit of all sorts, of most gentlemen in England' in the gardens. Johnstone built the Octagan room to entertain George II and Caroline; the queen was friendly with Lady Catherine Johnstone and used to come downriver from Hampton Court in the early mornings to breakfast in the beautiful gardens.

Marble busts of George II and Caroline are placed high up near the gilded ceiling of the Octagan Room where they came to enjoy musical entertainments. They were an extraordinary couple; the king difficult, ill-tempered and when angry capable

44

of kicking his coat and wig round the room and swearing at his ministers. The queen, a blonde with a milk and roses complexion, had a character of steel. Her friend Lord Hervey remarked that 'her predominate passion was pride, and the darling pleasure of her soul was power', but Caroline managed her husband with consummate skill. The king might flaunt his mistresses and be rude to her in public but she had what Thackeray called an 'inscrutable attachment' to him, and they remained deeply attracted to each other. After years of marriage, when he was apart from her in Holland, he wrote her passionate love letters 30 pages long.

In 1800, Louis Philippe came to live at Orleans House when he was the exiled Duke of Orleans; the name of the house was changed in his honour. He took a fancy to Twickenham, and later his son, the Duc D'Aumale, lived there when Louis Philippe was once again in exile. A collection of the Orleanist emigrés settled round Twickenham at that time. Louis Philippe was at Esher (Queen Victoria assigned Claremont to him), the Comte de Paris was at York House and the Duc de Nemours at Bushey Park.

The picture gallery built on to the Octagan Room shows Mrs. Ionides's pictures, and combines these with attractive exhibitions with a local interest. There is a new Spring and Winter show every year. The Arts Council also puts on exhibitions of children's art here.

Five minutes' walk along the towpath from Orleans House is the riverside edge of *Marble Hill*'s park. The eighteenth century Palladian villa stands at the top of sloping lawns, with the Thames below as part of its magnificent view. Pope's villa, pulled down years ago, was also on the riverside and did not look unlike Marble Hill. Pope, who was an expert on the theory and design of eighteenth century gardens, designed both his own and those of Marble Hill. He was Lady Suffolk's neighbour and a close friend.

Henrietta Howard, later the Countess of Suffolk, began to build Marble Hill in 1724 with money given her secretly by George II whose 'exceedingly respectable and respected mistress' she'd been for years. Pope wrote a little verse about her:

'I know a thing that's most uncommon
(Envy by silent and attend!)
I know a reasonable woman,
Handsome and witty, yet a friend.'

Henrietta's portrait in the National Portrait Gallery shows a woman with smoky-blonde hair, almond-shaped, swimmy eyes and a slight double chin. Her dress of pink satin displays a fine neck and bosom. She looks, and was, stylish, clever and gentle. She was unhappily married when very young to Charles Howard, whom Lord Hervey described as 'a wrong-headed, ill-tempered, obstinate, drunken, extravagant, brutal young brother of the Earl of Suffolk's family' and had been George II's mistress for ten years before he came to the throne. Henrietta didn't enjoy Court life. Her royal lover kept her with him more for show than passion and Queen Caroline used her as lady-in-waiting with the 'servile offices', said Walpole, 'of dressing the Queen's head'. Poor Henrietta, also a little deaf, was no match for Caroline of Anspach. But she was charming and dignified, 'civil to everybody, friendly to many, and unjust to none; in short she had a good head and a good heart', said Lord Hervey. Because of her tact and prudence at Hampton Court her apartments were nicknamed the 'Swiss Cantons': political rivals met there on neutral territory.

When George II rather surprisingly (he was famously mean) gave her £11,500, some jewellery and furniture, Henrietta began to build Marble Hill. She was filled with relief at the thought of escaping from the slavery and boredom of the Court. She wanted her new home to be peaceful and harmonious, a place to entertain close friends and where, she wrote, she might have 'more happiness for the latter part of my life than I have yet had a prospect of'.

All her friends helped. Lord Herbert, a man of high taste, advised and worked on the architecture. Pope worked on the garden. Dean Swift stocked the cellar. Marble Hill took four or five years to finish and Henrietta ran out of money. Swift wrote:

> 'My house was only built for show
> My lady's pocket's empty now
> And *now* she will not have a shilling
> To raise the stairs or build the ceiling.'

The villa was finished at last and Henrietta left Court and made her home here.

The mansion is like its owner, quietly elegant. The floors shine like dark water, the rooms are full of space, the windows have cool river views. The carved staircase was built of mahogany, a wood which had only once before been used in

England. George II had it cut for Henrietta in the Honduras Forests and shipped back by naval vessel.

At Marble Hill Henrietta entertained her friends, the writers, painters, wits and poets. Pope 'dangled here', as Swift described it. But so did Swift. For all his fierceness and severity, his habit of dismissing women as 'beasts in petticoats', the Dean could be a tender mentor and Henrietta was his friend.

John Gay who wrote the Beggar's Opera, a fat good-humoured creature spoiled by everyone and called Johnny, visited Marble Hill often; so did Horace Walpole, a steady friend throughout Henrietta's life. When he was in London he wrote to her to 'lament the roses, strawberries and banks of the river'.

Alexander Pope was Henrietta's neighbour. His villa, exquisitely landscaped gardens and underground grotto with walls covered with semi-precious stones, was on the river near Marble Hill. It was pulled down in 1807 by its owner, Baroness Howe, who resented people visiting and admiring it.

Pope was devoted to Henrietta; he was a frail, vivid little person, often in pain from blinding headaches and backache. His growth had been stunted by grave illness as a child; 'Little Pope', people called him. He had close deeply-felt relations with women friends—the greatest was for Lady Mary Wortley Montagu. She lived at Twickenham and came to Marble Hill too, but couldn't have visited it when Pope was there; by the time Marble Hill was built, they had quarrelled.

Lady Mary was small and dark with a pock-marked skin, brilliant eyes and a sharp wit. Pope had adored her, calling her the Second Eve; she was married with two children and her close relationship with Pope had been a society scandal. By 1723 they'd fallen out. Later Pope attacked her bitterly in verse, calling her lascivious, mean with money, and saying she suffered from the pox. Although the two were never reconciled, he kept Kneller's portrait of her in his drawing-room until he died.

Kneller was a Marble Hill friend, and so was Molly Lepell. John Gay called her 'youth's youngest daughter, sweet Lepell'. Molly and Henrietta had both been maids of Honour at Hampton Court; she was a merry, stylish, exquisite creature, everybody fell in love with her. She seemed to attract poems:

> 'Oh were I the King of Great Britain
> To choose a minister well
> And support the throne of Great Britain

I'd have under me Molly Lepell
Should Venus now rise from the ocean
And naked appear in her shell
She would not cause half the emotion
That we feel for dear Molly Lepell' . . .

Molly was secretly married to Queen Caroline's confidante, Lord John Hervey, about whom Lady Mary remarked that there were three sexes, men, women, and Herveys. But Molly and he married for love—and had eight children.

The Palladian house, its exterior beautifully painted in coffee and cream, the gardens, the spreading park which these people knew, are little changed. In the garden are dark ilex trees, a rare black walnut and the tallest Lombardy poplar in Britain. Another huge tree said to be the biggest weeping willow in the country grows in nearby Radnor gardens where the Earl of Radnor had a mansion. There'a a story about weeping willows and Marble Hill. Pope once watched Henrietta unpacking a parcel from Spain and noticed some twigs in the packing. Pope took the twigs back to his riverside villa and planted them. One grew to be the first weeping willow in England.

In Regency times, Mrs. Fitzherbert lived for a time at Marble Hill: another respectable and respected mistress.

From Marble Hill, the towpath follows the bends of the river to Richmond.

Kingston Market Place—early 19th century

3 RIGHT BANK
Clattern Bridge
Kingston
Ham House and Ham Walks
Petersham, St. Peter's Church
Sudbrook House
Richmond Bridge
White Cross Inn
Asgill House
The White Swan
Old Richmond Palace
Trumpeter's House
Richmond Green
Maids of Honour Row

It's true that there are chain stores and roaring traffic here, but down the old High Street is the market town which has existed for hundreds of years.

To the right of the Guildhall the little Hogsmill river flows busily under one of Britain's oldest bridges, the *Clattern Bridge*. 'Clatrung' is the Saxon word for 'clattering'. Three arches of the original bridge, under the present parapet, were built in the twelfth century. They each span 12 feet and still carry a quarter of the width of the present road. Near the bridge are the foundations of a palatial thirteenth century building.

Kingston's most famous monument is opposite the bridge outside the Guildhall. This is believed to be the Coronation stone on which seven Saxon kings were crowned. The stone is prehistoric, a kind of Druid stone once part of a sacred circle; this may have been why the kings chose Kingston as their crowning-place. A silver penny of each of their reigns is set in the plinth. The chronicles of Kingston begin with the crowning of Athelstan in 924. There is a tradition that as a child he was given symbols of his future power by King Alfred—a belt set with jewels, a Saxon sword with a gold hilt, and a scarlet cloak.

The High Street has clapperboard and timbered houses, a charming eighteenth century house (now an Angus Steak House) and some antique shops. The path by the river is along the road, and a new riverside walk is being made which will eventually lead as far as Richmond Bridge.

In the old market-place is an Italianate town hall with ornamental turrets and a lead statue (1706) of Queen Anne. All around are market stalls, fruit, vegetables, mounds of fish and flowers and a cheerful noisy press of people. The square has two Tudor buildings which belong to Boots the chemist. The smaller has a Tudor timbered front, the taller building was opulently restored in the 'twenties, with statues of Kings and Queens and varied coats of arms.

Ham House (National Trust)

Evelyn described it as 'furnish'd like a great Prince's . . . flower gardens . . . groves . . . statues . . . fountains, aviaries, and all this at the banks of the sweetest river in the world'.

Ham House was built, within easy river reach of Hampton Court, in 1610. There is the statue of a river god on the lawn at the entrance. The heads of Roman emperors decorate the formal façade.

The house is marvellously cared for by the Victoria and Albert Museum and shines as if its Restoration owner, the Countess of Dysart, still lived here. The rooms are lit with candles in silver candlesticks, and although the flames are electric the effect is still right. There are wonderful things to see ... rooms with walls covered in embossed leather ... ceilings painted with goddesses ... portraits and treasures in every room. The unique quality of Ham is that the things chosen by the families who lived in the house, the Dysarts and Lauderdales and Tollemaches, are still here.

The couple who created Ham were Elizabeth Countess of Dysart and her second husband the Duke of Lauderdale. Elizabeth had previously inherited Ham from her father (and the Dysart title in her own right). She was a red-headed beauty; Lely's captivating portrait of her as a girl is in the Round Gallery. There was a belief among contemporaries that Cromwell had been her lover—she was a close friend of his in her youth. After the Restoration she married Lauderdale, 'a great gorilla of a man, with uncouth body and a shambling gait, a massive head crowned with a disorderly tangle of red hair'. He had been a leader of the Scottish Covenanters but went over to the Royalists and had a strong influence over Charles II. In spite of Clarendon's opposition, Lauderdale became Secretary of State and was 'never from the King's ear nor council'. He was learned and clever, but unscrupulous, crafty, licentious and had a will of iron. He was described as 'the coldest friend and the most violent enemy that was ever known'. Many people tried to oust him from power; none succeeded. He was a member of the notorious Cabal (called after the initials of the five ministers who dominated it). When Secretary of State for Scotland he was loathed for his ruthless policy.

His duchess was also hated by the Scots who believed her as guilty as he was. She had as strong a character as her husband. Bishop Burnet described her as a 'woman of great beauty ... [with] a wonderful quickness of apprehension, and an amazing vivacity in conversation; had studied not only divinity and history, but mathematics and philosophy; but what ruined these accomplishments, she was restless in her ambition, profuse in her expense, and of a most ravenous covetousness; nor was there anything she stuck at to compass her end, for she was violent in everything—a violent friend, and a much more violent enemy'.

Together, the Lauderdales enlarged and altered Ham. They

lived there at a vast rate, Elizabeth 'carrying herself with the haughtiness that would have been shocking in a Queen'. In the Round Gallery there is a portrait of them together by Peter Lely. Sensual, arrogant, debauched, they look with lofty irony across a chasm of 300 years. Their twined initials 'J.E.L.' (John and Elizabeth Lauderdale), together with a ducal coronet, are set in the panels surrounding the fireplace in the Queen's closet, and also lie together in the marquetry floor of the same room.

Six years after Lauderdale died, in 1688, when William III had landed in England and the peers wished to be rid of James II, they wanted him to go to Ham. Macaulay wrote: 'Ham . . . decorated by Lauderdale on the banks of the Thames, out of the plunder of Scotland and the bribes of France and which was regarded as the most luxurious of villas, was proposed.' James objected. He didn't like the place which was cold and comfortless and lacked furniture; he preferred to go to Rochester.

In the years that followed, the great house grew neglected and shabby. The Dysarts who successively lived at Ham were, without exception, mean and spent nothing on the place. It became so gloomy, overgrown and ghostly that people were frightened of it. In the eighteenth century Horace Walpole's favourite niece Charlotte became Countess of Dysart. A full-length portrait by Reynolds in the Great Hall at Ham shows her to be a tall graceful creature with a high powdered wig. Walpole longed to see the old house but Charlotte's husband could not bear visitors; he even refused to allow George III to visit the house. Walpole managed to visit his niece and Ham with difficulty. He wrote:

'The old furniture is so magnificently ancient, dreary and decayed . . . that at every step one's spirits sink . . . I expected to see ghosts sweeping by; ghosts I would not give sixpence to see, Lauderdales, Talmachs, and Maitlands . . . in this state of pomp and tatters my nephew intends [the house] shall remain.'

The house is a fascinating place to visit. There is the candle-lit chapel where the worldly Lauderdales cannot have prayed very piously (Queen Charlotte visited it in 1809 and found it 'so dark and dismal that I could not go into it'.). In a roomful of miniatures and engravings is a ring made of two jewelled hearts fixed to two locks of fine blonde hair: Queen Elizabeth had the hair cut from Essex's head on the morning he was executed.

There are cases of robes belonging to the Lauderdales,

embroidered bedcovers, riding coats, the Duke's brocade-handled shaving brushes and hair-brushes. These things give Ham its satisfying, intense reality.

Ham Walks

These 'walks', as they used to be called, were avenues 'all overarched with lofty elms' which are constantly mentioned by writers of Queen Anne's time who lived in or visited Twickenham. Horace Walpole often wrote in his letters of promendading in Ham Walks. Pope, Swift and Gay all enjoyed walking under the trees.

But where are Ham Walks?

There's a very pleasant country walk from old Twickenham ferry, which faces the Ham House grounds, along the towpath in the direction of Twickenham. The meadows and country views are beautiful; in summer there are fields of wild flowers, thistles, rushes, butterflies. On the Twickenham river bank one can see the Octagan room at Orleans House through chestnuts and willows. There are trim gardens and white painted houses along the river bank.

But this towpath cannot be the old Ham Walks. They were supposed to run in front of Ham House just as far as the old ferry and there's not one lofty elm by the river here, only new-planted trees. It's unlikely that every large tree in the last 200 years has vanished. But there is a long green pathway, 'over-arched with elms', on the edge of the Ham House grounds. It is exactly where the wooden fences of Ham House have been placed: standing by the end of the fence one can see the expanse of an old avenue.

The towpath from Ham House, with Richmond Hill in the distance, leads to *River Lane, Petersham* on the right. The road, hazy with copper beeches and facing a little isle of willows in the river, leads up to the Petersham road, passing the Express Dairy where visitors may watch cows being milked every afternoon.

The Petersham road is traffic-ridden; lorries roar past the beautiful Stuart façade of Montrose House, which has two splendid wrought-iron gates. Beyond two more large old houses is a footpath on the left leading to *St. Peter's, Petersham*. It is very small, with a wooden steeple and a bell dated 1620 in-scribed 'Bryan Eldridge made mee'. Royalty and aristocrats have belonged to its congregation; the vicar believes this began when Ham House was built and many other members of the nobility, following suit, built great houses in Petersham. The Lauderdales were married in this church, and so was Charles II's cousin Prince Rupert. In the present century the parents of the Queen Mother, the Earl and Countess of Strathmore had their wedding here. The Scots tradition, dating from Lauderdales and Argylls, persists.

Inside the church are tall box pews and galleries; there is a scarlet and navy coat and a staff once belonging to a Beadle, and the arms of George III over the doorway. In the north wall of the chancel is an amusing Jacobean monument to George Cole, a lawyer, who lies on one elbow, wearing a long black gown and holding a scroll. Below is his wife, dressed to the nines in ruff and headdress, also balanced on her side. A flag-draped memorial, by the Hudson's Bay Company, commemorates Captain George Vancouver for his 'valuable and enterprising voyage of discovery'. Vancouver went round the Cape of Good Hope and the North Pacific and discovered the island which has his name; he came back to Petersham, wrote his *Voyage of Discovery*, and died at the age of 40. Other memorials, on the walls, and gravestones in the churchyard, show familiar, famous names . . . Argylles, Hydes, Montagues. The Earl of Cardigan, notorious for his part in the charge of the Light Brigade, was a member of the congregation. So was the eccentric Lady Mary Coke, reputed to have invented the top hat, who died in bed wearing one.

The church is cared for and full of flowers. In the churchyard are the graves of Hannah, Mary and Richard, the great-granddaughters and great-grandson of William Penn, the founder of Pennsylvania.

Mary and Agnes Berry are also buried here, with an inscription by the Earl of Carlisle. These sisters were the youthful friends of Horace Walpole. Later they were tremendously successful hostesses, travelled everywhere and met everybody from Madame de Stael to Dickens and Thackeray. They even met Napoleon. At their receptions, if they called to the servant 'No more petticoats', the front door lamp was extinguished to discourage further lady visitors. Male visitors continued to be heartily welcomed.

Both ladies lived to be almost 90.

The church has two services every Sunday; weekday visitors may get the key from the Vicarage in Sudbrook Lane, five minutes' walk away.

At the end of the same lane is the gateway to an eighteenth

century Palladian mansion, *Sudbrook House*, now a golf club, with a course which has a view of the Thames. It is possible to visit the house on Mondays.

It was designed by James Gibbs in 1726 and built for a family connected by marriage to the Lauderdales. The second duke of Argyll (whose portrait as an exceedingly handsome young man is at Ham), was the son of Elizabeth Lauderdale, the Countess of Dysart's eldest daughter. Unlike his father who was responsible for the Glencoe massacre, this Campbell was a fine soldier, an attractive man, a good orator, and much loved. His second wife, whom he met at Court, was a plain little maid of honour without a dowry, called Jenny Warburton; they were completely happy. The Duke fought under Marlborough at Oudenarde and Malplaquet; it was said that Marlborough was jealous because Argyll's troops adored him. Argyll and his wife settled at Sudbrook and reared a large family including four hoydenish daughters known by the local people as the 'bawling Campbells'. There is a covered passage leading to an annexe which the Duke built for his family . . . possibly to escape the noise.

Sudbrook has a portico with a double flight of steps leading to a beautiful park. On the first floor of the house is the Cube Room which is 30 feet long, broad and high; it has carved pine panelling and an ornamental plaster ceiling.

Long after the Argylls, Lady Horton lived for a while at Sudbrook. She was related to Byron and the story goes that he met her at a ball one evening. She was in half mourning, wearing a soft black dress spangled with stars. Byron wrote a poem about her which begins:

> 'She walks in beauty, like the night
> Of cloudless climes and starry skies;
> And all that's best of dark and bright
> Meet in her aspect and her eyes:
> Thus mellow'd to that tender light
> Which heaven to gaudy day denies.'

Richmond Bridge was built in 1777 and is the oldest of the bridges of London river, an enchanting five arched bridge with semi-circular buttresses and gilded lamps which match its character. The river here is about 300 feet wide.

Artists and writers have always been attracted to Richmond: in 1712 Sir Richard Steele rose at 4 in the morning and travelled with a fleet of gardeners taking fresh apricots to London. In 1791 Walpole went to the Richmond boat race and wrote of the scene upriver and down: 'The crowds on those green velvet meadows . . . the yachts, barges, pleasures and small boats, and the windows and gardens lined with spectators, were so delightful that when I came home from that vivid show, I thought Strawberry looked as dull and solitary as a hermitage.'

Wordsworth wrote a dreamy poem by the bridge:

'Glide gently, thus for ever glide
O Thames! that other bards may see
As lovely visions by thy side
As now, fair river! come to me.'

And Dickens, in a different mood, begged a friend to come and join him when he was living in Petersham. The air was so reviving and there were 'swimming feats from Petersham to Richmond Bridge . . . achieved before breakfast, I myself have risen at 6 and plunged head foremost into the water to the astonishment and admiration of all beholders'.

On the crest of Richmond Hill in the distance is the Star and Garter home for disabled soldiers. It stands on the site of a famous inn which somebody described in the eighteenth century as more like the mansion of a nobleman than a house for the public. Kings dined or stayed there. Dickens gave a yearly supper to celebrate his wedding anniversary. The house was burned down and the present square brick building was built in the 1920's.

The Richmond towpath is wide and lined with trees and there are boatyards on the two small islands. These islands are called Aits or Eyots which people believe originally meant osier islands.

Facing the bridge is the *White Cross Inn* with a terrace overlooking the river and a bow window with the same view. The pub stands on the site of a sixteenth century monastery of the Observant Friars (an engaging name for an order of monks). Beyond the bridge is a jetty where motor-boats may be hired by the hour. It takes an hour to get to Teddington and three hours to Hampton Court—a lovely way to spend an afternoon.

On the left, along the towpath towards Richmond Bridge, is a honey-coloured villa at the end of Old Palace Lane: *Asgill House*. It was built in 1758 on what was once the river frontage of old Richmond Palace, for Sir Charles Asgill, a wealthy banker who became Lord Mayor of London. Asgill entertained friends from the City Livery Companies at his villa; they came upriver in splendid barges, accompanied by bands of musicians. The guests were dressed in velvet, wore their City decorations and were received with rich hospitality. The house was a happy place until Asgill's son, another Charles, who was in the army, was sent to America during the War of Independence. He was taken prisoner. George Washington directed as a reprisal that one of the captured British officers should die, and they were forced to draw lots. The lot fell on Charles. His father was dead but his mother sent a heartrending appeal to France, and Louis XVI and Marie Antoinette interceded for him with Washington. An Act of Congress was actually passed to save his life; he was allowed to come home to Richmond on permanent parole.

By the entrance gates in Old Palace Lane is a plaque on the site of the grounds of old Richmond Palace. Opposite is the *White Swan*, one of the most attractive of Richmond's pubs, built in the 1700's on the site of a much older inn. The building, made from stones which came from the old Royal Palace, is small and beamed, with a courtyard. An upstairs dining-room has a view of the statues and gardens of Asgill House and a flash of boats going by. The pub is much used by local people and food and service are both good.

A short walk up the lane brings you to *Old Richmond Palace*.

Is there anything to see? Precious little. One is lured by drawings and paintings of the lost Tudor glories. Nothing is left of Nonsuch, even the foundations excavated in 1961 are under the earth again. Richmond Palace has not quite disappeared. Facing Richmond Green is the original Tudor gateway over which are the defaced royal arms of Henry VII; through the arch on the left in what was once Wardrobe Court are some Tudor houses. The house called 'The Wardrobe' was used to store royal furniture and hangings. The court is peaceful, grassy, shaded with chestnuts; little enough of a palace which covered ten acres and was more magnificent than Hampton Court. The buildings which stood by the water were turreted and ornamented, topped with 14 pinnacles; there were galleries and courtyards, apartments, quadrangles, tennis courts and gardens to the river.

In Medieval times it was the palace of Shene, the Saxon word for 'sparkling'. Edward III kept a brilliant court here and Richard II and his young beloved queen liked it best of all their palaces. But she died here of the plague. Her funeral procession came downriver from Richmond to Westminster. The king 'all distraught and disordered' with grief cursed the place and 'caused it to be thrown down and defaced'.

Henry V rebuilt Richmond Palace and came to hunt here. Later, after a great fire, Henry VII rebuilt it. The first Tudor King, an odd combination of miser and spender, made the palace sumptuous, with courts and towers, fountains and a chapel; he renamed it Richmond after his own previous earldom.

Henry VIII lived at Richmond Palace with Katharine of Aragon, giving masques in which he acted himself. But when she had a baby son who died at only 7 weeks old, the king left the palace as his ancestor Richard II had done and rarely came back.

Elizabeth, although she was imprisoned here in her sister's reign, loved Richmond Palace. In her old age she called it her 'warm winter box' and when in her sixties still danced with her Courtiers. 'I assure you,' wrote one of them, 'six or seven gallyards of a mornynge, besydes musycke and syngynge, is her ordinary exercise.'

She died at Richmond Palace in 1603. Richmond people believe she died in the room over the existing gateway. The dying queen at one time stood on her feet for fifteen hours. She died on a heap of cushions on the Palace floor. It's said that Lady Scrope dropped a ring from the window over the archway when the Queen was dead as a signal to Sir Robert Carey waiting below. Carey rode straight to Scotland to King James who knew the news to be true when he saw the ring.

Elizabeth's body was taken with great pomp in procession on the river; a poem by William Camden, written two years afterwards, describes:

> 'The Queen was brought by water to White-hall
> At every stroke the oars did tears let fall:
> More clung about the Barge, fish under water
> Wept out their eyes of pearl, and swam blind after.'

Clarendon's granddaughters, future queens of England, were brought up at Richmond Palace—Mary and Anne. They learned to dance, sing, play the viol and the lute. Pepys wrote that Mary could 'dance most finely so as almost to ravish one—her ears were so good'.

George II lived here as Prince of Wales but the palace was diminishing and needed repairs; its glory was fading. Finally, all the Tudor magic was razed to the ground and houses built on the site. Only the gatehouse and Wardrobe Court remain.

At the end of the court, now called Old Palace Yard, is *Trumpeters' House,* named after two stone figures of heralds in Tudor dress which used to stand at its gateway. The building has a stately eighteenth century façade seen best on the towpath to Richmond Bridge, from which there is a view of the Palladian and pillared front of the house set in parkland of lawns and fine trees. Metternich lived here after escaping from Vienna during Austrian upheavals. Disraeli wrote: 'I have been to Metternich on Richmond Green in the most charming house in the world . . . it is sweet, charming alike in summer and winter.'

Facing the Palace gateway is *Richmond Green,* where Henry VII and later Henry VIII held jousts and tournaments. The green became a favourite resort of the nobility in the eighteenth century. 'Today,' wrote Walpole, 'as I passed over Richmond Green, I saw Lord Bath, Lord Lonsdale and half a dozen more of the White's Club sauntering at the door of a house they have taken there . . . it made me smile to see Lord Bath sitting there, like a citizen that has left off trade!'

George III liked to watch cricket matches on the Green and once ordered a dinner for the cricketers at a local inn, generously tipping both teams.

Along the edge of the green is the line of elegant Georgian houses called *Maids of Honour Row,* built in 1723 by command of George I for the ladies attending the Princess of Wales, who was living at the old Palace.

The maids of honour were extremely pretty and some had to fend off the advances of the sex-conscious Prince of Wales, afterwards George II. An epigram by Swift was found in a prayer book belonging to one of the girls:

'When Israel's daughters mourned their past offences,
They dealt in sackcloth and turned cinder-wenches;
But Richmond's fair ones never spoil their locks;
They use white powder and wear Holland smocks.
O comely Church! where females find clean linen,
As decent to repent in as to sin in.'

Another maid of honour gave her title to a special kind of Richmond cheesecake which is supposed to date back to Henry VIII's time. The king found one of his maids of honour eating a

59

certain little cake, tasted it, and commanded that in future such cakes should be eaten only in Royal circles.

George III was very partial to the "maids of honour cakes" as they were named and had them sent to him when he stayed at Kew Palace or Windsor. These delicious pieces of edible history are still made daily, but at a distance from Richmond. Newens, an attractive shop in the Kew Road by Kew Gardens, use the original recipe for their Maids of Honour which contain sweet curds left for 24 hours before cooking.

Gates of Syon House (the Michaelangelo Lion), Brentford

4 LEFT BANK
Twickenham Bridge
The London Apprentice, Isleworth
All Saints Church
Syon House and Gardens
Ferry Lane, Brentford Ford
Kew Bridge
Strand-on-the-Green
Steam Packet
Zoffany House
City Barge

RIGHT BANK
Kew Church and Green
Kew Gardens
Kew Palace

Isleworth is a curious part of London. The river is lived-by and enjoyed at Richmond, but the roads to Isleworth and Syon Park run through a no-man's-land, with only faint traces of where villages used to be.

Twickenham Bridge, built in 1933 of concrete but balustraded with an oddly old-fashioned look, crosses the river before Richmond Lock. Syon Reach is pleasantly countrified, seeming a thousand miles from the dusty landscape up the road.

The *London Apprentice* is in Church Street, by the river and very close to the church. The pub is 500 years old and was a stopping-place for lightermen and boatmen. It was also appreciated by smugglers who hid their swag in the church vault and carried it to the inn at night by an underground passage.

The young apprentices of the City Livery companies used to row upriver to this inn on the one day they had off from work in the year . . . Isleworth was a kind of apprentices' Southend.

Painters have always appreciated the London Apprentice and its view of the Thames. Constable and Turner came here; Zoffany painted a portrait of his friend Richard Wilson in the bar, holding a tankard of porter. Wilson never admitted he liked to drink and was so offended that Zoffany painted the tankard out again.

In the usual way of old London taverns the pub claims some pretty high-ranking visitors including Henry VIII and Charles II. There is a nice Rowlandson drawing near the door of the ground-floor bar well-suited to an inn close to a church. A publican on his knees prays:

'Strengthen, I pray you, the digestive faculties of our worthy Vicar, so that he may be able to repair to my little bar parlour, and measure out his money to my advantage.'

The London Apprentice is very pleasant, very old and stylish. The Eights Room on the first floor is a restaurant where rowing eights sometimes dine, a room with bow windows overlooking the river and a beautiful Italian plasterwork ceiling of 1600. Downstairs, the Thames bar has a view of the willowy Ait. (There's fishing at Isleworth, incidentally, for carp and dace, bream and roach.) The food at the London Apprentice is good and not overly expensive and in the bar there are salads, sandwiches and excellent wine by the glass.

Little is left of the fifteenth century parish church of *All Saints* facing the river, except the tower with its painted sundial. A small modern church with a certain elegance has been built inside the old grey ruins and there is a beautiful brilliant stained-glass window. The churchyard is shady with limes and in summer full of flowers. A terrace of pleasant eighteenth century houses runs from the church to the pub. Across the river is the Old Deer Park leading to Kew Gardens.

Ideally, *Syon House* should be visited by river if this were possible. The dukes of Northumberland arrived this way and their enchanting eighteenth century boathouse is on the river front of the house ... it is more a summerhouse or a gazebo than a mere place to keep a boat. For everybody else, the way to Syon is by bus, train or in a car through the sprawling urban growth of Isleworth.

Syon, named after the Syon in Palestine, was a convent built in the fifteenth century by nuns of the unfamiliar-sounding Bridgettine Order. The sisters stayed until the Reformation when Henry VIII claimed the place. A friar preached against this Royal desecration, prophesying that dogs would lick the king's blood. The words came true; when Henry died his coffin was brought by river from London to Windsor. The cortège spent a night at Syon House and during the night the coffin burst open, and servants found the dogs licking up certain remains which had fallen on to the floor.

After its convent life, tragedy haunted Syon. Henry had imprisoned Catherine Howard here before her execution. When Henry was dead, Syon became a rich prize for the powerful, many of whom died violent deaths. Edward VI granted Syon to his uncle the Protector Somerset who extended it into a magnificent Tudor mansion, but soon Somerset was accused of treason and went to the block. His great enemy Dudley, Earl of Warwick (later created a duke of Northumberland) had Syon for a while. After the young Edward VI died, Northumberland and a group of nobles offered the English crown to Lady Jane Grey at Syon. She was a distant heir to the throne, but more to the point was Northumberland's daughter-in-law. Jane is a forlorn figure in history—quiet, religious, learned, innocent. There is a prim-faced portrait of her and one of her father-in-law in the Print Room at Syon. From Syon she was taken in state downriver to the Tower and proclaimed Queen. Nine days later Mary Tudor was on the throne and Jane and her father-in-law were imprisoned for high treason. Later they were beheaded.

As a Catholic monarch, Mary gave Syon back to the nuns but

they had little time to enjoy it for soon after their return Mary
Tudor was dead. Elizabeth suppressed the monasteries and
convents again, and this time the nuns left for ever.

They settled in Lisbon, taking Syon's keys as a symbol
that the house was still theirs. Centuries later a duke of Northumberland visited them and presented them with a silver model
of Syon.

'We still hold the keys,' said the Abbess.

'Ah, but we've altered the locks,' said the Duke.

Today there is a Bridgettine convent in Devon—called Syon
Abbey.

Syon had a time of glory in Elizabeth's reign when Francis
Drake came to meet the queen on his return from going round
the world in the *Golden Hind*. He spent six hours alone with her.
Most of the treasure he had captured was brought to Syon
before being taken to the Tower; Drake's haul was so rich that it
was enough to pay 'for seven years' wars'.

In the early 1600's, James I gave Syon to Henry Percy,
Earl of Northumberland but no relation to the Northumberland
who had proclaimed Lady Jane a queen. Percy was the first
member of this family to own the house; the Percys were
created Dukes by George III. Syon House still belongs to them
and they live here part of every year.

The House stands in a park and water meadows which stretch
along the riverside opposite Kew Gardens. It is a quadrangular
building with a square tower at each corner, the top of the
building battlemented like a child's sandcastle. On the east
front stands the lion which came from the Northumberland
Mansion in the Strand, demolished in 1874. The lion, used in the
family's crest, was modelled from one by Michelangelo. The
shell of Syon House is still that of the Protector Somerset's but,
inside and out, Syon was entirely remodelled by Robert Adam.
In 1762 he was invited by the then Earl to alter Syon which its
owner considered 'ruinous and inconvenient'. Adam worked at
Syon for years, changing the old Tudor mansion steeped in the
sad past into a place of classical magnificence. But his grand
design was never finished and the north of Syon was virtually
untouched.

The entrance to the house is through the *Great Hall* which has
been called the grandeur of Adam's conception realized, a
marvellous room floored with patterned black and white
marble and graced with statues and busts ... Cicero, Ceres,
Apollo. The ceiling is stucco in exquisite geometric decorations.

1 *Hampton Court—the Great Gatehouse, with the King's Beasts in the foreground (see Chapter 1).*

2 *View of Ham Ferry and Twickenham riverside from the towpath in front of Ham House (see Chapter 2).*

A flight of steps leads to the Roman-styled *Ante-Room*; its green columns came from the bed of the Tiber, its brilliantly coloured floor is scagliola, a method of working coloured marbles into patterns often seen in the great houses in Italy. Beyond the Ante-Room is the *Red Drawing Room*. There is gold and pink as well as red in this Adam room, the walls covered with Spitalfields silk, the carpet and furniture designed by Adam himself.

The room is also called the *Stuart Room* because of its portraits. It's interesting that the Northumberlands should have such a range of Stuart pictures for they were not on the king's side during the Civil War. It's true that the tenth earl, Algernon, was a friend of Charles I and tried to act as peacemaker between king and parliament. Charles was eager to have the influential earl on his side ... but Northumberland chose Parliament in the end.

During the war the Royal children—the young dukes of York and Gloucester and the princess Elizabeth—were sent to Syon to be under Northumberland's care. When Charles I was a prisoner at Hampton Court he was allowed to ride over to see them. There is a Lely picture of the meeting between Charles and his young son James who afterwards became James II. The tradition is that Charles is asking his son to swear not to escape. The king looks wooden and blank, a man suffering from shock, perhaps. The young prince gazes at his father from the corners of his eyes; James broke his word—he escaped to Holland.

There are portraits of many Stuarts famous in history ... Elizabeth of Bohemia, the Winter Queen with whom the world fell in love ... Charles II's sister Minette; people said she was poisoned by her husband, the French king's brother, at Versailles. The painting of Queen Henrietta Maria shows a pretty Frenchwoman, with an angel holding a crown suspended over her head. Trevelyan calls this queen 'the mother of many troubles to England and more to the House of Stuart'. Her enormous influence over Charles I made her disliked and later detested. The soldiers hated her for being both a foreigner and a Papist.

Beyond the Stuart Room is the *Long Gallery*.

Adam altered this old Elizabethan gallery to create a place for the 'variety and amusement of the ladies'. It is very like the gallery at Strawberry Hill and Walpole claimed the idea was copied from his. The long stately room, with eleven windows, is painted and decorated with wonderful style and cunning; the books inset into carved cupboards are made to seem part of the design and so are landscapes painted on the walls and along the edges of the ceilings. There are concave and convex mirrors for fun . . . the gallery is beautiful and cheerful. Standing here and there are present-day photographs of the Northumberland family at Coronations and Royal Weddings.

A panelled corridor leading out of the gallery is lined with portraits—rows of narrowed-eyed, impassive Tudor faces. Not a trace of Adam elegance here. A portrait of Elizabeth's Leicester shows him to be a startlingly handsome man for the queen to dote upon.

Aristocratic and powerful families living in the same place for hundreds of years seem to collect a hotch-potch of relics in their houses, and Syon is like this. There's a massive Sèvres vase, far too huge for beauty, standing on a pedestal. There is a sedan chair. A painted family tree takes up an entire wall. A 300-year-old map. And an oak stake dug from the river bed in Syon Reach, part of a palisade built by the Britons when fighting the Roman legions. The Romans crossed the Thames at Brentford half a mile away.

In the *Print Room* is a portrait of Algernon who took Parliament's side against Charles I and was keeper of the Royal children. He himself had a curious childhood, growing up in the Tower where his father had been a prisoner for years, suspected of being part of the Gunpowder Plot. Algernon wears the Stuart silks and velvets with a careless elegance. But leather and mail would be more suited to a man with so guarded and wary a face.

Syon's gardens and grounds

In the sixteenth century, the nuns cultivated 30 acres of gardens and orchard at their Syon convent—the venerable old brick wall by the car park once enclosed one of their gardens. The Protector Somerset created the first botanical garden in England when Syon was his mansion and two of the mulberry trees planted by him are still in the gardens and bear fruit. The Percy family continued the tradition of cultivating rare plants. John Evelyn came to Syon during the Plague Year of 1665 when Charles II was conducting his state business at Syon House, safely out of infected London. 'I viewed the seat belonging to the Earl of Northumberland builte, out of an old Nunnerie, of stone, and faire enough,' wrote Evelyn, 'but more celebrated for the garden than it deserves; yet there is excellent wall fruit and a pretty fountaine, yet nothing extraordinarie.'

In the eighteenth century, working for the first Duke, Capability Brown transformed the gardens much as Adam did the house. He cleared away the Tudor walls, made two lakes and created spacious views set about with trees . . . he planted cedars and oaks, beeches and chestnuts. An old black walnut which Brown planted now measures 17 feet in circumference round its mighty trunk. Syon's park and gardens today are Brown's, more or less unchanged.

The delightful *Conservatory* which rather resembles the domes of Brighton Pavilion was built in the 1820s; Paxton was so taken with it that he used it as the model for the Crystal Palace. It is more than just a conservatory for flowers . . . there are butterflies, birds and fishes here.

The *Rose Garden* is a marvel—six acres of roses of every size and colour, every kind and variety, flowering richly from early summer; this is a place of pilgrimage for the English rose-lover. There is also a Garden Centre, opened at Syon in 1968, which is a permanent gardening exhibition with plants, shrubs and trees for sale which come from nurseries all over the country.

Although Syon was built to be close to the Thames, visitors to the house cannot see the river from the rooms open to the public. (Apparently the family's upstairs rooms have river views.) The river banks are high and in summer thickly growing with grasses and reeds on the banks. The birds living in the Syon water meadows are protected by the Nature Conservancy.

Beyond Syon on the same bank the Grand Union Canal joins the Thames. Going towards London, the riverside is a maze of docks and wharves; there are plans to open up this stretch of the Thames but nothing is yet settled. *Ferry Lane*, off Brentford High Street, leads down to the old ford where the river Brent enters the Thames. A boy dived into the river at this spot, and came up with an Iron-age dagger in his hand. On the right near the water is a granite column put up in Edwardian times to commemorate many historic happenings at this ford. In 54 BC the British tribesmen fortified the river crossing and unsuccessfully fought Caesar's troops here. In 780 there was a Council of the Christian Church (it was to settle disputes between the Saxon kings of Essex and Wessex). The Danes were beaten by Edmond Ironside at the same river ford in 1016. The final inscription records the Battle of Brentford during the Civil War. The

Royalists triumphed temporarily, beat Cromwell's troops and drove many of them into the river.

Downriver from the pleasant little stone *Kew Bridge* (1903) with its carved stone coats of arms, the village of *Strand-on-the-Green* is on the north bank by the river. It is a delightful unspoiled place with rows of balconied houses, many with bay windows or flights of worn steps. In spring and autumn, the river invades the village and the towpath is often under water; lamp posts and willow trees are surrounded by swimming moorhens. Many of the houses have anti-flood measures; some have steps leading straight into first floor windows, others stout protecting boards in front of doors or gates.

Either the village's position is very sheltered or it has a gardening tradition borrowed from Kew, for its gardens are fine. There are mimosa trees, passion flowers, figs, wisteria, vines, roses and peach trees. The district used to be famous for producing some of the best barley in England and malthouses faced the river, loading the barley on to barges which went direct to taverns brewing their own ale. There is still a malthouse at Strand-on-the-Green.

The Steam Packet is the pub nearest to Kew Bridge, a pleasant Victorian building with an iron balcony, awnings and pots of flowers. A comfortable place for a drink and a snack in the panelled bar parlour.

Zoffany House has a small red lion over the front door; it was the painter's home for the last twenty years of his life. He was born in Germany, came to London as a boy and nearly starved in a Drury Lane garret before getting a job painting landscapes on the decorated faces of clocks. Zoffany became famous for his portraits of actors and scenes from the drama, and was a great friend of Garrick's. He was taken up by the Royal family at Kew and his strong, vigorous portraits of both George III and Charlotte are in the Royal collection.

Zoffany had a passion for travel and almost went on Captain Cook's second voyage of discovery, but cancelled it at the last minute because conditions in the ship were too cramped. He went to Italy. He spent time in Vienna where they made him a baron. He travelled as far as India. He made a great deal of money and enjoyed using it; when he came to live at Strand-on-the-Green he dressed his servants in scarlet livery and bought a sloop (he called it a shallop) which he painted green and pink. He moored his sloop opposite the house, gave musical evenings on board, built a summerhouse in a tree which reached out over the water for the Prince Regent to sit in willowy green comfort listening to the music.

Zoffany married a girl of 14 who was considered socially beneath him, but she was beautiful, good-natured and a universal favourite. Strand-on-the-Green was a fishing village then. When the painter was working at his picture of the Last Supper for Old Brentford Church he used the local fishermen as his models, with himself as the figure of St. Peter. The fishermen became known locally by their apostolic names, much to the annoyance of the wife of Judas.

All the houses along the towpath have a riverside air. There are model ships in the windows or skiffs drawn up in front gardens.

The City Barge is a pub much loved by local people and visitors as well. It was built in 1497 when Henry VII was on the throne and gets its name from the City of London barge which had its winter moorings here. The Lord Mayor's barge was a pleasure craft in every sense of the word, it had a state room, bedrooms and a kitchen. The bars in the City Barge are crowded and lively, one low-ceilinged room leading into another. The pub serves good wine and sandwiches, or luncheon at the small tables in both rooms—a speciality is chicken with mushrooms and herbs, cooked in white burgundy.

Two minutes away from the City Barge is the *Bull's Head*. There is an old tradition that Cromwell held a council here during the Civil War and was forced to escape by an underground passage to the islet in the river still called Oliver's Eyot. Historians deny the story; but when the landlords were recently modernizing the cellars they found traces of what could be steps leading to an underground passage. People having a meal at the Bull's Head often sit with the Thames lapping at the windows, particularly when there is a high surging tide. There are little carved figureheads of ships on the walls and the bars are built on two levels, with wooden settles and views of the sometimes-uncomfortably-high Thames.

The pretty village is safe from developers and bulldozers; in 1968 it was declared a conservation area.

Kew

Easily the best way to Kew is by Thames launch on a fine day; the pier is a ten-minute walk from the gardens and the green.

Kew used to be called Kai-ho, which despite its Japanese sound may have meant 'quay'. Queen Elizabeth visited her

Keeper of the Great Seal at Kew in 1594; he knew his ageing sovereign's relish for costly presents and in a single visit gave her a diamond-decorated fan, a diamond pendant, some virginals, a dress and petticoat, and a spoon and fork made of agate.

St. Anne's Church on the Green was the beginning of eighteenth century Kew's Royal connexions. Queen Anne gave £100 towards building a new church here. When George III lived in his palace at Kew he added the church's gallery to make room for his large family of children crowding in to divine service every Sunday. The sweet-toned organ was Handel's, given to the church by George IV. And in the late nineteenth century Queen Mary's parents were married at St. Anne's, and lived at the delightful Cambridge Cottage in Kew Gardens. Many of the old houses facing Kew Green were used to board out George III's sons with their tutors.

The church, of yellow brick with arched windows, is pleasantly stylish and light and beautifully looked-after. The hundreds of embroidered kneelers . . . little cushions for the congregation . . . make the place colourful. These cushions are embroidered by the local tapestry guild to commemorate long-dead or recent members of the parish and the designs are symbolic. There are embroidered houses and trees, ships, birds, telescopes, flowers, coats of arms. Cushions also commemorate every member of the Royal family since the church's patroness Queen Anne.

Two painters are buried in the churchyard—Zoffany and Gainsborough. Zoffany lived at nearby Strand-on-the-Green but Gainsborough was not a Kew person; he left a request to be buried beside his great friend Joshua Kirby who had worked at Kew Palace and had taught 'perspective drawing' to the young George III. Kirby also designed part of St. Anne's. Gainsborough, the favourite Court painter of the century and the 'father of English landscape painting', was an attractive man but quick-tempered and jealous; he quarrelled with Joshua Reynolds and was jealous of Reynolds' greater success. Before his death, Reynolds came to see Gainsborough and they were reconciled; 'We are all going to heaven,' said the dying painter, 'and Van Dyke is of the company.'

Kew Gardens

Queen Anne began the history of modern Kew with the building of the church on the Green, and it was George III's father Frederick Prince of Wales and his wife Augusta who began Kew

Gardens. Frederick lived at Kew in the 1730s, keeping a kind of rival court there . . . his parents George II and Caroline detested him. His mother called him 'the greatest ass and the greatest liar . . . and the greatest beast in the whole world'. His enemies merely called him Poor Fred. But to his friends he was the 'amiable Prince of Wales' and the people loved him. He visited the poor in their cottages, walked unattended in the streets. 'My God,' said Caroline 'Fritz's popularity makes me vomit.'

Frederick was a mixture of art connoisseur and country gentleman. He went to Bartholomew Fair wearing ruby velvet and gold lace, his long hair flowing round his shoulders. He wrote a bad play and some pleasant music, and Swift and Pope were his friends. He also liked village cricket, fishing, and rowing races on the Thames. He and Augusta began creating some gardens round their palace at Kew—they planned a royal pleasure ground. But Frederick died nine years before the king and Augusta was left a dowager and a widow at 32.

The Princess was not an attractive person; she was plain, with a long nose and a double chin. She was ungracious, censorious, certainly not clever—the only nice things people said of her were that she was civil and prudent. Yet we owe the existence of Kew Gardens to this princess. Kent had already began to design the gardens for the Prince of Wales, but Augusta had green fingers and a vision of making the garden 'exotic'. She started to collect rare and foreign plants and trees . . . she employed the most brilliant botanist and gardener of the day, William Aiton. Though the gardens were only nine acres in size, in her lifetime Augusta made them famous.

When she died, her son George had been king for 12 years. He decided to live at Kew and to use it as a country home for his growing family; from mid-May he spent as much time as possible there. Fanny Burney who attended the Queen described the quiet life at Kew where the Royal couple lived as the simplest country gentlefolk. George's homely taste amused the great world: his short modest meals of mutton chops and pudding, his four glasses of wine and no more, his barley water after hunting. Once a week the king and queen with the children in pairs like a school crocodile trooped through Kew Gardens.

In 1772, George built Charlotte the *Queen's Cottage* on the edge of the gardens, which the family used as a summerhouse, having tea and sometimes breakfast there. The small thatched cottage is open to the public; there is an enchanting room on the first floor designed to look like a tent, with a ceiling painted to represent canvas, and bamboo supports on the walls twined with convolvulus. It's believed that George III's daughter Elizabeth, who loved painting, decorated the room. The Queen's Cottage stands among trees in a dell, and in spring floats in a lake of bluebells.

George and Charlotte were enthusiastic about Kew Gardens, and William Aiton continued his work there, building hothouses and adding rare plants. He wrote a botanical work 'Hortus Kewensis' which became famous all over Europe. Darwin wrote a verse in its praise which included the lines:

> So sits enthron'd in vegetable pride
> Imperial Kew, by Thames's glittering side.

George III was soon nicknamed Farmer George; he had already turned Windsor Park into three farms and now he used Kew Gardens for breeding a flock of Merino sheep. He was happy at Kew. He liked an unaffected simplicity and strolled alone through Kew village as his father had done. When the village people spoke to him he answered kindly: 'Good morning, friend.'

The aristocracy might smile and make jokes but they still thronged to Kew when the Court was there. Carriages lined up in the drive, and many visitors came by river in boats bright with awnings, and musicians playing on board. The King opened the gardens to the public on Thursdays in summertime 'for the amusement of all persons genteelly dressed, by His Majesty's express order'.

Among the many famous gardeners of Kew, Capability Brown designed and planted the wonderful Rhododendron Dell which in early summer is one of Kew's famous sights; some of the rhododendrons, crimson, scarlet, apricot, purple, are over 20 foot high and covered with enormous flowers.

After its Georgian fame and fashion, the princesses tripping through its gardens, the parties and fun and fireworks, Kew waned. Royalty left the old Dutch House. But the gardens were enlarged in Victoria's reign and later they grew from 11 acres to 75. Today they cover over 300 acres.

The world's flora are studied at Kew and in the *laboratories* all the known forms of vegetable life are identified and examined. There is a *Herbarium* where dried specimens of the world's plants are preserved; the natural history library is vast. Plant diseases and pests are also studied at Kew and experts working at Kew have helped to found great industries. The rubber plantations in the East were begun by Kew botanists and it was from Kew that the first quinine was sent to India. Commonwealth countries have been encouraged to grow crops they have never grown before, with enormous success—coffee beans and pineapples, bananas and breadfruit.

Kew Gardens today gives a marvellous open-air entertainment, costing the visitor almost nothing. There are acres of green lawns, the rarest of trees, hothouses full of orchids, lakes studded with flowers or busy with English and foreign water birds. The woodlands are full of wild flowers. Fountains play. The Thames flows by.

Kew is a haven for wild birds; blackbirds and thrushes, chaffinches and tits are so tame they will sometimes feed from the hand. The nuthatch and chiffchaff nest in the gardens, and so does the handsome great green woodpecker.

A fine weather visit

Distances are deceptive in Kew Gardens and it is wise to buy a map sold at any of the garden gates. At any time of year there are flowers at Kew: Christmas roses in December and January, acres of snowdrops, crocuses, primroses, daffodils in spring. In summer it is the azaleas and the rhododendrons, later there is gorse and broom, blazing poppies, every kind of wild and cultivated rose.

The variety of trees in the gardens seems endless. The vast Maidenhair tree was planted by Kew's own Princess Augusta, and there is a turkey oak, a pagoda tree and a false acacia from George III's time. There are deodars from the Himalayas, bamboos, metasequoias from North East China. Many trees in later summer hang with unfamiliar, curiously-shaped seed pods.

A pleasant walk starts from the pond facing the Palm House where the two Chinese lions, Ming symbols of longevity, sit on guard. Behind the Palm House is a broad path planned by George III and leading to the *Syon vista*—a view of Syon House standing in its water meadows across the river. The towpath runs under great shady trees.

Another summer walk is to the Queen's Cottage. The land has been kept as a reserve for wild flowers and plants; it was presented to the nation by Queen Victoria who hoped it would remain in its beautiful and natural condition. Robins and butterflies live here and on warm days the rose-bay willowherb seeds float in a mist in the still air.

73

At Kew, too, there are the classic temples and ruins beloved of people in the eighteenth century. There is the *Temple of Bellona* and the *Ruined Arch*, both built in 1760. A year later the *Pagoda* which has become the symbol of Kew was begun. Horace Walpole wrote from Strawberry Hill at Twickenham to his friend the Earl of Stratford: 'We begin to perceive the tower of Kew from Montpellier Row; in a fortnight you will see it in Yorkshire.' The Pagoda is 163 feet high and used to be covered with red Chinese dragons on all its tiered roofs.

Behind Kew Palace is a replica of a garden in the seventeenth century in which only the plants grown at that time have been used. Most of these are herbs used in cooking, or to strew on the floor indoors to make the air smell good, or as medicines. Some of the herbs had real curative properties—others were believed to have practically magical powers. It was good news to make an infusion of rue in the seventeenth century:

> Such broth doth staie the belly gripes
> It helpth brest and loong
> It cures the sickness of the sides
> Cald Pleursie in Greek toong.

And a low-growing shrub, Ruscus Hypoglossis, was said to cure 'headache and yellow jaundies'.

An avenue of hornbeams leads up a steep path to the Mount, a feature of seventeenth-century gardens designed to give a view of the patterns made by the intricately-planted bushes of the knot garden. From the Mount there is a view of the river.

For a dull, cold or wet-weather visit

There are 24 plant houses in Kew—a bad-weather visit is best in the afternoon as the houses open at 1 o'clock; they range from tropical to cool, from steamy and humid to hot and dry, and there are some very strange, very marvellous things to see.

Most famous of the hot houses is the *Great Palm House* built in 1848; its fascinating shape is that of a ship's hull, keel upwards, with two smaller ships, one at each end. Inside the Palm House is a mini jungle, damp and sweet, full of exotic trees, ferns and plants, the air moist and dripping, the plants sometimes flowering with rare, brilliant blooms. In July and August, in Number Ten plant house, the Giant Water Lily is in flower . . . it is the direct descendant of the Victoria Amazonica brought to Kew in 1850. Some of its leaves measure 7 foot across and the waxy flowers are 15 inches from petal tip to petal tip.

Across the pond from the Palm House is the *General Museum*, where there are many models of rare flowers not found in the living collection. These include a wax model of that strange flower, the largest in the world, found in Sumatra in 1818 by Colonel Raffles. It is a parasite, growing on the roots and stems of the forest trees, a dusky red flower more than a yard wide, spotted with white. When it is living it has a sinister beauty and a horrible smell.

Cambridge Cottage where Queen Mary was born is now a museum of all kinds of woods. The pleasant old house near the tall flagstaff is the *Marianne North Gallery*. Miss North was a Victorian lady who spent her life travelling the world, painting flowers, trees, birds and butterflies; she left all her work to Kew, and some of it on display in the gallery is rare and curious.

Kew Palace

The smallest of all the Royal palaces, this is simply a comfortable old house built by a Dutch merchant in 1631; it is one of the earliest examples of the gabled style which the English came to love. The palace has recently been attractively redecorated. Much skill and care has been taken to recreate the rooms as they were when George III and his queen lived here, using the paintings and furniture, books, musical instruments, fans and games of the royal family who made Kew famous.

The house was always excessively cold. When Fanny Burney was lady to Queen Charlotte, she said they always started the Kew autumn with a houseful of servants and finished the winter with the Queen and herself nursing the entire staff who were all ill in bed.

From every window in the palace there are views of lawns, herb gardens, paths, distant groups of high trees. The rooms are artfully hung with Georgian colours . . . acid yellow taffetas, apricot stripes. *Queen Charlotte's Bedroom* has a sweet, absurd ceiling patterned with medallions representing the Five Senses. The whole of George III's family was passionately musical and the central figure is Hearing, a girl with a mandolin. But to look at the other figures one must stand on one's head.

There are portraits of George and Charlotte in almost every room, and their presence too. The king loved the queen devotedly; twenty-two years after their marriage, he wrote to his son 'your mother, whose excellent qualities appear stronger to me every hour.'

George III was tall and well-built; Boswell thought that he spoke 'with dignity, delicacy and ease'. Lord Hervey, comparing him to his grandfather George II, remarked: 'the levee room has lost so entirely the air of a lion's den. This Sovereign dont stand on one spot, with his eyes fixed royally on the ground, and dropping bits of German news . . . he is graceful and genteel.'

Charlotte of Mecklenburg was considered extremely plain when she arrived to be married to George. When somebody at Court thought perhaps she was looking a little prettier, the reply was 'Yes, I do believe the *bloom* of her ugliness is going off.' To modern eye, her wide mouth and button nose are rather attractive—but to the eighteenth century a woman's beauty had to be classic, flawless. Charlotte was a cultured and religious person and she and the king shared a great love of music. They both had their own orchestras, she played the harpsichord, the king, the flute. 'A love of music to distraction runs through our family' wrote the Princess Royal. In the *Drawing Room* the royal family and their guests listened to music in the evenings.

The Royal couple had fifteen children. The queen was a despot to her daughters who loved her in spite of that, and her sons worshipped her. But she was in awe of the king and was never allowed a finger in politics.

The *King's Privy Chamber*, where he sometimes received visitor leads to his *bedroom*, which has a beatiful embroidered picture of Christ on the wall. The married life of George and Charlotte was darkened and finally destroyed by the king's recurring fits of madness; the poor man was sometimes locked in this room during his illnesses. When the fits left him he was moody and difficult, but Charlotte became difficult too. Her kind daughter Mary thought her mother's changed, strained attitude to the stricken king was partly a fear of violence. But she also believed that her mother's nature lacked warmth and tenderness. Charlotte locked her door and refused to share her room with the king again, even when formally requested by the Cabinet. The Royal couple who had been so known, so reverenced, for their married happiness, still attended public functions together, but the queen would never see him without one of her daughters being present.

'It was melancholy,' wrote Lord Hobart, 'to see a family that had lived so well together for such a number of years completely broken up.'

The *Queen's Bedroom* is very charming and there is no trace of sadness to come in his choice of pictures of her royal babies. On the ground floor, too, is a roomful of evocative treasures of a family with many children; there are ivory alphabet counters from which the little princes and princesses learned to spell; a Royal high chair; one of the princesses' spangled fans.

When the king was in his last illness at Windsor he knew no more about his family; he did not even know that Charlotte had died at Kew. The queen had recently attended the marriages of two of her middle-aged children at Kew—her daughter Elizabeth was a bride at 48. Charlotte had sat in her arm-chair, holding the hand of her favourite son, and wept, wishing that she was near 'the dear King'.

Barnes Terrace in 1823

5 RIGHT BANK
St. Paul's School
Barnes Terrace
White Hart
St. Mary's, Mortlake
Burton's Tomb at
St Mary's Magdalenes's
Ship Inn, Mortlake
Chiswick Bridge

LEFT BANK
Chiswick House and Gardens
Hogarth's House
St. Nicholas's Church
Chiswick Mall
Hammersmith Terrace
Upper Mall
The Dove Inn
Furnivall Gardens
Lower Mall
Rutland, and Blue Anchor pubs
Hammersmith Bridge

Upriver from Hammersmith to Barnes is the most rustic of riverside walks by the London Thames. It's possible to wander for three-quarters of an hour on a bright morning in seemingly deep country without meeting a soul.

From the bridge, the towpath passes the new home of *St. Paul's School*, a group of low cream-coloured buildings in fields which used to be reservoirs. Elms, willows and poplars grow by the river path which widens into a lane full of wild sorrel, willowherb and the button flowers of the aromatic yellow tansy. In summer there are sometimes butterflies. Across the water are eighteenth century houses with gardens and moored boats, and in the distance the tower of St. Peter's church with its blue clock. Fishing along the river here is tidal; with luck there are catches of the usual Thames roach and dace, bream and eels.

The riverside walk continues under magnificent trees until it opens out to join first the lawns then the road to Barnes with the three-hooped railway bridge in the distance, and the lamb-emblazoned flag flying on top of the White Hart.

Barnes often comes into the conversation of Londoners, perhaps because by a small miracle the village and its atmosphere has survived. Some of the shops are old and small, a mixture of greengrocers, ironmongers and interesting antique shops. In Church Road is a village green and a pond with an island in the middle where swans occasionally nest. In Regency times three Shropshire girls raced round that pond for the prize of a 'Holland shift'.

In *Barnes Terrace* there are pleasant eighteenth century houses. In one of these Gustav Holst lived for a while, long before he composed The Planets. In a house almost next door lived the Scottish poet Henley, whose poem 'What shall I do for you, England, my England?' stirred and moved the Victorians.

An iron railway bridge (1849) which is also a footbridge crosses the river here, and the road continues past some modern flats and a few Georgian houses in walled gardens. In the last century people came to stay in Barnes for summer holidays, spending their days in yachts, steamers or punts—it used to be a boating paradise.

The Thames curves widely and in the centre of the curve is the Victorian *White Hart*, with marvellous views up and downriver —its three balconies are packed on Boat Race day. The bars are pleasant enough but only the exterior of the pub has kept its Victorian charm.

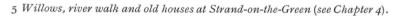

4 Richmond Bridge, built in 1777, is the oldest of the bridges over London river (see Chapter 3).

5 Willows, river walk and old houses at Strand-on-the-Green (see Chapter 4).

A short distance beyond the White Hart is the low Medieval building of *St. Mary's*, parish church of Mortlake. There's little of the thirteenth century building to see; the cupola'd tower was encased in brick in late Elizabethan times. But there are two Medieval carvings, one on either side of the church door, sculptured heads of a boy and a bearded man.

It is worth leaving the riverside at this point. On the right of *St. Mary's* is a path and another right turn leads into North Worple Way. The Catholic Church of *St. Mary Magdalene* is a few yards further on, standing in a courtyard graced by a massive cedar tree. Behind the church is a mild suburban churchyard; children shout and laugh in a nearby school playground. The churchyard is full of well-tended and unremarkable graves. But on the left among these is an 18-foot-high Arabian tent, the tomb of *Sir Richard Burton* and his wife Isabel. The tent-folds are patterned with sickle moons, two gilt stars are stuck above the flat top of the tent . . . it seems as if the stone flaps will part and there will be Burton at a table, planning his journey to the source of the Nile.

Burton has fascinated many people and still does. He was a scholar, an explorer, a great Orientalist; his life was vivid as that of an Elizabethan adventurer. He was full of curiosity and restless energy, made great and dangerous voyages, wrote learned, sometimes erotic books. His looks were astonishing, his face burned by sun and scarred in battle by a spear which transfixed it from one cheek to the other.

His wife, Isabel Arundell loved him for years before they finally married; she was companion and secretary, swam with him, rode and fenced with him. She was his dedicated champion. She also destroyed a considerable amount of his unpublished work after his death because it was obscene.

Burton's tomb was paid for partly by subscription from the public; inside the tent is a massive sarcophagus in front of a consecrated altar. After Burton died, Isabel came to live at Mortlake to be near the tomb, and held seances inside the tent. When she died she was buried beside him. The epitaph on the tomb begins:

> Farewell, dear friend, dead hero, the great life
> Is ended, the great perils, the great joys
> And he to whom adventures were as toys
> Who seemed to bear a charm 'gainst sword or knife
> Or bullet, now lies silent from all strife.

The lettering needs repair and some words are hard to decipher,
but there are plans, supported by the Royal Geographic Society,
to restore the tomb and to build a small viewing platform so that
visitors can see inside it. At present a tin window obscures the
interior of the tomb, which nobody has seen for some years.

Spreading along the Mortlake road, apparently growing as
one watches, is Watney's Brewery on the site of a manor
belonging to the Archbishops of Canterbury. The tradition of a
Mortlake brewery is very ancient; there has been one near
the river since 1487. Ship Lane runs between huge Watney
buildings and leads to the river and the little *Ship Inn*. The pub
is beside the Thames just where the Boat Race used to finish;
the race now ends slightly further upriver near Chiswick
Bridge.

The Ship belongs to Watneys and probably doesn't mind the
giant looming on three sides of it. From its windows there is a
long curving river stretch and across the water a line of tall
poplars and a boat house in *Duke's Meadows*. Local folk and
brewing folk come to the Ship, which is cheerful and popular;
inexpensive hot meals are quickly served and can be enjoyed at
tables with a river view.

Chiswick Bridge can be seen from the windows—it is the
Thames bridge with the longest concrete span, 150 feet wide,
the centre of three graceful arches.

Five minutes from the quiet riverside of Chiswick Mall, in the
suitably-named but traffic-ridden Burlington Lane, are the
walled grounds of *Chiswick* House. There are a number of gates
to the beautiful gardens but the Burlington Lane entrance is
best for its view of the mansion, set at the end of an avenue
lined with trees.

Chiswick House is a little work of art created in 1725 by
the Earl of Burlington and his friend William Kent. Burlington
was among the first English aristocrats to make the Grand Tour
of Europe and he became so fascinated by Italy that he went
back for a second visit. On returning home he began to design a
villa based on the classic country mansions designed by Palladio.
A hundred years earlier, Inigo Jones had also modelled his
work on Palladio; when Chiswick House was finished, Sir Hans
Sloane gave Burlington the gateway designed by Jones for the
old mansion of Sir Thomas More in Chelsea; the house was to be
demolished and Burlington re-erected the gate in Chiswick
House gardens where it is today. Pope wrote a little verse
about it:

I was brought from Chelsea last year
Batter'd by wind and weather;
Inigo Jones put me together;
Sir Hans Sloane left me alone;
Burlington brought me hither.

Chiswick House stands in a courtyard ringed by box hedges and a half circle of plinths topped with busts of fawns and satyrs. The house is two storeys' high with a lead-covered dome flanked with obelisk-shaped chimneys copied from an Italian villa.

The smallness of the house's interior is a surprise. It surprised Burlington's friends, and Lord Hervey remarked that it was 'too small to inhabit, and too large to hang on one's watch'. Hervey, like Pope, wrote a poem about Burlington's doings:

Possess'd of one great hall for state,
Without one room to sleep or eat:
How well you build let flattery tell
And all mankind how ill you dwell.

But Burlington did not build his little masterpiece to live in. It was intended as a kind of temple of the arts . . . a gallery for his paintings and sculptures, fine books and architectural drawings. A place to entertain friends as involved with the arts as he was—Pope and Gay, Swift and James Thomson. Wits and philosophers, men of thought and men of taste, came to visit Burlington at Chiswick House. But the actual business of living was carried on in a comfortable old Jacobean mansion which used to be a few steps across the courtyard, the old house which the first earl had bought forty years earlier.

After Burlington died, Chiswick House went to his heiress who married the fourth Duke of Devonshire. The fifth Duke in 1764 decided to demolish the old Jacobean manor and make Chiswick House into a home instead of just an artistic show-place. He added bedrooms and living-rooms in a fine new wing. It is interesting that Chiswick House has never lost its look and feel of being a classic temple dedicated to the arts. Burlington, not Devonshire, has the final say.

But it is curiously difficult to recreate the people who enjoyed the villa's stately room. On the ground floor there are some contemporary engravings which show the old Dutch-styled mansion standing beside Chiswick House, and men of fashion in wigs and three-cornered hats wandering in the classical gardens; there are peacocks on the lawns, waterfalls, a grotto, long avenues of clipped yews. But there isn't a single painting or drawing in the house showing Burlington and his friends sitting in any of the marvellous, now-empty rooms.

The centre of the villa is the *Domed Saloon* on the first floor; doorways are arranged to give long vistas of the succeeding rooms. The ceiling in the Saloon is plasterwork, elaborate as knobbly ochre-coloured lace and worked in octagonal panels gradually decreasing in size to the dome's top. William Kent, Burlington's friend and fellow-artist, had already used this design successfully in Kensington Palace and repeated it here.

On the left is the *Red Velvet Room* hung with flocked paper to replace the original ruby velvet. The ceiling was painted by Kent, whom Walpole considered a painter 'below mediocrity'; Hogarth also despised Kent's painting, calling him 'contemptible dauber'. Kent had considerable talents and as a designer of gardens was unparalleled, but painting and sculpting were by no means his forte. Yet a large number of great country houses have ceilings and walls painted by Kent and he sculpted the statue of Shakespeare in Poet's Corner at the Abbey. Walpole derided that statue too.

Through a door on the left is the *Blue Velvet Room*, its walls restored with turquoise flock paper. The room has the most elaborate of all the villa ceilings, painted by Kent in blue and gold patterns with the figure of Architecture in the centre accompanied by cherubs obligingly holding drawing instruments.

Walpole said the Earl of Burlington was a man who 'possessed every quality of a genius and an artist except envy'. The Blue Velvet Room shows this; Burlington hung a portrait of Inigo Jones, his patron saint of style here, and also a picture of William Kent, as though to say 'here are the men to whom I owe the house'. There is no painting of himself. Kent's portrait shows a plump self-confident man well satisfied with everything he put his hand to. Kent, Yorkshire-born, was a coach-builder's apprentice who went to Italy to study painting. When he came home he became enormously successful in the great world. With his knowledge and his pleasing manners he became quite the Oracle for fashionable people to consult 'for furniture . . . frames of pictures, glasses, tables, chairs . . . for a barge, for a cradle'. Pope liked him and christened him 'The Signior'.

Near the ceiling in a cherub-decorated frame is the haggard sickly face of Pope himself, a constant visitor and friend. Pope was crippled, often in pain, spirited, funny and brilliant. He was a devoted friend and a savage enemy. He described himself as 'a lively little creature, with long arms and legs. A spider is no ill Emblem of him'. One of John Gay's poems gives a picture of Pope sprawling in the gardens of Chiswick House, reaching out to eat the grapes and plums from the trees.

Beyond the Blue Velvet Room is a little place called the *Red Closet* which has one specially enchanting water-colour; Edward VII used to spend his summers at Chiswick House with his children and the picture shows the Royal children romping in the garden. They are wearing toy helmets and beating drums, and two of the little figures are the future George V and Queen Mary.

The Domed Saloon is the centre of the villa, but the most important apartment, a little architectural masterpiece, is the *Gallery*. Burlington and Kent succeeded in making a gallery which is grand in manner yet miniature in size. Everything is in the high Roman fashion; statues of Mercury, Venus and Apollo stand in niches, there are graceful arches beyond which the long corridors stretch, yet although the effect even of the statues is nobly large the whole has been artfully scaled down and is, in fact, quite small.

A doorway leads to the Green Velvet Room and beyond is a small plain room called *'the bedchamber'* where both Charles James Fox and Canning died.

At the end of the eighteenth century Chiswick House was the centre of politics and fashion, ruled over by the dazzling Georgiana, Duchess of Devonshire. Charles James Fox was one of her closest friends. Deeply loved by his many friends, a brilliant and learned statesman who fought for the abolition of slavery, Fox was hopelessly extravagant and often in debt. When he was seriously ill, Georgiana brought him down to the country to stay at Chiswick House. It was September 1806. There was a mountain ash growing by the window of his bedroom . . . there is no sign of it now. Fox looked at its orange berries every morning during his illness; the little tree seemed to fascinate him. 'His last look at that mountain ash,' wrote Bulwer, 'was his last look on nature.'

Twenty years later Canning came down to Chiswick for a 'change of air' when he too was ill. After Fox's death he had become the foremost man in Parliament, the legendary orator with an incomparable manner, tone and command of language. He died in the same room where his friend Fox had died.

The villa made history in English architecture by its Palladian style; the gardens made history in English landscape gardening. William Kent set out to design a garden to match the classic villa. He wanted to create the kind of dream-like beauty seen in the paintings of Claude Lorraine—a view of high trees, statues glimmering at the end of long avenues, a flash of water. He succeeded in an almost magical manner; 'as a gardener,' said Walpole, 'Kent is an inventor of the art, which realizes painting and improves nature.'

The Chiswick House gardens have changed in the last two hundred years but they still have Kent's vision of the Roman campagna. There are the temples and the water, sphinxes, stone lions, tree-lined avenues, distant obelisks. There is an exact model of St. Paul's church, Covent Garden standing like a little temple in front of a small lake. There is Jones's own weatherbeaten Jacobean gateway brought from Chelsea.

During the Regency, brilliant entertainments were given in the Chiswick House gardens; the Duke of Wellington, Blucher and the Czar of Russia walked on the lawns; in 1828 Sir Walter Scott wrote of a party where the gardens were 'dignified by the presence of an immense elephant, who, under the charge of a groom, wandered up and down, giving an air of Asiatic pageantry'. The elephant lived in a paddock near the house and was remarkable for her cleverness, docility and affectionate nature.

Famous people planted some of the magnificent cedars which still flourish on the lawns; one was planted by Garibaldi, one by the Czar, others by Queen Victoria, Edward VII and Queen Alexandra. When Edward VII as Prince of Wales lived at Chiswick House with his young family in the summer, part of the garden on the right was used by the children to cultivate their own patches of flowers. The future George V and the Duke of Clarence gardened there; it is still called *The Princes' Garden*.

Chiswick House's gardens are perfect for a summer afternoon; there are deck chairs on the lawns and under the cedars planted long ago by Royal princes. Ducks and rare geese nest on the ornamental waters . . . children play hide and seek among the trees. Burlington's little temple stands by, a classic but not severe presence.

It is ironic that Hogarth lived so close to Chiswick House, for he detested both Burlington and Kent as the leaders of a false and foreign taste. Hogarth had known Kent at drawing-school when they were both young, and disliked his showy ways. Later he thought him a pretentious social climber and never lost the chance to attack Kent and Burlington in his satiric drawings.

The lane where *Hogarth's House* stands is named after him but a lane no longer—it's the first stretch of the M4 and fast with traffic. The little eighteenth-century house manages to cling on, surrounded by a comfortable wall, graced by a venerable mulberry tree, and overlooked by tall buildings that have nothing to do with the arts.

Hogarth brought his little country box as he called it, in 1749. It was 'close to that amiable creature, the Thames', and he lived here with his family until his death in 1764. By the time he came to Chiswick he was already acclaimed as the greatest pictorial satirist of the age. Many people were afraid of his savage gift. He himself described his work as paintings made to work like acting.

He lived a decorous life at Chiswick; Hogarth liked a well-run home and his stately undemonstrative wife Jane gave him the formality and order that pleased him. Jane was the daughter of Sir James Thornhill, artist of the Painted Hall at Greenwich and the paintings inside the dome of St. Paul's. Hogarth's sister and Thornhill's widow also lived with them at Chiswick.

Hogarth worked in a stable converted into a studio in the garden and—in the way of most clever eighteenth century men—escaped from his virtuous life for flavour and savour to London where he and his men friends visited the taverns, coffee houses and brothels. The painter was short and pugnacious, with a round face, bright blue eyes and an expression described by Leigh Hunt as 'a sort of knowing jockey look'.

The house today is neat and pleasing; all the rooms are panelled and painted white, and there are engravings of many of his most famous works . . . Industry and Idleness . . . Marriage à la Mode . . . the Harlot's Progress. There is a copper-plate engraved by Hogarth, and delightful tickets which he designed for a Royal Masquerade at Somerset House. There is the famous portrait of Hogarth with his dog Trump, who looks so like him.

The garden outside, once much larger, has shrunk nowadays; the studio where he worked vanished a hundred years ago. Buildings loom. But the old mulberry tree is still alive; it was there in Hogarth's time and Jane Hogarth used to invite local children into the garden to pick the fruit or eat special home-made mulberry tarts. Both the house and the tree were damaged by bombs in 1940 but have quite recovered; the tree was coaxed back to life by an expert from Kew and is now healthy and green.

When Hogarth died, his widow lived on in the Chiswick house; she had less money but she kept up the style that her husband would have liked. She wore silk on Sundays and went to church preceded by her manservant who carried her prayer book and opened her pew door.

Church Street is really a country lane leading to the river. Old houses on both sides lean close to each other—one is decorated by the figurehead and wheel of a ship. At the end of the lane is *St. Nicholas's Church*, dedicated to the patron saint of fishermen, which stands almost by the water. The flint and stone tower is fifteenth century, but although there are still some parts of the ancient building remaining, most of the church is eighteenth century or Victorian; the interior is attractive and there is a Jacobean monument or two. Two of Cromwell's daughters, Mary and Frances, are buried in the church, but alas, without monuments. His third daughter Mary, said to have looked very like him, came to St. Nicholas's for five years and presented the church with its bells. The Earl of Burlington is buried in the family vault and William Kent beside him 'in a very handsome manner' said someone at the time.

In the churchyard is Hogarth's monument, paid for by a group of his friends. There is an urn and a pedestal decorated with the symbols of his art—a mask, a palette, pencils, a laurel wreath. Garrick wrote the verse which begins:

> Farewell, great painter of mankind,
> Who reach'd the noblest point of art;
> Whose pictured morals charm the mind,
> And through the eye correct the heart.

People still come to visit Hogarth's grave and lay flowers on it sometimes.

Another artist, Philip de Loutherbourg, is buried in the churchyard. There are details about him on a following page describing Hammersmith Terrace.

Chiswick Mall

It is a beautiful walk, at any season, from St. Nicholas's church by the river all the way to Hammersmith Bridge. One walks for more than a mile by seventeenth and eighteenth century houses, gardens, an island, a pier and many pleasant pubs. *Bedford House*, an imposing Georgian mansion at the beginning of Chiswick Mall, was for years the home of the Redgrave family, Sir Michael Redgrave, his wife Rachel Kempson, and their children Vanessa, Lynne and Corin. Further along is *Walpole House*, a sixteenth to eighteenth century mansion where Barbara Villiers, Countess of Castlemaine and Duchess of Cleveland spent the last years of her life. She was 'the fairest and the lewdest of the Royal concubines', a beauty with dark auburn hair and melting eyes; Charles II was devoted to her and she was mother of three of his sons. Many portraits were painted of the beautiful Barbara—it was a quirk of hers to be painted either in the role of saint or mourner. People who knew Barbara loved her but the nation deeply disapproved of her. Pepys once watched her at a Royal pageant in Whitehall when some scaffolding fell on the crowd. She was the only one of the great ladies to run into the street to see if anybody was hurt and to look after a child shaken by the accident. There she stood, talking with some young man; she was hatless and borrowed his hat to keep off the wind. 'It become her mightily,' wrote Pepys, 'as everything else do.' She managed to keep the king's affection for years in spite of exquisite rivals; on one occasion the king, his queen and Barbara spent a merry evening together. The people of England were greatly shocked.

Dryden wrote poems to Barbara; Wycherley fell in love with her. When she died her funeral was magnificent, two dukes and two earls were pallbearers. She is buried at St. Nicholas's but without a monument.

Walpole House became a school in the early nineteenth century and Thackeray was a pupil there. It's said that he used the house in *Vanity Fair* as Miss Pinkerton's Academy, at which Becky Sharp hurled her dictionary when she drove away in triumph. An eighteenth century house near Hogarth's, called *Boston House*, also claims to have been Becky Sharp's school.

The Walpole House gardens are open on one Sunday in late April: there is an iris garden and a wealth of spring flowers. Next door, in the less stately, more delicate *Strawberry House* the gardens are opened on the same Sunday and are rich with camellias and magnolias.

In summer the front of Strawberry House hangs with wisteria; all the gardens on *Chiswick* and *Upper Mall* are full of flowers. There are lavendar hedges, tall magnolias, a palm tree, a great many vines. Hammersmith vines used to make famously good wine. Opposite the island of *Chiswick Eyot* are more gardens and lawns. River and road sometimes join when the Thames floods; local children enjoy that. They splash through the shallows in rubber boots and ride bikes through water lapping on the pavement. The houses facing the island are of mixed centuries . . . Georgian . . . Victorian . . . Edwardian. Some are rather like houses in Worthing built to face the English Channel.

Until recently there was a bakery at the end of Chiswick Mall and ghostly figures white with flour came out for an occasional breath of air which was sweet with the smell of new bread. The bakery is gone and handsome new brick houses stand in the aptly-named Miller's Court.

Beyond Chiswick Mall is *Hammersmith Terrace*, a row of houses built in 1755 with gardens going down to the river. The oddest of the terrace's inhabitants was Philip de Loutherbourg who lived at Number 13. He was a painter and an R.A. (there are some dramatic pictures of his at the Tate), and he also worked as chief scenic designer at Drury Lane. Then he took to prophecy and healing. Walpole, very amused, wrote in 1789: 'Loutherbourg is turned an inspired physician and has 3,000 patients. His sovereign panacea is barley water; I believe it is as efficacious as mesmerism . . . I am glad of it. The more religions and the more follies the better.'

Hammersmith Terrace was crowded on de Loutherbourg's 'Healing Days' with people hoping for cures from blindness, deafness, lameness and loss of speech. When one of his so-called miracles failed, the crowds turned into a mob and rioted, breaking his windows. He had to escape by a back door.

At Number 7, further along the terrace, Sir Emery Walker lived for many years. He collaborated with William Morris as founder of the Kelmscott Press. Walker was an antiquary as well as an expert typographer and had a big collection of Medieval books from which he took some of the beautiful Kelmscott types—one is fifteenth century Venetian. He used to walk down the road every day to visit Morris at his house in Upper Mall where they worked at the Press together.

The Thames's friend and patron, Sir Alan Herbert, lived at Nos. 12 and 13 for more than 50 years until his death in 1971. He was author, poet, M.P., playwright, essayist, wit and sailor. The Thames lost one of its best friends and poets when he died.

At the end of the terrace is a new stretch of gardens created on the site of a factory which used to stand on the river bank. The gardens, imaginatively designed, have kept part of the old building as a sort of arched wall. There are broad paved walks and lawns, seats by the river and a low-set patio with slides and climbing frames for the children. Some new houses beyond the gardens have an open arcade running beneath them, with views of the water. The arcade leads to the expanse of *Upper Mall* and the pleasing front of *Linden House,* an old Queen Anne house now the headquarters of the London Corinthian Sailing Club. At week-ends the courtyard and quay are crowded with people in sweaters, jeans and rubber boots, bending over damp sails or busy with their dinghies and surrounded by the irresistible clutter of sailing. The club's starting box is a circular wooden eyrie raised on a stout pole by the water, from which the judge watches the red or white sailed boats scudding by.

Two famous houses in Upper Mall have gone for ever. Charles II's widow, Catherine of Braganza, lived here in a house celebrated for its flowers, though someone (it sounds like John Evelyn) said they were 'mostly of the common kind'. Near by was Hyde Lodge where Queen Anne's physician Doctor Radcliffe lived. He had planned to turn his house into a hospital but died before the work was finished. His famous library went to Oxford.

Kelmscott House (1790) is at the end of Upper Mall. Two well-known people lived here—Francis Ronald and William Morris. Ronald invented the electric telegraph in this house in 1816; when he offered his invention to the Admiralty they turned it down because, with the Napoleonic wars over, 'telegraphs are now totally unnecessary'. The 8 miles of cable which were in his garden can be seen in the South Kensington Museum.

There is a plaque, hidden by a large magnolia, to William Morris who lived in the house for the last eighteen years of his life. Most people know that Morris was a leader of the Pre-Raphaelites, an artist and a poet, and that he designed fabrics and wallpapers graceful with Medieval figures and flowers. But his vision is probably more important today than ever before. He foresaw, in the first industrial age, the dangers of machine-made objects becoming dull and monotonous: he wanted to use machines to make beautiful things.

Morris moved to Chiswick Mall in 1878, delighted by its peace and nearness to the Thames, 'the situation' he wrote 'is certainly the prettiest in London'. He changed the house's name, calling it Kelmscott after his old Oxfordshire home. At Chiswick, he founded the Kelmscott Press with Emery Walker —it was based in the next door studio now over the garage.

Together they revived the art of fine printing as it was done in the fifteenth century, designing and printing remarkable books. All Morris's work shows his love and knowledge of nature, of birds, flowers and trees, and the type faces, borders and ornamental letters of the Kelmscott books are rich with a natural invention. The Kelmscott Chaucer is said to be the finest printed book ever produced. There is a copy in the British Museum and another in the library at Hammersmith. At Kelmscott House some of William Morris's wallpapers are still on the walls.

A narrow alley at the end of Upper Mall runs alongside the famous seventeenth century *Dove* inn, usually called the Doves. In the eighteenth century it was The Dove Coffee House and 'wits and citizens resorted to it . . . to sip their coffee, enjoy the sweet prospect of the river and talk over the literature and politics of the day'.

In an upstairs room, the eighteenth century Scots poet James Thomson wrote the first part of his poem on *The Seasons*. It was a poem of winter; he wrote while the Thames was frozen and the country outside covered with snow. Thomson's poetry was admired by all the great literary people—Doctor Johnson praised him, so did Coleridge and Hazlitt. *The Seasons* began a new era in English poetry. In the same upstairs room he wrote the words of *Rule Britannia*; Doctor Arne set them to music and they were sung for the Prince of Wales.

Thomson was a sociable person but famously lazy—a friend once saw him in his garden, hands in pockets, munching only the 'sunny side' of some peaches hanging on the trees. One of his poems is called *The Castle of Indolence*. But he also liked long fast walks from his home at Richmond to visit Pope in Twickenham, or to London. On one of these walks he took a boat at Hammersmith Mall and was rowed to Kew in the biting cold; he caught a chill and died soon afterwards at the age of 48.

Watermen used to land their cargoes from barges by the Dove. H. G. Wells came here and the pub is featured in A. P. Herbert's novel *The Water Gypsies*—it's called The Pigeons. The Dove has three low-ceilinged bars which don't seem to have changed for a couple of hundred years, and a vine-covered terrace overlooking the river. At lunchtime or in the evening it is usually lively with people, many of them sailors or rowing men. There is hot or cold food, including delicious hors d'oeuvres and—a rarity in pubs—a cup of coffee. Which seems only right for an eighteenth century Coffee House.

The wide stretch of *Furnivall Gardens*, with lawns and flowers and cherry trees, is popular in fine weather. There used to be a creek here where the barges unloaded; in 1936 the creek was filled in and the *Hammersmith Pier* built for local boats. Doctor Furnivall was a scholar and literary critic and a Victorian philanthropist—he founded 'The Hammersmith Sculling Club for girls and men' in 1896; he used to spend jolly Sundays on the river with his protégés.

A massive elm stands on the path by the river, large enough to hide behind in a game of hide-and-seek; a survivor of scores of giant elms which grew on both sides of the Thames from Hammersmith to Twickenham. On the left is a prim little Queen Anne house once a vicarage, and now belonging to the local Council, called *Westcott Lodge*. An old-fashioned iron lamp on the wall of the house was presented by Willy Brandt when Hammersmith was linked with West Berlin as twin communities. The lamp used to light a street in West Berlin. But why isn't it lit in the evenings in Hammersmith?

On the Hammersmith reach Roman relics have been found in the river—two Roman keys, some money and a number of long iron strips made to standard weights, these were the Roman currency bars.

Facing the water in *Lower Mall* are two pubs which are very much part of the local riverside—the *Rutland* and the *Blue Anchor*. The crews of the rowing clubs crowd into them, people sit at tables by the river wall and at week-ends everything is very lively and social. The Rutland is the larger, with a Victorian atmosphere and an open fire in wintertime. The Blue Anchor is small and brightly painted, not unlike the interior of a ship.

There are some eighteenth and early nineteenth century houses along Lower Mall; one with a balcony, Number 9, was the home of George Devine, founder of to-day's Royal Court Theatre; he lived and worked in this house.

Stretching along the riverside at this point was a very celebrated mansion and its gardens built in Charles I's reign and 'famous for its splendour'. During the Restoration Prince Rupert bought the mansion for his mistress Pegg whom Pepys kissed, remarking that she was pretty but not modest. The house was enlarged and altered in the eighteenth century, made even more splendid with a gallery of statues, doorways with lapus lazuli pillars, gardens brimming with flowers and fruit. Doctor Johnson was a guest at the mansion sometimes. In the late 1790s the English-born Margaravina of Brandenburg-Anspach came to live in the house. She called it by her own name,

Brandenburg House, and lived in great style attended by 30 liveried servants. She kept a stud of 60 horses, built a theatre in the gardens where she acted herself to invited audiences of the nobility—'her talents . . . captivated every heart'.

The last person to live at Brandenburg House was the Prince Regent's unhappy wife Caroline. He had only married her so that Parliament and George III would pay his debts; he had always disliked her. When the couple separated, Caroline wandered round Europe, a royal exile. The Prince Regent became king and Caroline came back to London, to be refused entry at the Abbey on Coronation Day. There was a national scandal. While she lived at Hammersmith the Prime Minister introduced a bill to dissolve the Royal marriage and take away her title and rights as Queen. The country was horrified. Thousands of seamen demonstrated, marching in columns, 'each man with a white cockade in his hat'. Scores of Thames watermen and lightermen arrived by river in decorated barges which they moored by Brandenburg House's garden walls. They presented an address to the Queen, accompanied by cannon fire and music. Because of the people's indignation, the bill was abandoned; but Caroline died soon afterwards. When George IV heard of her death he was perfectly indifferent and 'partook most abundantly of goose pie and whiskey'. A few months afterwards the house was pulled down.

Hammersmith Bridge, now protected as a monument, was built in 1887; there was another bridge at this point designed by Tierney Clarke in 1827, the first suspension bridge over London river. It was simple and impressive with stone towers and an arched entrance described as 'Tuscan'. Clarke later made an enormous reputation by designing the bridges at Buda-Pest.

The present Hammersmith bridge is loved by Londoners for its fanciful decoration and pinnacles; it was designed by Sir Joseph Bazalgette, the engineer who created the Thames Embankments. Only the superstructure of the bridge was new— it stands on the piers of Clarke's chain bridge. The low pillars which mark the two entrances are decorated with coats of arms. People sometimes think these have an exotic significance; there was a local story that the bridge was intended for Canada and the coats of arms were French-Canadian. In actual fact they are the arms of the then-Metropolitan Boards of Works and of Middlesex, Kent and Guildford.

In the centre of the bridge, looking upriver, is a bronze plate on the wooden hand-rail. It commemorates a Lieutenant

Charles Campbell Wood, R.A.F. of Bloemfontein in South Africa who dived into the Thames at this spot at midnight in September 1919 to save a drowning woman; he later died of his injuries.

Boys fish on the beaches by the bridge when the tide is right. Although the water still looks pretty dirty, it is coming alive again; between the reaches of Hammersmith and Barnes there are those Thames inhabitants, roach and dace, eels and bream.

*Detail from Battersea Shield—2,000 year old Celtic treasure
found in the Thames.*

6 RIGHT (SOUTH) BANK
Barn Elms
Duke's Head and Star & Garter
Boat Race
Putney Bridge
St. Mary the Virgin
Wandsworth Park
Wandsworth Bridge
Old Swan, Battersea
St. Mary's Battersea
Battersea Bridge
Battersea Park

The last countrified walk beside the Thames is on the right (South) bank, walking from Hammersmith Bridge towards Putney. After this, except for a short stretch in Wandsworth Park, the Surrey riverside is built up as far as Battersea Park.

The towpath passes that TV landmark during the boat race, the *Harrods Depository*, very like its Knightsbridge parent in ochre-coloured brick with elaborate twin towers. The nearby reservoirs can be fished for a small fee (for big roach and perch), and ducks and gulls feed there. The Barnes Reach runs by the fields and playing fields of *Barn Elms*. These were the grounds of a mansion owned by the Tudor statesman, Sir Francis Walsingham; Elizabeth visited him often at Barn Elms and brought her entire Court with her. It is said that Walsingham died penniless as a result of entertaining his Queen.

For hundreds of years the grounds and lawns of Barn Elms were popular both with the nobility and the people. Charles II and the Duke of York swam in the river here, 'and take great delight in it and swim excellently well' said a watching Londoner. In 1667, the Lord Mayor and his City dignitaries moored their barges by Barn Elms, danced, ate a costly supper and listened to music. Pepys often took a boat from Tower Wharf and was rowed to Barn Elms for 'merry talk and good singing'.

Near the old Tudor mansion was the house of the publisher Tonson, the friend of eighteenth century writers and artists. He built a gallery next to his house and founded the *Kit Kat Club* (his landlord's name was Christopher Kat). Kneller painted portraits of all the club members, a notable group of worldly men in velvets and full-bottomed wigs. The National Portrait Gallery has a whole room full of them; there is Tonson, and Pope, and Kneller himself with a wild head of chestnut hair and a painter's sharp eyes.

Along the towpath by Barn Elms are elms and blackberry bushes, tansy and some venerable old ash trees. Rowing crews go by in scarlet sweaters. An obelisk to Steve Fairbairn, 1862–1938, marks one mile from the start of the Boat Race. Fairbairn founded the *Head of the River race* which takes place every March in the opposite direction to the Boat Race, beginning at Mortlake and ending at Putney. Any rowing club in England can take part and recently as many as 370 Rowing eights have competed . . . the race takes over an hour and it is amusing to watch the succession of skimming boats.

On the north bank of Fulham Reach are wharves and quays with country names, Willowhaven, Crabtree. Many are closed and there are hopeful plans for opening up this river stretch, building houses and flats, a restaurant and a riverside walk. The *Fulham Football Ground* dominates the river bank just before the park. The new stand, which is very fine, cost a quarter of a million pounds. Fulham's team hasn't yet achieved a celebrated history but its players have dash and style.

Treasures have been dredged up in this part of the river. The famous legionary short-sword, the *gladius*, now in the British Museum, was found in the river at Fulham in 1873. And on the Surrey side a small black pottery cup was dredged up; experts believe it is Trojan, possibly brought by traders from Phrygia who came up the Thames selling their wares to riverside settlers. The cup has large looped handles and is one of the oldest and most mysterious treasures found in the Thames.

The towpath ends by a row of boathouses, ships' chandlers and clubs in attractive old buildings facing slipways to the water. Swans are plentiful and in winter there seems to be a large gull standing sentinel on every riverside post. The black-headed gulls arrive from September onwards—they find the living and feeding easier at Putney than in the cold North Sea. In bad weather there are herring gulls too, and greater and lesser black-backed gulls as well as the gentler mallard ducks. Most of the gulls leave the Thames sometime in April.

Two riverside pubs just by Putney Bridge are the *Duke's Head* and the *Star & Garter*. The Duke's Head has windows of engraved glass and a riverside bar, but the redecorated Star & Garter (which has nothing to do with the building on Richmond Hill) is more luxurious and food and wine are excellent. The pub has a revived Edwardian ambiance, with orange globes like gas lamps, richly-coloured curtains and window-seats on a raised gallery. Outside is the river, two churches and the wide sky.

The *University Boat Race* starts just below Putney Bridge; it is rowed every year on a Saturday around Easter and has been raced annually since 1856 and before that, intermittently, right back to 1829. Sometimes in bitter cold and wind, sometimes in blessed sunshine, the crews row 4 miles and 374 yards from Putney to Mortlake. It is still the big event of the London Thames, crowds gather to line both banks of the river and cheer encouragingly as the crews go by. The University boats are followed by a launch with the TV cameras trained on them, then by a mass of steamers, launches and private boats in a great jolly flotilla which creates a rocking tidal wave as it passes; one sees how the Thames pageants used to look. TV has cooled down some of the Boat Race fever of the past. In 1876 the crews came to Putney a week before the race for preparatory trials, and interest in them was so great that the whole of Putney was crowded with people and became 'like a fairground'. Fifty years later, in 1927, the whole country was passionately involved with the Boat Race, wearing the colours of either University and having fierce arguments over who would win. It was London's festival; crowds travelled to Putney, Hammersmith or Mortlake where they stood eight deep, scarcely able to catch a glimpse of the boats when they finally flashed past. 'Then they struggle back amongst the crowds . . . and buy a paper to find out who has won.'

Putney Bridge, built in 1886 of solid Cornish granite and widened in the 1930s, is another of Bazalgette's bridges. There is a church and a tower at each end of the bridge. On the Putney side it is *St. Mary the Virgin*, a landmark for Boat Race crowds for generations though now crowded round with tall blocks of buidings. The church was badly damaged by fire in 1973 but is to be restored. It will look very different from the past—it is planned to design the interior as a large central room with small rooms leading off it to be used both for divine service and for parish affairs. *Bishop West's Chapel* in the church, by a stroke of fortune, escaped the fire. The bishop was the son of a Putney baker and built the chapel early in the reign of Henry VIII; the lovely fan tracery of the vaulting has the bishop's arms and initials.

Before the Thames was bridged at Putney, St. Mary's was a place of prayer for people getting up their courage to ford the river at low tide. And in the seventeenth century Cromwell—no respecter of churches—used it as a meeting place when discussing strategy with the General Council of the New Model Army.

Downriver by *Putney Railway Bridge* a labourer saw a sword sticking out of the mud. It turned out to be a Viking sword; 9 inches of the blade were missing but later these were found in Wandsworth reach. Beyond the railway bridge is the smallish stretch of *Wandsworth Park* by the riverside and further downstream the river Wandle joins the Thames. The Wandle, for all its lovely name, is sadly polluted but there are heartening G.L.C. plans for cleaning up all the little rivers which flow into the Thames. When Izaak Walton wrote *The Compleat Angler* he used to fish in the Wandle, catching trout with 'marbled spots like a tortoise'.

Wandsworth Bridge, plain and red, built in 1938, replaces an iron lattice girder bridge with five spans. The bridge is wide and busy with traffic, the district much industrialized. It seems incongruous that at Wandsworth a German duelling dagger was found in the Thames, its hilt inlaid with gold and silver. A curious fact is that there have been many many more knives and daggers than swords discovered in the river. Nobody knows why.

Beyond the bridge is a long stretch of the river with no riverside walk, towpath or embankment. Travelling by launch along the river here, there is the sharp roasting smell of hops from the local Breweries.

A railway bridge crosses the river from the districts of Hammersmith to Battersea. In the Battersea Reach a magnificent shield was found in the river—it is called the Battersea Shield and was made either in the first century BC or the beginning of the first century AD. It is now in the British Museum and is strikingly beautiful, with a swirling Celtic pattern and red enamelled studs like jewels.

On the right at Vicarage Crescent in *Battersea* is the *Old Swan*; there was an inn by that name here years ago. The swan is old no longer, the new version is built of white clapperboard in soaring shapes, rather pleasant, rather stylish. Inside the pub is not unlike a pier with massive wooden beams, lobster pots and fishing nets. A bench runs the full length of the windows and has dramatic industrial river views. Upstairs is an attractive restaurant with an interesting menu which includes a number of fish dishes.

Battersea is known for its park and funfair, for a certain vanished timber bridge which Whistler painted, and for the Dogs' Home. One of the few churches actually by the Thames is *St. Mary's* in Battersea Church Road, a pillared Georgian church with a lawn by the water and a barge moored by the church wall.

There was a church here before 1777, and when it was pulled down the old monuments were saved and placed on the walls of the Georgian church. Up in the gallery are many monuments to the St. Johns who lived in Battersea. One of the most interesting, in green, white and grey marble, is to Henry St. John, Viscount Bolingbroke and his French wife. There are cameo portraits of Bolingbroke and his beautiful wife by Roubiliac. This Bolingbroke who was baptized in Battersea and inherited the manor there, was a gifted and remarkable man much involved in politics; a man of influence and power and a writer on both politics and philosophy, many people think he was one of the most brilliant of English political writers. But he had a sympathy and goodwill towards France and towards the Jacobites, and in 1715 was impeached and forced to leave the country. He was allowed to come back in 1723. He became friends with Pope and this friendship inspired some of Pope's poetry. Voltaire also visited Bolingbroke and dedicated a play to him. Goldsmith was fascinated by Bolingbroke and wrote his life. He described him as 'ever active, never depressed; ever pursuing Fortune, and constantly disappointed by her . . . [we] find him an object rather more proper for our wonder than our imitation'. His Battersea mansion was demolished in 1778 to build a malt distillery.

On the south of the gallery is the quaintest of St. Mary's monuments with an epitaph to Sir Edward Wynter who died in 1685. He was related both to the Wynter who fought in the Armada, and the other Wynter implicated in the Gunpowder plot. Sir Edward was apparently a heroic soldier and fearless traveller:

> Alone, unarm'd, a tyger he oppressed,
> And crushed to death the monster of a beast;
> Twice twenty Moors he also overthrew,
> Single on foot; some wounded; some he slew
> Dispersed the rest. What more could Sampson do?

The gallery congregation in a church usually have a view of the top of the preacher's head, but in St. Mary's the pulpit is exceptionally high—practically a lookout post just below the gallery's level. The pulpit once had three decks but the lower two were removed.

William Blake, the poet, artist and mystic, married Catherine Boucher at St. Mary's in 1782—she was the daughter of a local market gardener. Wilberforce, the great abolitionist of the Slave Trade, was witness to a marriage here. Turner used to come to St. Mary's to paint the river view. He sat in the small bay window of the vestry and painted the clouds and sunsets of Battersea Reach. The chair he used is on the left of the altar; it has unusually high legs to give the painter a good view out of the window in comfort.

Behind the altar is a Jacobean stained glass window given to the church in 1631 by the St. John family and illustrating, in the way of the nobility obsessed with their genealogy, the family's connexion with the Tudors; there are portraits of Henry VII and Elizabeth and family coats of arms. On either side are two charming circular eighteenth century stained glass windows, one of a dove and one of a lamb, in soft fine colours. The dove window was shattered during the 1944 bombing but the fragments were collected, new glass cut and painted and the window made a perfect whole again.

Beyond Battersea and Albert bridges (covered in a later paragraph) is *Battersea Park*. The park has only been here since the 1850s. Before that time the district was known as Battersea Fields, 'one of the darkest and dreariest spots in the suburbs of London. A flat unbroken wilderness of 300 acres, the resort of costermongers, roughs and vagabonds calling themselves gypsies.' Battersea Fields were rough and dangerous, a kind of no-man's-land where fights broke out and on Sundays the police were powerless to control the hordes of people wandering across the fields and marshes. Duels were sometimes fought—it was far enough out of London for privacy when breaking the law. The Duke of Wellington, of all people, actually fought a duel in Battersea fields in 1829 with the young Earl of Winchelsea who had attacked him with violent abuse over the Catholic Relief Bill. Neither man was hurt.

In 1851 it was finally decided to make the fields into a park 'with an ornamental lake, walks and parterres for the recreation and enjoyment of the people'. Perhaps, also, to tame them and to stop the fighting. The area was wet and marshy, and the whole surface had to be raised by unloading earth excavated from the Victoria Dock which was being built at that time. A million cubic feet of earth was carried along the Thames in barges to raise up the land for the new park.

The park was popular from the moment it opened, and soon famous for its flowers, waterfalls and landscaped prospects. In 1951, a hundred years later, something was added to the park for the Festival of Britain. John Piper and Osbert Lancaster designed the new Festival Gardens as a twentieth century version of the old pleasure gardens of Cremorne and Vauxhall.

The new design included a Funfair bordering on to the river— 'the biggest and best fair we've ever been to' Londoners said. The fair, with its ghost trains and big wheel, was very much part of an old-fashioned London fairground tradition. It was finally closed in 1974. At the time of writing it has not been

103

decided how it shall be replaced. One suggestion is for a new pleasure ground on the lines of the American 'Disneyland', described as 'a sophisticated fairground with historical scenes'. But many people living in Battersea would like to see new gardens running down to the river: others would prefer to continue with a new version of the fairground, but keeping it to the English tradition.

The gardens themselves have magnificent trees and flowers, and—a luxury in a great city—tennis courts.

Albert Bridge

7 LEFT BANK
Fulham Church of All Saints
Sir William Powell's Almshouses
Fulham Palace and Bishop's Park
Hurlingham House, Battersea Bridge
Chelsea Embankment
Cheyne Walk, King's Arms
Crosby Hall
Chelsea Old Church
King's Head and 8 Bells
Cheyne Row, Carlyle's House
Albert Bridge, Physic Garden
Royal Hospital, Chelsea
Ranelagh Gardens
Chelsea Bridge, Vauxhall Bridge
Tate Gallery, Millbank Tower
Lambeth Bridge, ICI building

On the north bank by Putney Bridge is Fulham's *Church of All Saints* which faces the park belonging to the Bishop's Palace.

The church looks very plain despite its fifteenth century tower, but although it was rebuilt in the late Victorian period it has marvellous monuments of earlier centuries. At the foot of the tower is a sumptuous monument to Lord Mordaunt of Avalon, 1675; he is dressed in a Roman toga, has curling hair and a moustache, and holds the baton of Constable of Windsor Castle. On either side is a little marble pediment, one for his coronet, the other for his gauntlets. Alas, the long epitaph is in Latin. There is also his pedigree showing 600 years of blue blood back to William the Conqueror.

Beside this monument is a plaque to Theodore Hook who is buried in the churchyard. Hook is almost forgotten now; he was the kind of eccentric practical joker and outrageous friend whom eighteenth and nineteenth century aristocrats enjoyed. He wrote novels, edited John Bull in its heyday and was famous for his wit, his pranks and sociability—statesmen, authors, even Royal Dukes enjoyed being with him. After a lifetime of amusing the great, he died of brandy, a bankrupt. The bronze and marble plaque was put up by his granddaughters.

The ten bells in the church tower were cast by the eighteenth century master of the art, John Ruddle; each has an inscription. One is engraved 'Peace and good neighbourhood', another 'I to the church the living call. And to the grave I summon all.' One bell merely says 'John Ruddle cast us all'. The bells have a fine soft peal which people have always liked. One Thames waterman in 1829, discussing the bells of London, said: 'Of all the bells, give me Fulham, they are so soft, so sweet.'

Against the east wall in the south aisle is a lozenge-shaped Flemish brass to Margarat Svanders, a Flemish lady who died in 1529. The brass was buried during the Civil War and dug up again in 1770; it was found at the foot of one of the church columns. Margaret Svanders, shown in her shroud in a half-length portrait, was married to a painter from Ghent, Gerard Hornebolt. She and her husband came to England when her daughter married the Keeper of the King's Wardrobe. Margaret is mentioned by Dürer as being in Antwerp in 1521 when she was 18; this brass portrait is in a Dürer-like style.

Inside the communion rails on the right of the altar is a Tudor effigy (1603) to Lady Margaret Legh, elaborately dressed in farthingale and ruff, her hair in tight curls; she holds a baby muffled to his nose in swaddling clothes and another baby is propped up beside her. Lady Margaret bore seven sons and two daughters.

Near to the Flemish brass is a wall monument to William Paine of Pallenswick who erected the memorial himself. He and his wife, in Jacobean clothes, kneel in prayer, but there is no date of Paine's death. He bequeathed the little islet of Mackenshaw by Kew Bridge to Fulham church 'forever'; small dues from the moorings still come in every year from this bequest.

It is worth searching out one more marble monument tucked away on the left of the altar; this is to Katharine Hart, 1605. It shows her in a stomacher, a ruff, and wearing a delicious little hat. Her four children are kneeling round her; her hand is on the head of one of her sons who himself holds a skull, the symbol that he died as a child.

Outside the church, slightly behind it and facing a garden are *Sir William Powell's Almshouses*. They were founded in 1680 for twelve poor widows, rebuilt in the eighteenth and again in the nineteenth century. They are delightful, ornamented in brick and honey-coloured stone, with Art Nouveau statues, including one of Ruth with a sheaf of corn and the text 'God's Providence Our Inheritance'. The houses have a lawn and a hedge dividing them from the *Bishop's Park*, the grounds of *Fulham Palace*.

The palace was the summer residence of the Bishops of London for nearly 900 years; they only left here in the early 1970s. There are many interesting plans for the palace. Hopefully there will be rooms for concerts, a permanent exhibition of the pottery and paintings of William de Morgan, meeting-rooms, and in the park a botanical garden and an adventure playground for handicapped children.

Fulham Palace is built low and much hidden by a number of ancient brick walls and thickly-growing trees. There have always been tall trees round the palace; when one of the bishops thinned them down a wit remarked that he must be a man to throw light on dark places. The palace is part Tudor and built round two courtyards, one with a fountain in the middle. The remainder of the buildings are mixed eighteenth and nineteenth century. It is very peaceful near the Bishop's Palace, pleasantly far from busy Fulham whose traffic is scarcely heard. Birds sing from all the palace trees.

In the history of Fulham Palace, Bishop Juxon has an important place, for he was the friend of Charles I and attended him on the scaffold. Charles gave him his gloves—preserved at Lambeth Palace still—and spoke his last mysterious word:

'Remember'. The gardening bishop at the Palace was Bishop Compton whom James II banished to Fulham for two years. Compton spent his time filling the palace gardens with curious and exotic plants and trees never before seen in England, including an ilex and a huge cork tree.

There used to be a moat round the palace; it has been turned into a garden of lavender bushes and roses, heather rockeries and yuccas which flower in summer and autumn with thick, cream-coloured blossoms. A magnificent avenue of plane trees stretches into the distance beside the raised riverside walk known as *Bishop's Walk*, a favourite vantage point for watching the start of the Boat Race on the Surrey bank opposite.

Between Putney and Wandsworth bridges there is one eighteenth century mansion still on the riverside, *Hurlingham House*, a stately place with a pillared portico in a park of chestnuts, acacias and copper beeches; there is a good view of the house from a river launch. Hurlingham House was built in 1760 by a Doctor William Cadogan who refused to be worried by the fact that his grounds had been a pest house and plague pit as recently as 1736. The house was altered in 1803 when the neo-classical front was added to what the doctor called his 'cottage'.

Hurlingham became famous for polo, the game newly-brought from India by the army in 1869; the club became a visiting place for European royalty. At one gathering at the time of Queen Victoria's Diamond Jubilee, 40 Royal Highnesses . . . kings, queens, princes and princesses . . . came to Hurlingham in a single day. The grounds were a mass of noble guests and the Guards' Band played.

The glamour ended in 1939 when, at the beginning of the war, the polo grounds were turned into allotments. The game never returned to Hurlingham which is now a private club for tennis, golf, cricket and croquet.

Beyond Hurlingham, going east, the riverside is mostly wharves. There is the Heliport, and Fulham Power Station, and finally the river walks begin again just before *Cheyne Walk* in Chelsea.

Here by Cremorne Road is the site of the old *Cremorne Gardens* which used to stretch for 12 acres from King's Road to the Thames. The gardens must have been an enchanting sight; they sparkled with hundreds of lanterns and had a landing stage for the penny steamers which were crowded with good-humoured visitors. Cremorne opened in the 1830s and was at the height of its popularity and fun by 1860; it continued to shimmer with lights and crowds until 1877. There was a theatre, a concert room, a dining hall; there was an open-air dance floor round which the crinolined girls were swept in the waltz to music played from a bandstand shaped like a pagoda. Cremorne's great speciality was balloon ascents. One man was reported to descend from a height of 2 miles. Another, in a machine shaped like a bird with a peacock's tail, fell to his death.

The gardens were rowdy and loud with music, dazzling with fireworks. Among the famous Chelsea people who lived near by, Carlyle disliked Cremorne very much, Rossetti enjoyed it and Whistler sketched it. In the end the gardens' rowdy character was its downfall, it was called a place of immorality and was closed.

The elaborate wrought-iron gates with lions' heads which stood at the entrance to Cremorne now belong to the Chelsea Council who have them in store, waiting for a new home ...

Battersea Bridge.
When people think of a bridge at Battersea, they conjure up the timber bridge of 1772. It was built on a slight curve, lit by strings of lamps, and its slender-seeming outline was painted by Turner and Whistler. It was a very bewitching bridge and people say its disappearance changed the face of Chelsea.

The present iron bridge, built by Sir Joseph Bazalgette, is decorated with turquoise scrollwork and is pleasant enough. Bazalgette was the engineer of the *Thames Embankments*. He had previously worked for the Commissioners of Sewers and when he joined the Metropolitan Board of Works ... there was no GLC or LCC then ... he began his project of remedying 'the evils from sewage flowing into the Thames'. It was an enormous achievement—over 1,300 miles of new sewers were built as well as new pumping stations; the embankments were part of the plan for the two main out-fall sewers were built to run on either side of the river. While the sewers were being dug extraordinary things were found under London: bones of elephants, whales and oxon, flint implements, skulls, Roman coins, and stone and lead coffins.

The look of Bazalgette's Embankments are not much admired today (the job they achieved is accepted as a matter of course). The granite walls are heavy and ponderous; but the same engineer enhanced the riverside with dolphin-twined lamps, lions holding iron rings in their mouths and seats supported by camels and sphinxes.

Chelsea Embankment begins just before Battersea Bridge. Facing Chelsea Reach is the lovely *Cheyne Walk*. Traffic is heavy and sometimes deafening; it is a miracle that the row of marvellous houses where so many painters and writers and poets lived, manages to survive. On the river in front of Cheyne Walk is a colony of houseboats reached by unsteady gangways, a remnant of the messy romantic old Chelsea of the past.

The first house in Cheyne Walk going east is No. 119 where Turner lived, using the assumed name of Booth. He was already famous and had come to live and paint in Chelsea in anonymous peace. The Thames watermen took a fancy to him and nick-named him 'The Admiral' because of his sailorlike appearance and weatherbeaten face. Turner painted the river many times from the window of this house and often climbed on the roof to watch the dawn. He died in his room on the first floor in 1851; the river reach facing the house is sometimes called *Turner's Reach*.

A few doors along is the *King's Arms*, built two years before the Great Fire. There are traces of old ovens in the cellars—the house used to be a bakery for Chelsea buns; but it was not the legendary Bun House where on a single Good Friday the baker sold a quarter of a million fresh buns and even Royalty came to buy the hot spiced delicacies. The old Bun House was demolished in the last century. The King's Arms has a pleasant upstairs restaurant with a river view through the trees where one can dine by candlelight, and a cheerful ground floor bar, liked by the local Chelsea people.

Wilson Steer lived at No. 109 Cheyne Walk for 44 years until his death in 1942; there is some of his work at the Tate Gallery. His work was influenced by Whistler and more by Manet whom, he said, had a 'delayed action' on his way of seeing and painting. Steer was shy and inarticulate and his art students loved him; sometimes he would watch a student painting for some time then merely mutter 'I'd go on with that.' George Moore was his friend and made affectionate fun of him in his book *Conversations in Ebury Street*. Steer went shopping in Chelsea accompanied by his large cat; he walked around oblivious of traffic and was once knocked over by a car. Sickert sent him a telegram: 'Do be careful—I have no desire to be the greatest living painter.'

The odd-shaped corner house, No. 104 Cheyne Row, was the

home of Walter Greaves and later of Hilaire Belloc. Greaves has a special place in the hearts of local people, he has a Chelsea ambiance about him. He and his brother were boatmen; Whistler asked them to do odd jobs in his house, they decorated some rooms, prepared his canvases and gradually became fascinated by painting. Whistler agreed to teach them to paint in return for being taught to row with what he called 'The Watermen's Jerk'. Whistler and the two brothers were soon close friends. They rowed him out to Battersea at night and he sat in the boat making notes for paintings. But in later life, he became too grand for his old boating companions.

Walter Greaves painted Chelsea scenes for many years; he never became famous and his pictures only sold for a few shillings. Today experts see a touch of genius in his work and his comic spirited *'Hammersmith Bridge'* is at the Tate. A further irony is that in 1974 a collection of Whistler's paintings were established as actually having been painted by Walter. Whistler allowed him to paint in his studio and when Whistler went bankrupt in 1892, his model and mistress Mary Woods (whom Whistler wouldn't marry) went off with a load of eighty or ninety canvases which she believed were by Whistler. Now it's proved that most of them are by Greaves.

Lindsey House is set back from the road with a paved court-yard and wrought iron gates; it's one of the few manors left in Chelsea. It was built in 1640 by a Swiss doctor who had been physician to two French Kings and two English Kings, James and Charles I. His house had a wide river frontage and although plain, was magnificent; later it was bought by a Count Zinzendorff for the group of gentle religious brothers, refugees from Bohemia, called the Moravian Brothers. Their burial ground, with a mulberry tree descended from one of Thomas More's, is off Milmans Street. The Lindsey House mansion was later divided into six houses numbered 95 to 100; in the centre house the Brunels, father and son, lived from 1808 to 1824. Marc Brunel was busy planning the first tunnel under the Thames; Isambard was still a little boy.

The house next door to Lindsey House, in a paved courtyard, is No. 96, Whistler's home for 12 years and the place where he did some of his finest work. When he came to Chelsea he was already fascinated by Japanese art and he decorated the house with matting and Japanese prints and long shelves full of blue and white porcelain; to the Victorians used to plush and clutter the plainness of the Japanese style was staggering.

Whistler's mother came from America to live with him at Chelsea; an austere reserved lady, she deeply disapproved of her son having a mistress and Whistler had to pack the girl off as soon as possible. Of all the mothers of painters, she was destined to be known the world over . . . Whistler painted a portrait of her called merely: '*Arrangement in Grey and Black.*'

Carlyle was very impressed with the picture and agreed that Whistler should also do his portrait. Whistler's friends were pleased and relieved for he badly needed work, and it must surely enhance his reputation to paint the venerable and famous Carlyle, the Sage of Chelsea.

Carlyle was an old man and a brusque one; he arrived at Whistler's studio wearing a long overcoat and a wide-brimmed hat, sat himself down and said briefly: 'And now, man, fire away!'

It was definitely not the way Whistler liked to work.

The two never got on; Whistler had no interest in Carlyle's great works and Carlyle found the painter annoying and tiring. Whistler's portrait of him is in essence very much like the painting of his mother—austere and plain. The old man sits with bowed back, wrapped in a shawl; it is considered a work of genius.

Whistler's tastes, Whistler's gift, changed a great many things in London . . . most of all it altered the world's view of the city. He loved the dirty, poverty-stricken buildings in the filthy smoke-filled air; he painted them into poetry. 'They lose themselves,' he said, 'in the dim sky and the tall chimneys become *campanili*, and the warehouses are palaces in the night, and the whole city hangs in the heavens.'

A blue plaque on a small house, No. 93, commemorates the birth of *Mrs. Gaskell*, the Victorian authoress; but it was the briefest of times that she stayed here. Her mother died when she was a baby and the child was taken away from Chelsea and brought up by her aunt in Cheshire.

What is curious about *Crosby Hall* is that it was literally moved stone by stone to Chelsea from Bishopsgate in 1910. 'A marvellous monument transplanted' wrote Henry James who lived in Chelsea then. The hall was part of a huge old mansion in the City built by a wool merchant, John Crosby, in 1470. After his death Richard III took over Crosby Hall and made it a royal palace; the hall is the setting for some of the dark action in Shakespeare's *Richard III*. In 1501, Katharine of Aragon was entertained at Crosby Hall and fifteen years later Thomas

More bought the mansion; some historians say he lived here. It is a coincidence that Crosby Hall now stands on land which was part of More's gardens in Chelsea.

The Hall belongs to the British Federation of University Women and is used as their dining-room, but it is possible to visit it. The hammer-beam roof has carved pendants like coloured lanterns; there is a minstrel's gallery and a high oriel window with John Crosby's crest. Near the door is a huge old Jacobean table and a set of stamped patterned leather chairs; these are Spanish and belonged to Katharine of Aragon's doctor. They were given to the University by Lady Astor. There is also a Holbein of the More family; the painter made three copies of the picture for More's three daughters.

Thomas More came regularly to *Chelsea Old Church*, his riverside manor was only a short distance away, and he built a chapel here where his first wife is buried. The church was badly damaged by bombing in 1941 but fortunately the chapel on the right, near the altar, survived. Holbein was living with the Mores at Chelsea when the chapel was built and he's said to have designed the capitals of its pillars. Here is a long wall inscription composed by More, his coat of arms (with a Moor's head) and those of his two wives. Written in Latin he wishes his second wife and himself to be buried in this vault.

When he was beheaded for treason his head was taken to Canterbury; but there is a Chelsea tradition that Margaret Roper somehow conveyed his body back to Chelsea for burial.

The church is well-restored and cared for and its history has not been destroyed. But its ghosts have gone. Henry Kingsley, the Victorian writer, knew the church well when his father was its rector and his description of it creates a place of haunting memories: 'The dead stand thick together there, as if to make a brave resistance to the moving world outside, which jars their slumber ... I cannot fancy anyone being married in that church—its air would chill the boldest bride that ever walked to the altar.' Now the sun floods through windows of plain glass, and marriages are frequent and festive.

On the north side of the chancel is the Lawrence chapel where, according to Wriotheseley's Chronicle, Henry VIII secretly married Jane Seymour some days before the official Royal marriage in 1536. Thomas More, the man Henry had loved and later imprisoned and executed, was gone from Chelsea. The king began to build a Chelsea palace for his new young queen.

113

Some of the monuments which crowded the walls when Henry Kingsley shivered in the old church are still in their places. There is Sara Colville, who died in 1631, wearing a shroud and rising heavenward 'in ye 40th yeare of her age received ye glorious rewards of her constant piety being ye happy mother of 8 sons and 2 daughters'. Under a window, with daylight falling on her shapely head, is the monument to beautiful Lady Jane Cheyne, a heroine of the Civil Wars. She was the Duke of Newcastle's daughter and she and her sister, besieged in their home and surrounded by Cromwell's soldiers, buried the family silver and hid the paintings; when the house finally surrendered, the girls were made prisoners. Jane managed to sell her jewels secretly and smuggle the money to her father who had escaped to Holland. After the Restoration Jane's large dowry bought Henry VIII's old Tudor palace in Chelsea. Jane and her husband lived there and she also helped to rebuild the church. When she died, at 48 years old, she was deeply mourned. Dryden wrote:

> Make much of her, ye saints, for God knows when
> Your Quires will ever have her like agen.

Her husband asked the sculptor Antonio Raggi to make her monument 'in her habit as she lived'. So there is Jane, leaning gracefully on her elbow, dressed in a stylish seventeenth century gown and pendant earrings. The architect of the monument is believed to have been Paolo, the son of Bernini.

The many embroidered kneelers in the church commemorate people with Chelsea connexions—there is one to Bartholomew Nutt who ferried the congregation across the Thames before there were bridges. There are kneelers to the More family, including one to Margaret Roper. Thomas More's love for his daughter Margaret and hers for him echo down the centuries. On the day before he died he wrote her a letter from the Tower, using a piece of coal, 'I never liked your manner towards me better than when you kissed me last, for I love when daughterly love and dear charity hath no leisure to look to worldly courtesy.'

Near the door of the church on the right are the only chained books remaining in a London church; they include the *Vinegar Bible*. This is the name given to the 1717 edition which contains a printer's error: the parable of the vineyard is printed as the 'parable of the vinegar'. The books were given to the church by

Sir Hans Sloane, whose fine monument is outside the churchyard; Sloane was a famous physician and a great collector whose books and treasures were the beginning of the British Museum. He was also a well-known botanist, and it seems suitable that cherry trees and flowers and lavender bushes grow round his stone urn.

When Whistler lived in Chelsea he used to walk with his mother every Sunday morning to Chelsea Old Church. When they arrived at the door she went into the church and Whistler walked home.

In front of the church is an impressive statue, a black-robed figure with a gilded face and hands; a modern sculpture of Thomas More by L. Cubitt Bevis. Three words are carved round the pedestal: Scholar, Statesman. Saint. More sits, with the Chancellor's gold collar which he surrendered for conscience sake in his lap. When the statue was put up in 1967 the saint united three churches for a little while; the church of England and of Scotland, and the Catholics were all represented at the ceremony. A More sermon is preached in Chelsea Old Church every July and a Catholic Mass is said in a church in Cheyne Row dedicated to him. It is followed by a procession and a pilgrimage to the Tower where he died.

The site of Beaufort Street and the land surrounding it and running down to the river was Thomas More's house 'the greatest hall in Chelsey' and his gardens. It was a fine Tudor mansion built, as they usually were, round courtyards, with gardens and orchards and a home farm. Down by the riverside was a flight of steps where the Chancellor kept his barge—he had eight watermen to row him to Westminster.

The family and their friends lived a close united life in the Chelsea house; there was time for prayer, for conversation, for study and for fun. More had a little zoo in the garden and kept rabbits, a ferret, a fox and a monkey; the monkey is in Holbein's painting of the family. More is an enigmatic character; he had an austere taste, wore no silk, drank only water, but his nature was 'rather, to mirthfulness than to gravity'. In person, he was described by Erasmus as 'neither tall nore short, but well proportioned, white skinned and pale ... deeply set eyes which have specks in them—indications of a happy disposition'.

The More mansion, that 'sweete place in Chelsey' as John Evelyn called it, survived until the eighteenth century. It belonged to many noble families and must have been very beautiful, with long lawns sloping to the river, orange trees, flower gardens and luxuriantly growing orchards. But when in

1737 Sir Hans Sloane bought it, it had already begun to crumble. Sloane in any case only bought it to extend his own property (he owned Henry VIII's old Manor). More's house was demolished during the 1740s, and the Inigo Jones gateway erected in Jacobean times was given to the Earl of Burlington.

It is teasing and annoying to read about great houses and realize there isn't a trace, not a wall or tower, remaining today. But a visitor to Chelsea may at least like to know that Henry VIII built a Royal mansion on land which is now Cheyne Walk. Henry had taken a fancy to the healthy riverside when he used to visit Thomas More in Chelsea—he thought that the country air would suit his children. The year after More died the king began to build a mansion in Chelsea; it was to be the nursery for his baby son Edward and for his young daughters. At the end of his life the king gave Katharine Parr the Chelsea house as part of her dowry and she lived there. A hundred years later the gallant Lady Jane Cheyne bought the manor.

Hans Sloane moved to the Royal manor in 1712 from Bloomsbury and brought his famous collection with him. He was already in his eighties and intended to leave Henry VIII's manor to the nation as a place to house his library of 50,000 priceless books, his vast collection of statues, Egyptian mummies, gold and silver, porcelain, instruments. He also had a Natural History collection of fish and butterflies, insects, snakes and lizards. But when he died in 1753 the parsimonious Government were not in the least interested in preserving Henry VIII's manor. They moved the collection back to Bloomsbury where it became the nucleus of the British Museum. The historic house was pulled down. Many houses in Cheyne Walk have, as part of their garden walls, old portions of Henry's nursery palace.

Further down Cheyne Walk is the *Kings Head and 8 Bells*, a lively pub from which one can see the river. The food and snacks are good, the leather settees comfortable, and there's an amusing series of silhouettes showing naval uniforms from 1787 to 1822.

The pub is on the corner of *Cheyne Row*; a short walk up this road is No. 24, *Carlyle's home* for fifty years. Of all the houses of the famous on the riverside this is perhaps the most satisfying; it is more or less exactly as it was when the Carlyles lived here.

Carlyle came to London to househunt in 1834 and wrote to Jane about the Cheyne Row house enthusiastically . . . 'on the whole a most massive, roomy, sufficient old house; with places, for example, to hang say three dozen hats or cloaks on . . . Our

Row ... runs out upon a beautiful "Parade" ... huge shady trees; boats lying moored and a smell of shipping and tar ... the broad River with white-trousered white-shirted Cockneys dashing by like arrows in their long canoes of Boats.'

Do people leave an invisible mark in the air if their possessions are still there? The narrowish house is furnished with the chairs and desks, patchwork cushions, paintings, photographs and scrapbook screens which Carlyle and Jane chose and used. On the ground floor is the room they called the parlour where Jane welcomed Leigh Hunt so warmly that he afterwards wrote the enchanting poem which begins: 'Jenny kissed me when we met, Jumping from the chair she sat in.' Over the fireplace in the parlour is a painting of the room in 1857; it is the same today.

The most Victorian thing about the house is the dark colour of the wallpaper; a paper resembling mahogany was chosen by the Carlyles who covered up all the eighteenth century pine panelling. The pretty staircase is eighteenth century and so are the hand-turned spiral banisters.

When Carlyle became famous after the publication of the *French Revolution* the house was thronged with celebrated visitors; the Carlyles used the first-floor room as their drawing-room, as the parlour had become too small. Tennyson and Dickens came to visit them, and Chopin, and the dandified Count D'Orsay whom Jane rather disliked to start with but later described as a 'devilish clever fellow'. Tennyson became a family friend and he and Carlyle used to sit smoking clay pipes in the small back garden for hours.

At the top of the house is the room which the Carlyles called the *'garret study'*, prepared by Carlyle as a place for work and soundproofed against Chelsea's distracting noises. There were many noises to disturb him ... pianos and street organs, children shouting, cocks crowing, the barking of dogs. The room, unchanged like the rest of the house, is large but not light; there are photographs of him in his garden, a photograph of the room when he worked there, the fire cheerfully burning. There are the books Goethe sent him, a letter from Disraeli beginning: 'Sir—a Government must recognize intellect.' Some of the letters are from Jane in a dashing, impulsive hand ... 'And didn't Mr. C. kiss me wildly,' she writes, 'and call me his Guardian Angel.'

Carlyle lived in Chelsea to the end of his life. He used to go for long solitary walks and his figure was familiar, known to everybody. He was so deep in thought that he was quite unconscious of carriages when he crossed a road; cab drivers, seeing the tall bent figure would shout 'All right, Mr. Carlyle.'

When Carlyle was old an American pastor who visited him in Cheyne Row wrote a vivid description:

'We were shown into a plainly-furnished room on whose walls hung a rugged portrait of Oliver Cromwell. Presently an old man, apparently over threescore years and ten, walked very slowly into the room. He was attired in a long blue woollen gown, reaching down to his feet. His grey hair was in an uncombed mop on his head. His clear blue eye was sharp and piercing. A bright tinge of red was on his thin cheek, and his hand trembled as he took our own. This most singular looking personage reminded us of an old alchemist.'

A bronze statue of Carlyle, seated and looking towards the river, is in a small riverside garden near the end of the road.

The *Albert Bridge* crosses the Thames opposite Oakley Street; it is an enchanting suspension bridge, many people's favourite of the London bridges, built in 1873. A mass of lattice-work girders make it look rather like the superstructure of a sailing ship; its arches are decorated and painted in blue and ochre, and at night it is strung with lights. The *Cadogan Pier* is just east of the bridge with many smart craft moored here.

Cheyne Walk continues for a little further east with some imposing Georgian houses. The finest, in a paved courtyard with a blossoming jasmine, is No. 16; its iron gateway is topped with the decorated monogram 'R.C.' For years people believed these initials were 'C.R.' and that Catherine of Braganza, Charles II's queen, had lived here. Now it seems they are the initials of the house's first owner in 1717, Richard Chapman. The house became famous when Dante Gabriel Rossetti made it his home.

He was already a celebrated poet and painter and a leader of the Pre-Raphaelites when he came to Chelsea. He had recently lost his wife who had died from an overdose of laudanum. Elizabeth Siddall had been a milliner's assistant who became the model for Millais' painting of the dying Ophelia. Dante Gabriel fell in love with her strange mournful beauty and masses of coppery hair. She became his symbol, the Beatrice to his Dante. He painted her as Beatrice and as the Blessed Damozel. She was a strange girl, 'thinner and more deathlike and more beautiful and more ragged than ever' wrote Madox Brown.

After her death Rosetti was glad to come to Chelsea. He loved the old house and began to furnish it with lavish colour and decoration; there is a painting in the National Portrait Gallery of Rosetti in the drawing-room of this house, reading poems to his friend Walter Dunton. The drawing-room is beautiful, crowded with paintings, papered with Morris wallpaper, coloured turquoise and gold, with books, Dutch tiles and a sparkling fire.

Rosetti led a life of fun and sociability at Chelsea; he gave parties, collected animals and kept them in the garden. There were kangaroos and peacocks, owls and a fat wombat which was said to be the original of the dormouse in 'Alice in Wonderland'. Lewis Carroll came to Cheyne Walk to photograph Rossetti. Ellen Terry visited him and so did William Morris and his beautiful wife Janey for whom Rossetti had a romantic passion. Burne Jones and Millais were constant guests and Swinburne came to live with Rossetti for a while.

Towards the end of his life, Rossetti changed. He no longer enjoyed friends and company, he became melancholy and sad. He was wounded and upset by any criticism of his work and was convinced that he was persecuted. The old house began to decay, the garden where so many brilliant parties had been given was left to grow wild and covered with weeds. But his friends still thought him the most fascinating and magnetic of men. Among Rossetti's paintings at the Tate is his 'Beata Beatrix', the picture of Elizabeth Siddall painted the year after she died; it shows her as a beautiful woman with closed eyes sitting in a kind of trance; beside her is a red bird, the messenger of death.

At the handsome house near Rossetti's, No. 4, George Eliot died. She had lived for years with George Henry Lewes to the scandal of Victorian society; two years after Lewes died in 1878 she married John Cross who—as Lewes had been—was utterly devoted to her. They went for a long honeymoon on the Continent. In the winter they came hopefully to live in Chelsea, believing it would improve her health which was never good in London. Nineteen days after they came to live here she went to a concert, caught a chill, and died.

After Royal Hospital Road joins the Embankment there is a garden behind railings, with a pair of handsome old iron gates decorated with the sign of Apollo and a dragon. This is the Physic Garden begun in 1673 for researching into plants used in medicine by the Society of Apothecaries. Hans Sloane presented the gardens to the Society in 1723 'in perpetuity' and they have been here ever since. A statue to Sloane stands in the gardens.

The Physic Gardens had already become famous all over Europe by the late eighteenth century. Sloane was a fine botanist and gave many rare plants to the gardens; others came from abroad. The Physic Garden is not open to the public but walking by one can see the flowers and trees are not chosen as they are in ordinary gardens. There are many curious bushes, trees and shrubs. The Garden's work no longer concentrates only on plants used in medicine; most of its work is now botanical. Specimens of plants from the Conquest to the present day grow there—it is a living library. More than 30,000 specimens are sent out every year to colleges and schools for study.

On the east of the gardens is the delightful *Swan Walk* of eighteenth-century houses facing the Physic Garden's old brick walls. The balconies of the houses must have an interesting botanical view.

The road now passes the sloping grounds of the *Royal Hospital*, Wren's stately red brick building graced with stone faces the Thames. Everybody wants to believe that a wounded soldier hobbled up to Nell Gwynn's coach to ask for alms, and the warmhearted beauty was so shocked that a man should be forced to beg who had fought for his country that she persuaded Charles II to build the Royal Hospital. Historians say this story isn't true. Somehow it never gets forgotten and the historian Lysons believed it; he cited Nell's sympathy for the suffering and the 'known benevolence of her character'. Charles II had certainly been impressed with Louis XIV's Les Invalides in Paris and decided to found the hospital at Chelsea 'out of a tender and deep compassion for ye sad and deplorable condition of so many loial and brave men'. He was strongly supported by John Evelyn and much of the money was provided by the Army Paymaster, Sir Stephen Fox. The site by the river was chosen by Wren and the magnificent buildings first opened in 1692.

Five hundred pensioners live in the Royal Hospital. In summer they wear brilliant scarlet, in winter navy-blue coats designed in the Duke of Marlborough's time. The Hospital is open to the public, there are interesting things to see and a kindly welcome from a Chelsea pensioner who will show you round.

The pensioners eat in the Great Hall. At the end of the noble panelled room is a portrait of their founder Charles II, begun by Verrio and finished by Henry Cooke. The king is on horseback with the Royal Hospital in the background and Father Thames sitting nearby, a conch shell in his hand. The king's horse steps daintily through a mass of wriggling Thames eels. On a centre table in the Great Hall are six blackjacks, big jugs made of leather which used to hold the pensioners' beer.

The Duke of Wellington lay in state in the Great Hall in 1857; Queen Victoria and Prince Albert came here, followed by the pensioners who filed past to pay their last respects to the country's dead hero. For four days after that the public were allowed into the hall—the crush was so great that several people were killed trying to get in.

The chapel which Wren completed in 1687 is handsome, with a fine black and white marble floor. Over the altar is a wood panel designed with a star and IHS rescued from a church destroyed in the Great Fire. Above the altar is a dramatic fresco of the Resurrection by Sebastiano Ricci and his nephew painted straight on to the plaster—the fresco took them a year and a half and is in the Baroque Italian style; Christ is a Michelangelo figure rising from the tomb, surrounded by the figures of centurions, disciples and angels—every figure in movement of theatrical intensity.

The exquisite wood carving in the chapel is the work of two wood carvers, William Emmett and William Morgan; the altar rails are particularly beautiful, carved with delicate leaves and roses. The Queen's staff, topped with a crown, orb and oak leaves, is carried in procession at the Chapel's services; 'then we know,' say the pensioners, 'that the Queen is with us in spirit.' In a glass case by the altar is a prayer book open at a prayer of thanksgiving for the Restoration, placed there in 1690.

The spacious *Figure Court* is the Hospital's central quadrangle with long colonnades and two projecting wings of the hospital on either side. Facing the Hospital, with his back to the Thames, is a delightful bronze of Charles II by Grinling Gibbons. The king wears a festive Roman tunic and winged sandals and looks his unmistakable, sardonic self. Every year on Oak Apple Day the statue is wreathed in branches of oak to celebrate the king's escape from the Roundheads when he hid in an oak tree after the Battle of Worcester.

The Museum is housed in one of the buildings to the east of the main Wren Hospital; it was opened in 1971 and is full of fascinating things. There is a copy of The Times of 1815 with Wellington's dispatch announcing the battle of Waterloo. 'It gives me the greatest satisfaction to assure your Lordship,' wrote

Wellington to the Secretary of State, 'that the army never, upon any occasion, conducted itself better'.

Pensioners' uniforms from 1692 to 1703 are well displayed; and there are engravings and paintings of Chelsea's riverside past including oyster shells from some forgotten Ranelagh feast in the gardens next to the Hospital. There is a huge collection of medals, many thousands, all glittering with polish as brightly as the pensioners' buttons. And those sad, tattered remnants of war, the flags taken in battle, including a French eagle, the first of its kind captured and brought to England.

In the grounds of the hospital, full of sycamore trees and hollies and alive with blackbirds, the Flower Show is held every May.

On the left of the hospital's London Gate is the Old *Burying Ground* which visitors can see on request. It was consecrated in 1691 and closed for burials in the 1850s. Fanny Burney's father Doctor Charles Burney, organist at the Chelsea Hospital for 23 years, is buried here; the grave the pensioner-guides are most proud of is that of William Hiseland, the pensioner who lived to be 112 years old. There is a portrait of him in the museum, looking oddly like Voltaire. Hiseland's friends admired him and the epitaph on his gravestone describes 'A Vetran if ever Soldier was . . .'

'His Complexion was fresh and florid
His Health Hale and hearty
His Memory exact and ready'.

The poem ends:

'What rendered his Age still more Patriarchal
When above 100 years old
He took unto Him a wife.'

Hiseland, born in 1620 when James I was on the throne, died in 1723 when George II had already reigned for 5 years. He had lived through the Civil War, the Commonwealth, the Restoration, and the reigns of eight English sovereigns.

East of the Royal Hospital is a smallish garden of trees and lawns, the site of the wonderful eighteenth century pleasure-garden— *Ranelagh*. The Earl of Ranelagh leased the land from the Hospital and built a mansion there. After his death the house and gardens were sold and it was then that Ranelagh became the famous place of 'Polite Amusement'. The Rotunda, built of wood, stood in the centre; it was 'a noble edifice, somewhat resembling the Pantheon at Rome ... the interior elegantly decorated, and when well illuminated and full of company, presents a most brilliant spectacle'. A painting by Canaletto in the National Gallery shows the Rotunda at the height of its popularity. Walpole who went to the gardens' opening night remarked that there was 'much nobility and much mob'.

As a place of amusement Ranelagh was unequalled in Europe for beauty, elegance and grandeur. There was music and opera, masquerades and boating on an artificial lake, avenues of trees shining with lights. Shopkeepers, selling Dresden china in their boutiques, wore masks. The refreshment boxes were painted with goddesses and roped with fresh flowers. Walpole visited it nightly and said it was so fashionable that every step he took he trod on princes and dukes. 'Ranelagh is so crowded that in going there t'other night in a string of coaches, we had a stop of six-and-thirty minutes.'

There was a Venetian masquerade, with harlequins, masked dancers, gondolas on the lake and orange trees with a lamp in every orange. All Royalty, nobility and gentry went to Ranelagh to dance and gamble and wear fantastic fancy dress. Sometimes when the guests arrived by boat for a big party, the Thames looked like a floating town. At one musical entertainment a little boy of eight played the organ; it was Mozart.

There was a sigh in English hearts when the gardens were demolished in 1803. 'Ah Ranelagh was a noble place!' said an old nobleman, remembering, 'Such elegance! And such beauty.' There was the Duchess of A—the finest woman in England, sir; and Mrs. B—a mighty fine creature; and Lady Susan what's-her-name, who had that unfortunate affair with Sir Charles. Yes, indeed, sir, they came swimming by you like swans. Ranelagh for me!'

Nearly 70 years after the gardens were gone, a writer visited the place and wrote nostalgically: 'A single avenue of trees, formerly illuminated by a thousand lamps, and over-canopying the wit, the rank, and the beauty of the last century, now forms an almost solitary memento of the departed glories of Ranelagh.'

Under a circular shelter in the garden the site of Ranelagh is marked on a map; the Rotunda was situated somewhere 'between a snake-bite sycamore on the left and a tree of heaven on the right'.

East from the Royal Hospital and the site of Ranelagh is the functional *Chelsea Bridge*, rebuilt in 1935. When the old bridge was built in 1854 all kinds of debris was found in the river; experts think this proves there was a great battle here between the Britons and the Romans. There were iron spear-heads, human skulls and the sole of a Roman military boot.

From Chelsea Bridge to Vauxhall Bridge the walk is loud with traffic but the view of the *Nine Elms Reach* of the river is interesting and dramatic with the huge chimneys of Battersea Power station rising up, trailing tufts of smoke. *Vauxhall Bridge* (1906) has arches painted a sea-like blue and is decorated with enormous Art-Nouveau styled statues. A. P. Herbert, sailing under Vauxhall Bridge, was very entertained by these figures on the pier arches. There is a mighty figure of Agriculture with her scythe, Architecture clutching a model of St. Paul's cathedral, there is also Engineering and Pottery. 'On the lower side,' writes A. P. Herbert in his book on the Thames, 'counting again from the north is a lady who has been described to me as Local Government—or Learning, Education, the Fine Arts and Astronomy'. A. P. Herbert thought that Lambeth Bridge would be improved with some sculptured bishops on its piers.

Vauxhall Bridge was built in 1906—the previous bridge on this site was built in 1816 and called the Regent Bridge but the name was changed to 'Vauxhall' because it led to the Vauxhall Pleasure Gardens on the south bank.

The land which faces the Tate gallery was until 1890 occupied by a huge grim fortress, the Millbank Penitentiary, known to prisoners as the 'Tench'. It was a prison which looked like a Medieval castle and which many people called the English Bastille. It had been planned to follow theories of two prison philanthropists, but it was a horrible place, damp, unhealthy, and with a cruel staff hated and feared by the prisoners. The buildings were designed in the form of a wheel with rows of buildings like spokes coming into a central section, the Governor's house, in the middle; it was said that he could see into every cell from his window.

On the Embankment at this point is a buttress which stood at the top of some steps down which the prisoners were taken to ships bound for deportation to Australia. There is a fountain there now and riverside seats, and a great bronze by Henry Moore with the enigmatic title 'Locking Piece'.

Tate Gallery
Built in 1897 on the site of the hated Tench, the gallery has a cool neo-classic look. A bronze girl by Renoir, 'The Washer-

woman' kneels half-way up the flight of steps and other bronzes decorate the small terraces at either end of the building. The Tate contains two National collections; a superb collection of English painting from 1500 to 1900 and a foreign collection showing the work of painters and sculptures over the last hundred years. Only a sixth of the Tate's riches can be shown at one time and the work on view is constantly being changed.

The English collection, beginning in the sixteenth century with Nicholas Hilliard, goes through the centuries. There are portraits by Lely, Kneller and Hogarth. There are galleries glowing with the eighteenth century midsummer of English painting, Gainsboroughs and Reynolds and Stubbs. The collection of Turners is very remarkable, for he left the entire contents of his studio to the nation—300 oils and 19,000 water-colours and drawings. All the oils save ten are at the Tate, who also have many of his watercolours. There are Constables, Samuel Palmers, Cotmans and numbers of the extraordinary visions in paint and pencil by Blake.

There is also a vivid collection of Pre-Raphaelites, and many Victorian genre paintings; these seem to show, more than in literature, the chasm between Victorian morality and ours, particularly when the subject is a 'fallen' woman lying at the feet of a noble, unrelenting man.

The late Victorian and present-century period of inter-national painting is shown in many very beautiful Impression-ists and Post-Impressionists, including Monet and Degas, some wonderful Gauguins, Cezannes and early Picassos.

Modern English painting is strong, with Pipers, Sutherlands and Francis Bacons. Finally, there is the Sculpture Hall; there is a dancer by Degas, an impassive King and Queen by Henry Moore, some massive Hepworths. And the immortal embrace of Rodin's 'The Kiss'. It is impossible to list all the riches of the Tate in a short paragraph; the galleries are spacious and tempt-ing and the Tate attracts people of every age. There is a pleasant feeling of interest and vitality.

Just east of the Tate is the *Millbank Tower* which appears to be built mostly of glass; rather dull in daytime, it is an oblong of diamonds at night from across the river.

Two obelisks, on both river banks, mark the entrance to *Lambeth Bridge*, with its handsome red arches. The bridge, built in 1932, faces the Horseferry Road on the north bank. Before Westminster Bridge existed this was the only place along the river where horses were allowed to be ferried; the ferry-boat station was just by the palace of Lambeth on the south bank and the ferry was large enough to take a coach and six horses.

Beyond Lambeth Bridge is the tall building of *ICI*; its entrance doors are rather remarkable. They are 20 feet high, weigh 5 tons, open and close by electricity and have no locks; the doors sculpted in bas-relief are something of a curiosity. They show the history of scientific discovery and its effect on man. Each of the panels tells a story; there is man hunting the mastodon with ropes made of grass, prehistoric man's first way of farming . . . the panels trace progress right up to a scene of Faraday lecturing to the Royal Institute with Darwin and Huxley sitting in the audience. They were made in 1928 and designed by W. Fagan.

Houses of Parliament from Albert Embankment

8 RIGHT (SOUTH) BANK
Vauxhall Bridge
Albert Embankment, Old Father Thames
Lambeth Bridge
Lambeth Palace
St. Thomas's Hospital
The South Bank Lion
County Hall
South Bank Gardens, Shell Centre
Hungerford Bridge
Royal Festival Hall, other halls and
National Film Theatre
National Theatre

On the south bank after the green spaces of Battersea Park there is no riverside walk until *Vauxhall Bridge*, a mile down-river. *Vauxhall Gardens* were by the river bank where the bridge now stands. The gardens were opened in 1732 by a man called Jonathan Tyers who bought eleven acres which had been part of a riverside mansion. He decorated the gardens with taste and skill, added a statue of Handel by Roubiliac and engaged an orchestra. The gardens were popular from the first; Doctor Johnson was a friend of the proprietor's son and he and Boswell visited Vauxhall frequently, sometimes bringing Joshua Reynolds 'dressed in velvet, of course'. Johnson described Vauxhall as 'that excellent place of amusement . . . peculiarly adapted to the taste of the English nation . . . a mixture of curious show, gay exhibition, music, vocal and instrumental, not too refined for the general ear, for all which only a shilling is paid'. Later the price of entry to Vauxhall skyrocketed.

The gardens were filled with trees and flowers, a star-topped Chinese pavilion, a Fountain of Neptune with five sea horses. There were the long walks ending with picturesque artificial ruins. Hogarth decorated one of the pavilions; masked parties called Ridottos were the fashion. Guests arrived by river, landing at a flight of steps leading up to the gardens. Vauxhall was famous for two things—its nightingales and its pretty women. A poem of 1737 describes:

> '. . . the walks, orchestras, colonnades,
> The lamps and trees, in mingled lights and shades.
> The scene so new, with pleasure and surprise,
> Feasted awhile our ravished ears and eyes.
> The motley crowd we next with care survey,
> The young, the old, the splenetic, and gay,
> The fop emasculate, the rugged brave,
> All jumbled here, as in the common grave.'

Walpole never missed any fun or high fashion and came to Vauxhall constantly in the 1750's, describing with pleasure how: 'We minced seven chickens into a china dish, which Lady Caroline stewed over a lamp with three pats of butter and a flagon of water . . . She had brought Betty, the fruit-girl, with hampers and strawberries and cherries, and made her wait upon us, and then made her sup by us at a little table.'

In Thackeray's *Vanity Fair*, Rebecca Sharp and her friend

6 Hammersmith Bridge, designed by Sir Joseph Bazalgette in 1887—
fancifully decorated, much loved by Londoners (see Chapter 5).

7 *One of the few London churches which stands right on the river's edge—St Mary's, Battersea (1777) where Turner often painted the Thames (see Chapter 6).*

Amelia go to a party at Vauxhall where Jos Sedley, who accompanies them, gets sadly drunk on rack punch. The gardens were successful and festive for another hundred years; Dickens and Landseer came to Vauxhall together and watched the Duke of Wellington actually attending an entertainment called 'The Battle of Waterloo'.

The gardens lingered on until 1855 but they were losing their glitter. 'Low prices brought low company,' wrote John Timbs, 'the place seemed literally worn out; the very trees grew scrubby and shabby, and looked as if they were singed; and it was high time to say, as well as seen in letters of lamps, "Farewell".'

The *Albert Embankment* which runs between Vauxhall and Westminster Bridges now replaces the girls and the nightingales. The Embankment is similar to Bazalgette's other two, broad and heavy, with plenty of space and the river wall decorated with the dolphin-entwined lamps. In a modern block which it shares with the National Coal Board is *Old Father Thames*, a pub which is not old but modern and busy; one cannot see the river from the ground floor but there is a magnificent panorama of the Houses of Parliament's towers and pinnacles and the arches of *Lambeth Bridge*.

There was a pretty, three-span suspension bridge at this point built in 1862; the present bridge by Sir Reginald Blomfield and G. Topham Forrest was built between 1929 and 1932. It is painted red and gold and sometimes at night is beautifully floodlit.

When this was London's only horse ferry, on one bitter December night in 1688, James II's queen, Mary of Modena, escaped from Whitehall Palace and was rowed across the river. She left the palace secretly at midnight, accompanied by a French noble and taking her six-month old baby son, the Prince of Wales. The night was dark and stormy, they could scarcely see each other in the boat which was 'one frail plank between her and eternity'. When the queen landed on the Lambeth shore she stood with her eyes full of tears trying to see the lights of Whitehall reflected in the black, rushing river. She had left James at Whitehall.

The coach had not arrived for her and she had to shelter under the walls of Lambeth church for an hour before the coach arrived to take her to Gravesend on her journey to France. The baby asleep in her arms in the rain was James, later the Old Pretender.

Lambeth Palace 1708

Lambeth Palace is just east of the bridge, beside the old church of St. Mary which is now closed. The palace has been the London home of the archbishops of Canterbury since the twelfth century, and is the only palace except for Hampton Court and the Tower which still stands on the banks of the Thames. The gardens of the palace used to slope down to the water and the Archbishop kept his barge here, moored in readiness for river trips to Westminster and Whitehall. The last archbishop to keep a state barge at Lambeth was Archbishop Wake who died in 1737.

Edward the Confessor's sister Goda had a manor on this site; a pious princess, she gave it to the see of Rochester, and it became the residence of the archbishops in 1209. It is now an impressive mass of buildings of various dates with a number of ancient towers including the Lollards' Tower and Morton's Tower, which is the magnificent brick gateway at the entrance.

Like Westminster Abbey the palace belongs to nearly a thousand years of English history. Archbishop Chicheley built the Lollards' Tower in the early 1400s as a prison-place for the heretical followers of Wycliffe. Iron rings to which they were chained, their names and fragments of last messages are carved in a dusty prison high up in the tower. Cardinal Morton built

Morton's Tower in the early 1500s; Thomas More was his page and attended the cardinal in the chamber over the archway. It was at Lambeth that Cranmer helped Henry VIII to obtain his divorce and confirmed his marriage to Anne Boleyn. Cardinal Pole, Mary Tudor's archbishop, was the last Catholic archbishop of Canterbury. Mary often came to visit him and dine with him at the palace.

When Elizabeth became queen she too visited the palace to see her Protestant archbishop. Somehow Elizabeth, despite her good Protestantism, could never get used to the Reformation's law by which a priest could marry. Having been entertained by the archbishop and his wife, Elizabeth remarked to the lady:

'*Madam*, I may not call you, *Mistress*, I am ashamed to call you; yet though I know not what to call you, I thank you.' To this day the wife of the Archbishop of Canterbury has no official title. He is called 'My Lord' and takes highest precedence. His lady remains plain Mrs. It seems a long time for Elizabeth's prejudice to last . . .

The public are sometimes admitted to the palace; in July in recent years a garden party has been held in the grounds in aid of some of the churches in the district, and the Guard Room, Great Hall and Chapel have been opened to visitors.

The palace's handsome buildings are grouped round a wide courtyard. Along the wall of the Great Hall is a flourishing fig tree originally planted by Cardinal Pole in the sixteenth century. Today's tree was grown from cuttings of Pole's tree and bears many pounds of figs every autumn. Over to the right are the Abbey gardens and fields where boys from Westminster School are allowed to play football and cricket.

Inside the palace the old *Guard Room* is now a state dining-room; once it was the place for the arms and armour kept for defending the palace. The room has a fine timbered roof, oak wainscotting and a magnificent series of half-length portraits of the Archbishops of the past. The lords of the Church had taste as well as riches—the portraits over the centuries are by Holbein, Van Dyck, Hogarth, Reynolds and Romney.

The *Great Hall* built in the thirteenth century has a magnificent hammer-beam roof with pendants carved to look like hanging bunches of flowers. The Hall was badly damaged during the Commonwealth, but later was carefully repaired.

The great halls of Medieval and Tudor buildings were used for entertaining vast numbers of guests; there was a tradition of hospitality and generosity among the nobility. A list of

Cranmer's household staff gives an idea of the numbers of people working in the palace and the variety of their jobs; it begins 'steward, treasurer, comptroller, gamator, clerk of the kitchen, caterer, clerk of the spicery', and goes on with bakers and cooks, butlers and waiters, chandlers and ushers and yeomen, and at least a score more groups of servants. The Tudor Archbishop Parker commanded that all strangers who came to the palace should be given meals, entertained, given rooms and comfort. The Archbishop, said a contemporary writer, 'loved hospitality, and no man showed it so much or with better order'.

The Great Hall is now the library for the palace's famous collection of rare books and chronicles; there are many illuminated manuscripts, one from 900 AD, books printed in the fourteenth century by Caxton and books which belonged to Cranmer and to Charles I. In a glass case on the wall is a pair of fine suede gloves embroidered with gold and silver thread. They are the gloves Charles I handed to his friend Archbishop Juxon who attended him on the scaffold.

The palace was taken over by Cromwell's army during the Civil War, and the *Chapel's* wonderful stained glass windows which told the story of man from the Creation to Judgement Day were smashed to pieces. The soldiers used the chapel as a room for dancing. The chapel was destroyed, a second time, during the 1940 bombing. The windows have been remade in the original designs, edged with borders of blue gentians, lilies and birds. The Archbishop celebrates morning and evening service every day in the chapel and many foreign Church dignitaries, entertained at the Palace, come to the chapel. The Archbishops of Canterbury travel abroad to visit churches all over the world and the chapel is full of gifts . . . an ikon from Russia, a carved statue from the Philippines, a ninth century fresco of Christ from the Pope.

On the floor of the chapel are some tiles similar to those in the Chapter House of Westminster Abbey; they are very old, perhaps eleventh century, and may be tiles which were on the floor of the manor house which belonged to Edward the Confessor's sister. Some are patterned with leaping deer.

In the gallery which now holds the organ is a small balustraded room overlooking the chapel: it was Cranmer's study where he composed the Book of Common Prayer.

From Lambeth Palace it is a pleasant walk down the rarely-busy Albert Embankment past *St. Thomas's Hospital*, very much part of Lambeth's riverside though it has only been here for a hundred years. The hospital was originally part of the Abbey at Southwark founded by Augustinian monks. When Guy's Hospital began in Southwark in the eighteenth century the two hospitals worked side by side. St. Thomas's moved to Lambeth in 1862. The old operating theatre of St. Thomas's can be seen at Southwark in an old church in St. Thomas's street off the Borough High Street. The theatre, opened in 1821, is a plain gloomy room with banked seats for students and a wooden plank as an operating table. No anaesthetics then. No anti-septics. In an attic room next door is a display of herbs grown for medical uses in the hospital and an exhibition of photographs and drawings of nineteenth century surgery . . . enough to make twentieth century flesh creep.

Queen Victoria opened the eight turreted pavilions of St. Thomas's, opposite Parliament, in 1871. Florence Nightingale chose the hospital as the place for founding her nurses' training school; the nurses still wear caps shaped like hers but they wear them back to front. When they qualify, trained nurses are called 'Nightingales' and wear her badge. Florence Nightingale also took part in planning the Victorian hospital's pavilions, which are now disappearing . . . four have already gone and dramatic new hospital blocks are rising in their place.

Along the Albert Embankment the swan-decorated seats are raised on platforms to give a view of the river, the bridges, and the long panorama of Parliament. Below on the river wall are the lions' heads, which also line the river walls beyond West-minster Bridge in King's Reach.

On the east side of *Westminster Bridge* is the *South Bank Lion.* This robust but not aggressive beast was made in 1837 and used to stand on the river front of a Lambeth brewery—he was the brewery trade mark. The lion is made in something called Coade stone, an artificial substance invented in the eighteenth century and developed at a Lambeth factory by a lady called Eleanor Coade. Coade stone is almost impervious to weather; the secret of how to make it is lost. The South Bank lion survived the war and, by the particular request of King George VI, was preserved. He was first placed by Waterloo station and now guards Westminster Bridge.

It's often said that the old high-spirits and practical jokes of people like Theodore Hook in the last century have gone for ever. But not long ago some joker painted huge paw-marks in weatherproof red paint descending from the South Bank lion's plinth. The beast apparently gets loose sometimes; the pawmarks padded across the bridge and down the Embankment, finally climbing over the wall into St. Thomas's.

County Hall, palace-like, stands east of Westminster Bridge on the South Bank. When the site was being excavated in 1910 a third century Roman boat was dug up here. County Hall was designed by Ralph Knott in 1912 but was not completed until 1933. It is very much a building built by and for committees and as the headquarters of the GLC is a kind of mini-parliament. The public can attend meetings on matters which interest them. River lovers may like to visit the central foyer of County Hall where there are two aquaria full of healthy fish. These are fish caught recently in the Thames by Westminster bridge—a total of 63 species of fresh and sea water fish which have come back to the cleaner Thames. There are some beauties: the thin and thick-lipped grey mullet, sparkling sea trout, haddocks and herrings, and the lissom-swimming sole.

The *South Bank Gardens* run from beyond County Hall as far as Hungerford railway bridge. This is the best riverside walk in central London, with the King's Reach to the left and lawns and trees to the right. Even in the stuffiest weather there's a breeze, and in winter it is chilly but inspiriting to walk by the water and watch the police launches licking along at high tide. There's a sea-front feeling. Huge towers rear up but do not oppress because there's air and space. In the evenings the small trees are strung with lights.

The towering *Shell Centre*, with a fountain in the courtyard, stands back from the gardens just before *Hungerford Bridge*, a railway and footbridge; pedestrians cross from the South Bank to Charing Cross with thick latticed railings between them and the clattering trains. The bridge is built on the piers of the old Hungerford suspension bridge and the footway extends in a half circle above the piers, giving a magnificent view downriver of Waterloo Bridge's wide arches, the trees of the Temple, St. Paul's and the green dome of the Old Bailey.

On the Charing Cross side of the river, on the site of the Charing Cross Pier and the Embankment, was an ancient building called Hungerford Stairs. 'A crazy breakdown old house, abutting the river, of course, and swarming with rats,' Dickens wrote. When he was a little boy of ten Dickens was employed to sit in a room on the first floor, covering pots of paste-blacking with oiled paper.

A flight of steps from Hungerford Bridge leads to the raised walk in front of the *Royal Festival Hall*, one of the two most important concert halls in London (the other is the Albert Hall). The Festival Hall was designed by Sir Robert Matthew and Sir Leslie Martin, and built in 1951 for the Festival of Britain. It was much criticized at first, but it has now settled into the London scene and is accepted as one of the best of London's post-war buildings. It has wonderful acoustics, and is insulated against the noise of traffic, trains and planes.

On the same high terrace, overlooking the riverside walk, are the *Hayward Gallery*, the *Queen Elizabeth Hall* and the *Purcell Room*. Beside the river and partly under the arch of Waterloo Bridge, are the two cinemas and restaurant of the *National Film Theatre*.

The whole group of South Bank buildings is interesting and unexpected, with flights of steps, spiral stairways, terraces and galleries at different levels . . . there are few solid masses, all kinds of surfaces and many varied shapes of building. Perhaps the concrete is rather heavy and its colour a little sombre but even that has many versions of grey, from soft to dark. The buildings are on pillars, like trees in a stone forest, and real trees and a flower bed or two can be seen from beneath them. When the halls are crowded and busy with audiences they have an evanescent beauty. People walk by the river, the Festival Hall staircases and huge windows are bright with light, and figures are thrown into dramatic silhouette.

On the east side of Waterloo Bridge is the newest addition to the South Banks art centre—the *National Theatre*, designed by Denys Lasdun. It is a very dramatic addition to the riverside, with great splayed stanchions underpinning the many-levelled buildings, and walls of bleached white concrete ribboned with glass windows, topped by the fly-towers of the three auditoriums. The Olivier, with its open stage, is the largest of these; the Lyttelton is a more conventional proscenium auditorium; the Cottesloe is a small studio. Off the auditoriums and foyers are the many outside terraces all overlooking the river, and forming a large part of the public spaces, the three auditoriums being intimate in feeling. There are bars, a restaurant, and two self-service buffets. Set round an open courtyard in the heart of the building are the actors' dressing-rooms, and also backstage are two large rehearsal-rooms and a number of smaller ones. The workshops integrated with the theatres, include costume workshops, wigmaking, carpentry, scenic paintings, and even shops for metalwork, and an armoury.

135

Tomb of Mary Queen of Scots in Westminster Abbey

9 LEFT BANK
Victoria Tower Gardens
Jewel Tower
Houses of Parliament and Westminster Hall
Parliament Square
The Abbey
St. Margaret's, Westminster

The *Victoria Tower Garden* is a long thin triangle of lawns and trees stretching from Lambeth Bridge to the Houses of Parliament. Raised seats by the river wall give a view of passing launches, the towers of Lambeth Palace and the rising blocks of the new hospital.

Facing Millbank is a bronze figure, fur-collared and dressed in the fashion of Edwardian high society; it is *Mrs. Pankhurst*, a demure image of a leader for whom impassioned followers chained themselves to railings or nearly died, forced-fed, in prison. At the base of the statue in bas relief is Mrs. Pankhurst's daughter Christabel and the symbol of a Prisoner's Badge. Both Mrs. Pankhurst and her daughter were imprisoned many times while campaigning for women's suffrage.

On the lawn is a bronze replica of Rodin's *Burghers of Calais*—the original is in Calais. The figures wear ropes round their necks, one holds an enormous key. When Calais fell to the English after Creçy, Edward III intended to hang the burghers in revenge for their long resistance; but his queen, Philippa of Hainault, who came from Flanders persuaded the king to spare their lives.

The elaborate *Buxton Drinking Fountain* was put up in 1865, the year slavery was abolished in America. It commemorates the emancipation of slaves in the British Empire in 1834 and is in memory of Fowell Buxton, Wilberforce and the other M.P.s who helped to abolish slavery. The fountain is elaborate and Victorian, with statues of kings, decorated mosaic and coloured tiles, but is sadly in need of repair.

Facing the Victoria Tower on the other side of the road is a bronze by Henry Moore, *Knife Edge*, on the lawn in front of the *Jewel Tower*; this little low tower is one of the few remaining fragments of the old lost Palace of Westminster. The Jewel Tower, of Kentish ragstone, was built in 1090 and was originally a monastic prison belonging to the Abbey; Edward II bought it to house his jewels. Round the tower the moat is filled with water and in summer with flowering water lilies. The building is three storeys high, with a large and small chamber on each floor joined by a winding stone stairway. On the ground floor are a number of great stone bosses and capitals of pillars saved from old Westminster palace. They are curiously carved with the figures of knights, eagles, lions and birds. A watercolour by Alan Sorrel shows the Jewel Tower before the Reformation; the monks busy in walled gardens, a knight riding by. On the first floor is a Saxon sword found near

Westminster Hall, a slender-bladed weapon with a decorated bronze hilt.

The Royal treasure stayed in the Jewel Tower until the 1540s when it was moved . . . in the seventeenth century the tower was used for storing the House of Lords' records. These were removed to the Victoria Tower in 1864.

The old Palace of Westminster

Parliament sometimes uses the name 'palace' for its buildings which stand on the site of a Royal palace originally built by King Canute. Edward the Confessor rebuilt it when he founded the Abbey—he wanted his church and his house side by side.

William the Conqueror thought the palace very inferior to his palaces in France and rebuilt it again; his son William Rufus added the Great Hall, remarking that if people considered the new hall to be big, it was to be a mere bedroom to what he intended later.

Over the centuries, the palace was partially burned, rebuilt, burned and built again. Sometimes it was shabby, sometimes it was glorious. But after a fire in 1512 it was used by Royalty less and less, and when Henry VIII took Whitehall from Wolsey he moved out of Westminster Palace more or less for good.

The palace had been the meeting-place of Parliament for hundreds of years. In Edward I's reign the Commons were allowed to use the Abbey Chapter House (a great circular room also used for the monks' meetings). During the Reformation the Commons moved by the king's permission out of the Chapter House to St. Stephen's chapel in the palace. They sat here for 300 years until the chapel was destroyed in the 1834 fire.

St. Stephen's Chapel must have been a beautiful place; it had long galleries and walls painted with medieval frescoes of saints. Some historians say these were covered up with panelling in Edward VI's reign, others that Wren was the culprit. The Tudor cloisters and the crypt of the chapel are still used today.

The old *House of Lords* was also in the Royal Palace in an oblong pinnacled building; the Lords sat in a room decorated with magnificent tapestries given by the Dutch to Queen Elizabeth to celebrate the Armada—embroidered seascapes filled with blazing ships. Between Commons and Lords was a small stone building with arched church-like windows, the Painted Chamber; it had been the Confessor's bedroom and he was said to have died there. Round the walls of the Painted Chamber was a frieze of historic subjects, mostly scenes of battle, very

139

similar to the Bayeux tapestry. Walpole thought the paintings dated back to 1322 or even earlier. The Painted Chamber was used by both Lords and Commons; the witnesses for Charles I's trial were examined there.

Parallel to the river was the old Star Chamber, given its name because of its star-patterned ceiling. Henry VII started this Court which was answerable only to the king. It came to be hated by the people. The Chamber could hold secret trials and had the power to sentence men to torture though not to death. Just as prisoners were taken to the Tower by river, entering by Traitors' Gate, so the Star Chamber prisoners were taken by boat to the Fleet where there was a similar gate used only for the unhappy victims. During the Commonwealth the Star Chamber was abolished; by an irony of fate, this place hated by so many was responsible for the destruction of Parliament. The Star Chamber when it was old and decayed was used for rubbish. Thousands and thousands of tallies, the notched sticks still used until Georgian times instead of written bills in Government accounts, were piled into the Star Chamber. The tallies grew to such vast proportions that one night they were crammed into the stoves under the House of Lords. Burning sticks fell from the overfilled stoves, caught some panelling and started the great Westminster Palace fire.

London wasn't in the least horrified by the blaze; huge crowds gathered to watch, arriving in boats or standing knee-deep in the river. Every time a particularly large tongue of flame licked into the sky there was a loud cheer. Only the Great Hall and the crypt of St. Stephen's Chapel were saved.

The Houses of Parliament

It was decided to rebuild Parliament on the same riverside site. Characteristically the Duke of Wellington gave his approval for this decision because the seat of Government, he said, should always be strategically placed where it could never be surrounded by a mob.

A national competition was held and of the ninety-seven designs in a style 'to be Gothic or Elizabethan', Charles Barry's designs won. Barry was the right choice for the monumental task. He was a gifted, tough man of enormous energy who had a passionate desire for fame. As Wren had done when building St. Paul's, Barry gathered round him a group of talented artists . . . stone-workers and metal-workers, men who worked in mosaic, in tiles, cabinet-makers, wood-carvers, gilders. Barry moved to

Great George Street in Westminster to be near his work. Twelve years later Parliament was finished and he achieved his dream—fame.

The key artist close to Barry in creating Parliament was Augustus Pugin, whose knowledge of Gothic art has been described as 'unequalled since the Middle Ages'. He was 24 when Barry gave him the huge task of doing the detail drawings of the new buildings. Pugin was architect, illustrator, writer and archeologist; like Barry a man of untiring energy, and a brilliant, swift worker. Pugin used only a pencil, a carpenter's rule and compasses to produce his exquisite drawings; he could work anywhere, even on a steamer in a gale. Pugin loved the sea and sailing and always dressed like a ship's pilot. 'Nothing,' he said, 'is worth living for but Christian architecture and a boat.' His work harmonizes perfectly with Barry's, which is a curious fact, for during their great project the men often quarrelled bitterly.

Besides the massive task of his work for the new Parliament, Pugin wrote and illustrated many books, designed and enlarged churches. At 43, overwrought by the pressures of work, his mind gave way. He died insane a year later.

The Gothic palaces created by Barry and Pugin are world famous; no other English buildings have been painted so often or by such a variety of artists. They have become what Barry hoped, a symbol both of London and of the nation. The buildings look their stately best from the river, for then one can see the graceful whole, the pinnacles and towers, the long rows of sculpted kings, so very like saints standing in alcoves in a building dedicated to prayer long ago. To the west, when the flag flies over the Victoria Tower it shows that Parliament is sitting. To the east Big Ben in its tower burns a lamp to show the same. A bronze of Richard Coeur de Lion rides on horseback in front of Parliament; Cromwell, impassive as Richard is romantic, stands nearby.

Big Ben has become, by usage, the name of the tower as well as the enormous clock it contains. It's said to have been a nickname given to the clock in a debate when Sir Benjamin Hall was Commissioner of Works—he was very tall. Barry had included a clock tower in his designs for Parliament and the Office of Works promised 'a king of clocks'.

The hour bell of Big Ben was cast in 1856 near Stockton-on-Tees, brought to London by rail and schooner, pulled across Westminster Bridge in a cart drawn by sixteen horses and hung in New Palace Yard. It drew gasping and admiring crowds. But it had been dropped on deck during the journey and was cracked. It cracked a second time after it was placed in position in 1859. The Astronomer Royal was consulted in 1862, and from then onwards the clock has been a king. It is famous for its accuracy, and its solemn chimes have been included in the music of London by both Vaughan Williams and Eric Coates. The clock is in a tower 316 feet above the river.

Visiting Parliament

Visitors are only allowed round all the buildings when the two Houses are not sitting. But the public is admitted to the Strangers' Gallery during debates; in the winter it's easy enough to get in, there are small queues or no queues at all. The *House of Lords* is impressively Gothic. Even the notices are in scarlet and black Gothic script. Every corner of the Chamber is carved or ornamented; there are bronze figures of the eighteen Barons who forced King John to sign Magna Carta, a wealth of stained glass, dark carved panelling, wall paintings. The Lords sit on crimson leather benches; the Lord Chancellor as Speaker sits on the Woolsack, a scarlet divan stuffed with wool from British and Commonwealth countries. The custom goes back to Edward III's reign when England's wealth much depended on wool. There are two smaller woolsacks occupied by the judges at the opening of Parliament. All three woolsacks, incidentally, are excessively hard to sit upon. Commanding the chamber and noticeably empty is the canopied throne used only by the Queen at the State Opening.

Matching the detail and colour, the speech used in the Lords sounds curious to modern ears: 'I would like to remind the Noble Lord' being the prelude, perhaps, to sharp argument.

The *House of Commons* is more exciting to visit, particularly at times of national drama. But an unlucky visitor may well see a House poorly attended and find himself listening to a matter being discussed which appears ludicrously small.

After the elaborate decoration of the Lords, the Commons looks well-worn and faded, in spite of being rebuilt in 1950 after being gutted by fire during the war. The members sit or sprawl on green hide-covered benches, the room is panelled in dullish oak. Journalists in a gallery behind the Speaker's chair sit in rows, looking like Victorian students at a lecture in Medical School. On the table facing the Speaker is the Mace, some despatch boxes and two books of Common Prayer.

The two scarlet lines woven into the carpet down the centre of the chamber are intriguing; these measure two sword-lengths apart and no member may step over them during a debate.

In the Commons on an interesting day one can watch the Prime Minister and the Opposition Leader confronting each other and listen to the cheers and jeers, shouts of disapproval and ironic applause which hasn't changed much for centuries.

Visiting all the Houses of Parliament

Walking through the empty, Gothic building when the House is not sitting, it seems dazzling, romantic and a little absurd. A Gothic revival could go no further. Perhaps the Victorians saw themselves as living in Malory; in a shimmering world of pre-Raphaelite colour, gleaming with mosaic and graced with noble statues (sometimes of themselves). Everything in the building and decoration of Parliament works harmoniously. But the wall-paintings are surely the worst in the world.

Visitors go into the building by the Royal Entrance used by the Queen at the State Opening, and walk up the Royal Staircase to the *Queen's Robing Room*. The name is deceptive for it is a large panelled room of state decorated with bas-reliefs, a throne, and a pleasing portrait of the young Victoria; there are also paintings from the Arthurian legend, that favourite of the nineteenth century. The Robing Room leads into the *Royal Gallery* which is vast—110 feet long and built on the scale of a medieval Great Hall. The enormous frescoes (The Death of Nelson, Wellington and Blucher at Waterloo) are by Maclise; there are many Royal portraits of which the eighteenth century ones are best. There is also a model of the old palaces of Westminster in Henry VIII's time.

The ceiling is gold, the windows of brilliantly blue stained glass and there is a frieze of the arms of English and Scottish kings—the effect is beautiful and impressive.

The *Prince's Chamber* is the ante-room to the House of Lords; there is a large marble statue by Gibson of a charming, still-girlish Victorian holding a sceptre and 'supported by Justice and Mercy'. On the walls are copies, with gilded backgrounds, of portraits of almost every English sovereign and many queens from the Tudors onwards.

Beyond the House of Lords is the *Peers' Lobby*, its gilded gates patterned with Tudor roses. The same rose, worn out by many feet, is on the tiled floor. On the walls of the *Peers' Corridor* is a series of strictly impartial paintings of Stuart and

Cromwellian history. With rigorous fairness first Cromwell, then Charles I, is presented as hero. All the frescoes in the corridors were painted by various Victorian Academicians; they look exactly like naïve illustrations in an old-fashioned history book for children.

The *Central Lobby* is very magnificent with a glittering mosaic ceiling, graceful gilded Plantagenet kings and queens, and candelabra the size of young trees. The lobby is full of life on weekdays, crowded with M.P.s, staff, police, all busy in a Gothic setting of roses and crowns.

The *Commons' Corridor* is painted with more of the Stuart and Cromwellian frescoes and leads to the *Commons Lobby*, an impressive square room decorated with statues of twentieth-century statesmen. The best is a bronze of Churchill (Oscar Nemon, 1969) which stands beside the arch rebuilt at his suggestion with stones from the burned-out House of Commons. Churchill is standing in a characteristic attitude, hands on hips, about to address the house. Members passing the statue on their way into the House often rub the toe of the statue for luck—it's now a burnished gold.

After the 1834 fire, the only building in the old palace which survived was the *Great Hall*. This was incorporated into Barry's newly-designed buildings and is beyond St. Stephen's Porch.

William Rufus built the Great Hall in 1097. John Stow in Tudor times wrote: 'All the Kings of England since the Conquest . . . have they in the great hall kept their feasts of Coronation.' The Great Hall was a place of celebration. There were Christmas and Pentecostal feasts, Royal weddings at which 30,000 dishes of meat were served. The Hall's nearness to the river meant that it was constantly in danger of floods. In 1236 when the river flooded, men rowed wherries in the Hall; six years later at another flood they had to ride through the hall on horseback. After one flood the floor of the hall was covered with fish.

At Richard II's coronation feast in 1377 the King, dressed in a gold robe sewn with pearls, watched one of his nobles fully armed riding into the hall as the King's champion to challenge anyone who opposed the king's claim to the throne. The gallant custom lasted for 500 years and was carried out for the last time at the coronation of George IV.

Richard II rebuilt the hall, spent Christmas there with joustings every day and entertained huge numbers of guests. The Courts of Justice, including the King's Bench, were also

8 *The Royal Hospital, Chelsea, designed by Christopher Wren for Charles II's army veterans (see Chapter 7).*

9 *The National Theatre, designed by Denys Lasdun, seen from Waterloo Bridge: a dramatic addition to London's riverside (see Chapter 8).*

10 *The Houses of Parliament, with police launch from the Thames Division on patrol (see Chapter 9).*

established in Westminster Hall; so were the early Councils which later became Parliament. Both English justice and the governing of the country began in the Great Hall of Westminster.

The Law Courts continued here from the thirteenth century until 1825 when they moved to a building close by; they moved to the Strand in 1882.

All the great state trials were held in Westminster Hall. Thomas More was condemned to death here in 1535; the Duke of Norfolk—for championing the cause of Mary Queen of Scots —in 1571. Elizabeth's once-loved Essex was condemned to death here, and Guy Fawkes in James I's reign was tried here. In 1648 the English king was brought to trial.

Charles I's trial lasted just four days. Sitting in the Great Hall, the king remained impassive during the proceedings, though once when he was called 'tyrant, traitor and murderer' he laughed. He'd never been able to speak well in public for he had a speech impediment, but at his trial he spoke fluently and clearly. On his death-day he said: 'This is my second marriage day. I would be as trim today as maybe for before tonight I hope to be espoused to my blessed Jesus.'

Twelve years later Charles II was proclaimed king at the gate of Westminster Hall. The following year the Act of his father's trial was burned in the Great Hall by the common hangman.

In the eighteenth century Warren Hastings was tried here; the trial became such a fashionable event that tickets cost 50 guineas each. Hastings was on trial for seven years before he was acquitted.

One of the last century's great banquets held in Westminster Hall was for the Coronation of George IV. A contemporary engraving shows the guests seated in tiered galleries erected in the hall to make it like a theatre; trumpeters stand on the balcony. There are lamps hanging from the hammer beams and the floor is covered with rich carpets. The King's champion wearing armour gallops in to give his challenge. At the banquet the thousands of guests ate 7,000 lbs of beef and veal, washed down with Burgundy described by someone present as 'the source of wit and gay hilarity'.

During the 1834 fire, flames nearly burst through the windows of the Great Hall which in a few minutes would have had its wooden roof blazing; but the hall was saved.

Today Westminster Hall seems in a trance. It is very cold

even in summer. Certainly it is haunted. Overhead is the huge oak roof with carved angels at the beam ends. High up are bearded, centuries-worn statues of Plantagenets . . . William Rufus . . . John. Half-way down the vast flight of steps is a tablet marking the place where Charles I sat when he was condemned to death.

This medieval place rejects today, stays immovably in the past. The only time it seems in the present is during a great lying-in-state. Edward VII, George V, George VI, Queen Mary, and Winston Churchill all lay in state in the Great Hall. Then, when a catafalque is in the centre of the hall with burning candles at each corner, the soldiers stand with folded arms and silent crowds walk past, then it is the heart of England again.

A flight of low steps on the right leads to the undercroft of the chapel where Parliament sat for 300 years, *St. Stephen's Crypt*. This is now a chapel where M.P.s are sometimes married or distinguished babies christened. The crypt was built in 1327 but Victorian redecoration has transformed it—one could say spoiled it completely. The artist's aim may have been to create a Sainte Chapelle but it is simply Victorian gothic, the fourteenth century covered up under bright uncompromising reds, greens and mint-new golds. Even the bosses in the vaulted ceiling carved with scenes of the martyrdom of saints are cheerfully painted in white, red and green.

Parliament Square was designed by Charles Barry to match his Parliament buildings; it is a pleasant square of lawns and statues, but curdled with traffic. There is a bronze of General Smuts by Epstein which looks oddly as if the figure is skating; there is a statue to Disraeli which is faithfully decorated with primroses on Primrose Day, April 19; they were his favourite flowers. A great bronze statue of Churchill by Ivor Robert Jones stands facing Big Ben, looking larger and older than any of the other statesmen in the square.

Across the road from Parliament, surrounded by lawns and built to be close to the once-Royal palace, is *Westminster Abbey*. In this magnificent church every English sovereign but two has been crowned for a thousand years.

The Abbey's Beginning

There was a temple to Apollo on this riverside site in Roman times 'which being overthrown, King Lucius built therein a church of Christianity'. Later came 'a little monastery . . . with a few Benedict monks in it, under an abbot, serving Christ;

146

very poor they were, and little was given them for their relief'. Edward the Confessor decided to rebuild it as a noble church 'for that it was near the famous city of London and the river of Thames, that brought in all kinds of merchandises from all parts of the world'. The new church had an abbot and eighty monks. The king had planned the church also to be his sepulchre; very soon after its solemn consecration he died and was buried in front of the high altar.

Within a few weeks of the Confessor's death, his brother-in-law Harold was crowned in the Abbey—the first king to be crowned in the new church. Harold was a fine general, a commanding but rash leader, and might have made a good Saxon king but the year of his coronation, 1066, the Normans landed and Harold was killed in battle.

On Christmas day of the same year the Conqueror rode up to the Abbey for his coronation, accompanied by a great crowd of soldiers, monks and priests, and watched by a mass of the people. The new king, aged 38, was a hard, ruthless, lonely man who was to rule England for twenty-one years. Before the service he was introduced to the people in both French and English. The crowds shouted and the mercenaries among the soldiers mistook the noise for a riot and attacked. Chaos followed. Leaving the fighting, the king entered the Abbey and went straight ahead with the coronation, though at one time, he, the Archbishop of York and a few terrified priests were the only people present while a bloody riot went on outside.

The Confessor's church remained much as it was when he built it until the reign of Henry III. This king decided to rebuild the Norman church in a more magnificent style in praise of the Confessor, who was his patron saint. Henry III was buried in the church in 1272; a hundred years later the nave was rebuilt by Henry Yvele, architect of the nave of Canterbury, who also rebuilt Westminster Hall. All Yvele's work was done in Richard II's reign; both he and the king died in the same year, 1400.

There are only traces of the Confessor's church today—some walls and foundations, the Undercroft and the Chapel of the Pyx. The main Abbey architecture is pure Early English with moulded arches above the highest nave in England.

The Chapel of the Kings

It is perhaps best to begin an Abbey visit by going to the tomb of Edward the Confessor in the heart of the church behind the Sanctuary. The saint and many Plantagenet kings lie in a half-circular chapel approached through an arch, above which is the Chantry Chapel of Henry V. *St. Edward the Confessor's* coffin is in a curious oblong-shaped shrine of marble, with a carved wooden canopy said to have been placed there in 1557 when the shrine (mutilated during the Reformation) was reconstructed. But antiquarians now think the canopy so fine that it may be the actual cover to the gold chest which originally held the saint's coffin. Proof of our ancestors' avarice are the rows of empty sockets in the marble; they were filled with precious stones. The stonework is hollow and the saint's coffin is inside, in a strong iron chest.

The Confessor was revered by his people as a saint when he was alive, and canonized 100 years later. Pilgrims came from all over England to his shrine . . . the ground is worn away by their knees. The little recesses in the tomb's base were for the sick who were left during the night to pray for miraculous cures. The shrine looked wonderful in those days, sparkling with jewels, decorated with gold statues, a lamp always burning there. It was the custom to give offerings to the shrine. Thomas à Beckett brought an ivory statue of the Virgin, Henry V a ruby ring.

On a winter's day at ten in the morning it's possible to be alone in this chapel where five Plantagenet kings and three queens lie in a circle of Royalty. *Henry III* has the highest-placed tomb. He built most of the Abbey (keeping only part of the Confessor's Norman church), and created the saint's shrine. When Henry's tomb of polished porphyry was built, it was covered in jewels. The tomb is too high for one to be able to see the king's effigy.

Henry, the son of King John, reigned for fifty-six years. He was a weak petulant man, recklessly extravagant and deeply pious, but he had a great love and understanding of the arts. The most beautiful ancient parts of the Abbey are due to him.

Towards the back of the High Altar is a great oblong tomb the colour of hammered metal, without an effigy. *Edward I*, Henry's son, is buried here. Edward was a supple, manipulating king and a brilliant soldier, strong as his father had been weak. He was the only ruler of England in 200 years who controlled the Barons without civil strife. Edward conquered Wales and was drawn into wars with France and Scotland where he was named 'the hammer of the Scots'. The words are carved on the tomb which is close to the Coronation Chair made for him to contain the Stone of Scone which he captured from Scotland.

In 1774 the Society of Antiquarians, who believed that
Edward I's body had been 'done over with wax', opened the
tomb. The scene must have looked like the opening of a tomb
of the Pharaohs. The king's body was found wrapped in a
waxed linen cloth, the body almost entire and dressed 'in all
the ensigns of majesty, richly habited', with a tunic of red silk
damask, a crimson velvet mantle, a sceptre in his right hand,
the rod and dove in his left, and wearing a crown. In life he
had been called Longshanks; the body was 6 foot 2 inches tall.

His queen, *Eleanor of Castile*, is near the Chantry. She is
perhaps the most beautiful person in the Abbey and her tomb
and effigy, without a surrounding grill, are low enough to be
seen. Her figure is in gilt bronze and very graceful. Her long
wavy hair falls to her shoulders, she has a plumpish serene face
and wears a simple crown. Edward I loved her; she was brave
as well as beautiful, went with him on the Crusades, is said to
have saved his life by sucking poison from a stab wound. When
she died, the king ordered crosses to be built at every place on
her coffin's journey from Nottinghamshire to Charing Cross;
three of Eleanor's crosses, in Northampton, Geddington and
Waltham are still there.

Her grandson *Edward III*, who reigned for fifty years, is on
the other side of the chapel; many people think his effigy the
finest in the Abbey, an impassive medieval face bearded like a
Patriarch's. He wears curious pointed shoes and a long plain
robe. Round the sides of the tomb are tiny figures called
'weepers' which represent mourners. Edward's weepers are the
figures of his children. There were originally twelve of his fourteen children carved on the tomb but only six figures survive.
The figure on the extreme left is his son, afterwards the Black
Prince. Like his grandfather, Edward III was a soldier of lion-
like courage; his huge shield and sword of state are beside the
Coronation chair. His long life was darkened by sorrow at its
close; the Black Prince had died in battle and England was
ravaged by plague.

On the same side of the chapel is the tomb of *Richard II and
his first queen*. People know Richard II from Shakespeare's
play—he was deposed in 1399 by Henry IV of Lancaster and it
is believed that Richard was murdered when he was a prisoner.
Although the tomb is high, it is possible to see his gilded
effigy quite well. Richard's face is narrow, with a sharp
nose and pointed beard. It was his command that at his death
his effigy should lie hand-in-hand with his queen's . . . and

149

so they lay until the clasped hands and arms were stolen or destroyed.

Entering and leaving the chapel one passes the monument to *Henry V* under the arches of a high Chantry chapel built in his memory. The king's effigy was originally covered in silver-gilt armour chosen by Katharine, his French queen. But already by 1597 Stow says 'the head of this image, being of massy silver, is broken off, and conveyed away with the plates of silver and gilt that covered his body'. The king's effigy also wore a crown and held an orb and sceptre. All that is left is the ancient piece of oak roughly carved to which the armour was fastened. A new head based on the early portraits of the king was added in 1971. High overhead on a wooden bar is the battered black helmet he wore at Agincourt.

Henry's queen *Katharine* is now buried in the Chantry chapel overhead. Her tomb was even worse treated than her husband's. She had been buried in the old Lady Chapel but in 1438 'her corpse being taken up in the reign of Henry VII . . . she was never buried, but remaineth above ground in a coffin of boards behind the east end of the presbytery'. The unburied coffin was still there in 1669 and Pepys was present when it was opened. He took the body in his hands and kissed the Queen's mouth, 'reflecting . . . that this was my birthday 36 years old that I did kiss a Queene'. The bones were 'firmly united, and thinly cloth'd with flesh like scrapings of tann'd leather'.

The *Coronation Chair*, with pointed back and snarling lions at the base, is at the far end of the chapel facing the shrine. Originally it was painted with figures, animals and birds; it was specially made to hold that mystic lump of sandstone which Edward captured from the Scots and on which their own kings had been crowned for hundreds of years. The Scots and English were finally united when the king seated in the chair for his coronation was James VI of Scotland who became James I of England.

The single state occasion when the chair was taken out of the Abbey was when Cromwell used it on being proclaimed Lord Protector in Westminster Hall. At coronations the chair is covered with cloth of gold.

The people of the seventeenth and eighteenth centuries had none of the very ancient—and modern—reverence for relics. For centuries the Coronation chair was unguarded and people carved their initials on it—initials still very much there including a large 'VB' and a scripted 'A'. Even the celebrated Izaak Walton visiting the Abbey in 1658 thought nothing of carving his initials on a tomb.

When the Reformation came and the treasures and jewels were all stolen from the tombs, the monks hid the coffin of Edward the Confessor. It was put back in the shrine when Catholic Mary Tudor came to the throne, and she replaced the statues and jewels. But later they were all stolen or destroyed again, though the saint's tomb remained. In 1685 a choirboy noticed a crack in the tomb and actually saw the saint's head 'solid and firm, the upper and lower jaws full of teeth, a list of gold round the temples'. Putting in his hand he extracted a gold cross and chain which he gave to the Dean who promptly gave it to King James II. The king rewarded him and wore the cross. When he lost his throne and left England, the cross was finally inherited by Bonny Prince Charlie who gave it to the Pope. But the Vatican has never been able to trace it.

Henry VII's Chapel

Two kings planned the Abbey for their burial place; the Confessor and Henry VII. The Abbey was still a monastery when Henry VII decided to build a second shrine to a saint—this time for the holy king Henry VI. Henry VII's idea was to pay reverence to the saintly weakling who lost his throne during the Wars of the Roses; the king also wanted to show his own strong claim to being a descendant of John of Gaunt and therefore an heir to the House of Lancaster. But Henry VI was never canonized and the chapel has never contained the shrine of a saint.

To build his new chapel, Henry VII demolished the Lady Chapel built by Henry III and in its place built this beautiful Gothic chapel which was called 'the wonder of the world'. The magnificent roof has fanwork tracery and hanging pendants sprayed out like the stalks of flowers; numberless statues stand in richly-carved niches. Banners hang over carved stalls in the central chapel—these belong to the Knights of the Bath. The order was founded by Henry IV, revived by George I and reinaugurated by George V. Each knight has a decorated helmet and embroidered banner above his stall, his name and arms on the stall back. The insignia of chivalry are strange and beautiful, helmets decorated with dragons, banners with flying horses or castles. The hinged seats were used by the monks when this was their Lady Chapel and are decorated with grotesque little carvings of figures and animals—one shows a bear playing the bagpipes.

Beyond the altar is the black marble tomb of the Royal couple for whom this chapel was built. *Henry VII and his queen* lie side by side, their effigies enclosed by a bronze grill on which in Henry VIII's reign the poet laureate Skelton hung parchment verses praising the royal pair. Henry VII's queen Elizabeth was gentle, pious, kind and loved of the people who called her 'The Good'. Her kind heart helped to lessen the worst of the king's avarice. One of the strange things about the Abbey that Henry VII is still remembered for his miserliness, yet built the 'wonder of the world'.

Two of the most elaborate memorials in the Abbey are at the end of the chapel, one on each side. Neither is to a king. On the left is the tomb of the *Duke of Lennox and Richmond*, a cousin of James I, with enormous bronzes representing Faith, Hope, Charity and Truth. On the right is an even more excessive monument to *George Villiers, first Duke of Buckingham*. He began life as a penniless hanger-on, and grew to be one of the richest nobles in England. A contemporary writer describes 'his cloaths trimmed with great diamond buttons . . . diamond hatbands, cockades and earrings, to be yoked with great and manifold knots of pearl—in short to be manacled, fettered and imprisoned in jewels'.

Buckingham was the most powerful favourite of two Stuart kings; James I was devoted to him. And when Charles came to the throne Buckingham practically ruled the country for the first three years (Charles did everything he advised), even negotiating the royal marriage to Henrietta Maria. His advice to the king began to be disastrous and the people started to hate him as much as the king doted on him. On his way to a foreign war Buckingham was assassinated at Portsmouth by a subaltern who believed he was doing the country a service.

Buckingham was the first person not of royal blood to be buried in Henry VII's chapel, by the express wish of the king. The monument erected by his Duchess has an excess of everything. There is the Duke haughty even in death; angels; heartbroken soldiers; weeping bronze beauties, and a row of his sturdy little children praying for his soul.

The chapel is a place of Royal bones. Fourteen kings and queens are buried here, as well as scores of their kinsmen and children. In the north aisle is the white marble tomb of *Elizabeth I*. In death she keeps her closeness to the people and no grille encloses her. Her marble face is bony and as strong as a hawk's, she wears a wide ruff and lies with her head on two embroidered cushions. Her effigy used to wear a crown but it was stolen or lost. The Latin inscription calls her 'mother of this country . . . a Prince incomparable'.

Poor unhappy *Mary Tudor* is buried near her without a monument. During Elizabeth's reign her sister's grave was merely heaped with the stones from broken altars.

At the east end of the aisle is the *Innocents' Corner* where two of James I's children are buried. There is a black and gold cradle facing the wall and a mirror hung so that it is possible to see, tucked up fast asleep, the baby *Princess Sophia*. Sophia's little sister, two-year-old *Princess Mary*, lies on her elbow next to the cot, dressed in all her Jacobean finery. A sarcophagus against the East wall contains the bones of two children found at the foot of a stairway in the Tower. Charles II believed these were the skeletons of the *Little Princes* murdered in Richard III's reign and it was he who put up this monument to them.

Three graceful tapestries on the south wall are by William Morris, based on the medieval paintings on the Abbey high altar, of St. Edward, St. John, and Henry III.

Mary Queen of Scots is buried in the south aisle in a magnificent tomb, grander than Elizabeth's, but enclosed by a grill through which Scottish girls often throw bunches of heather or roses. The Scots queen has an impassive, worn face with only faint traces of its celebrated beauty. While there is history, people will argue about her guilt or innocence in the plots and murders surrounding her. Like her grandson Charles I she has become a Royal martyr.

When her son James I was king he had Mary's body moved from Peterborough, and erected this magnificent tomb for his 'dearest mother'. But with shrewd fairmindedness he also built Elizabeth's tomb. The queens lie opposite each other in the two aisles of the chapel. On a tablet in the wall near Mary Queen of Scots are the names of people buried in the vault . . . princes, princesses, and Charles I's sister, the Winter Queen.

At the far end of the chapel is the *R.A.F. Memorial chapel* to the memory of the R.A.F. pilots and crew who died in the Battle of Britain. The vivid window by Hugh Easton is patterned with badges of the squadrons who fought in the battle, and tall winged figures. At its foot are the words from *Henry V*— 'We few, we happy few, we band of brothers'. Below in the wall is a hole made by a bomb in September 1940, now covered in with glass. The *Roll of Honour* is in the adjoining chapel and has the names of 1,495 pilots and crew who died. *Trenchard, Father of the R.A.F.*, and *Dowding*, who commanded during the Battle of Britain, are both buried here.

In the pavement of the chapel a stone records that *Cromwell* was once buried in this place. He was buried 'amongst kings and with more regal solemnity'. But after the Restoration his body and those of two of his followers were dug up, dragged to Tyburn, hanged and beheaded, the heads set on spears above Westminster Hall. Pepys disapproved of 'the dishonour to a man of so great courage'. There has always been a mystery about where Cromwell is buried. It is said that his body was buried under the gallows at Westminster Hall, but there are legends that he had never been buried in the Abbey but secretly on the field of Naseby, his greatest victory.

There are *services in the Abbey* every morning and evening. The choir is very fine and visitors are not allowed to walk about, so the church is reverently quiet. At evensong the choir stalls in the dusk are lit with red-shaded lamps, the choir processes up the aisle in scarlet cassocks. Prayers and music follow.

When one has attended a service in the Abbey and at another time visited the Royal chapels, there still remain the other Abbey tombs and memorials in daunting numbers. *Poet's Corner* is more than a corner; it began when Spenser was buried near Chaucer's tomb and now includes not only poets and writers, but musicians and actors. *Chaucer*'s fine tomb, without an effigy, is in the eastern part of the Transept. The poet was a friend of John of Gaunt, worked in the Royal household and lived in a house where Henry VII's chapel now stands. Chaucer went to Italy as a diplomat, and his knowledge of Italy strongly influenced his poetry.

There is a bust of the Jacobean poet *Michael Drayton* who wrote the lovely 'Since there's no help, come let us kiss and part', there is a statue of *Milton* by Rysbrack and a much-romanticized *Tennyson* by Woolner. On the Abbey pavement is a plaque to *T. S. Eliot* on which people often place flowers; there is soon to be a tablet to *W. H. Auden*. In the chapel adjoining is *Shakespeare* by William Kent; the poet leans in an eighteenth-century attitude on a pile of books. Walpole thought this monument preposterous. There is also *Blake* by Epstein, and *Handel* listening to an angel playing the harp. There are scores of other poets, authors, musicians, some well and some badly sculpted.

It is impossible to appreciate in a single visit the many curious, interesting or beautiful monuments. In St. Michael's chapel, for instance, is the Roubiliac monument showing the skeleton Death aiming his dart at *Lady Elizabeth Nightingale* who droops in her husband's arms. In the south aisle is the monument to *Thomas Thynne* who was murdered in his coach in Pall Mall. A bas relief shows the scene of the crime; mournfully graceful above is the sculptured figure of Thynne glancing heavenwards as if to say 'Look what happened.'

There are crimson-robed effigies of bishops, marble girls in wigs, battles at sea, statues of soldiers and duchesses, Empire builders, dukes and children. And two Red Indian braves.

At the West door of the Abbey, with the glorious length of the nave's white arches and gold bosses stretching into the distance, is the plain black slab marking the tomb of the *Unknown Warrior*.

From the time the church was founded until Henry VIII dissolved the monasteries, a large community of monks lived in the Abbey. They met each morning in the thirteenth century *Chapter House* by the east walk of the *Great Cloister*. Each morning after early Mass eighty monks sat on the stone bench encircling the room and the abbot gave each monk his task for the day. The novices and junior monks then left the chamber and a conclave of senior monks discussed the monastery's work and business.

The Abbey monks were Benedictines and their life was silent and austere; they rose at two in the morning to say the Holy Office; they followed their three rules of poverty, chastity and obedience. The Chapter House evokes this life of order and prayer. The walls are painted with the figures of saints; the bearded heads beneath the arches are abbots and kings. But holiness doesn't reject gaiety and a love of nature, and all among the angels and saints are flowers and trees, a stout horse or two, a reindeer and many birds.

Visitors are given overshoes to protect the thirteenth century tiled floor, and one walks in a slippery shuffle across a great expanse of marvellous ochre and navy blue tiles delicately patterned with heraldic animals and designs and emblems. By the central pillar the tiles are miniature portraits; there is Edward the Confessor giving his ring to a beggar, Henry III with his hound, his queen with a hawk on her wrist.

On the right by the Chapter House doorway is a Roman sarcophagus, A.D. 300, found in the Abbey precincts; its inscription says that the sons of Valerius Amandinus made it in memory of their father. There is a cross on the lid which may mean that it was used later as a Christian coffin.

The *Cloisters* of the Abbey are beautiful and the *Little Cloister* which encloses a tiny garden with a fountain particularly so. Beyond the Chapter House is a Norman doorway with two doors and seven locks opening on to the vaulted chamber of the *Chapel of the Pyx*, a surviving part of the Confessor's Norman Abbey; like the Chapter House, it has a thirteenth century tiled floor. The monks must have used the chamber originally as a chapel for it has the only stone altar in the Abbey. In the fourteenth century, however, they used the room for storing the Abbey treasure and later the king's gold plate, jewels and money were stored here, which explains the double doors and many locks. For centuries it was a kind of strong room. The 'Pyx' which was kept here was a chest for the standard pieces of gold and silver. Annually, the Trial of the Pyx, similar to the official testing of currency at the Mint, was held here.

To the south is the eleventh century *Dark Cloister* and the door to the *Norman Undercroft*, another chamber of the old Norman abbey believed to have been the monks' Common Room.

It is now the *Abbey Museum*. There is a letter of Edward III's, a sword used by Henry V in battle and a fourteenth century chest for storing church vestments. But people mostly visit this museum to see the *Royal effigies*; these were figures carried on the top of the coffin at Royal or noble funerals and dressed to 'imitate life'. The effigy would be left on the grave until the monument was completed; some effigies stayed on graves for years and people pinned epitaphs on them.

The effigies have been in the Abbey for centuries—some were used at the funerals of the Plantagenets. By the eighteenth century they were in a sorry state, tattered, broken and pushed into cupboards in eerie rows . . . Walpole called them 'The Ragged Regiment'. They have now been identified by antiquaries and arranged in glass cases.

The early effigies are made of wood—there are two full-length figures, one of *Edward III* and one of Henry V's *Queen Katharine*. The queen, Shakespeare's 'Dear Kate', has a tiny waist, a doll-like face, and round her head a little groove which held her crown in place. The head and shoulders effigy of *Henry VII* is startling; it is a face lined, strong and sardonically alive, yet it was modelled from his death mask. There are numbers of full-length wax figures; *Charles II* is wearing his Garter Robes. 'It is to ye life' said someone who knew him. The pretty *Frances, Duchess of Richmond* is dressed in the robes she wore for Queen Anne's coronation, and has with her the West African grey parrot which lived with her for forty years. Pepys was fascinated by the Duchess and couldn't sleep for thinking of her 'sweet eye, little Roman nose, and excellent taille'.

The effigy of *Nelson* is dressed in his own clothes, frilled shirt and full-dress Admiral's coat. When Lady Hamilton saw the effigy she leaned forward and carefully rearranged a lock of his hair. In a nearby case is his cocked hat and green eye-shade. There is also a sardonyx cameo ring made for a woman's hand but later enlarged; this is the *Essex Ring* which has a strong but disputed legend. Forty years after Essex was dead, Clarendon dismissed the story as absurd; but now antiquaries are not so sure. The ring is believed to have been given by Elizabeth to Essex; if he were at any time under sentence of death and he sent her the ring, he would be pardoned.

Essex led a plot to raise the people, seize Whitehall and demand that the Queen should dismiss all her counsellors. The plot failed and he went to the Tower. He sent the ring to Elizabeth, but either it did not reach her or she had hardened her heart. She certainly loved him and was reluctant to sign his death warrant. But she finally did and he was beheaded. After his death she gave a curious order—his banner of Knight of the Garter should stay in St. George's Chapel. There is little evidence that she grieved over him.

The fourteenth century *Jerusalem Chamber*, now the Chapter Room of the Abbey, cannot be visited but should be mentioned. Henry IV died there; the incident used by Shakespeare in his play when the young Prince Hal placed the crown on his head when his father lay dying is said to have happened in the chamber.

After visiting the Abbey Addison's words seem to fit best: 'When I look upon the tombs of the great, every emotion of envy dies in me . . . when I see kings lying by those who deposed them . . . rival wits placed side by side, or the holy men that divided the world with their contests and disputes . . . when I read the several dates of the tombs, of some that died yesterday, and some 600 years ago, I consider that great day when we shall all of us be contemporaries and make our appearance together.'

Edward the Confessor built *St. Margaret's, Westminster* so

near the Abbey, according to Stow, 'for the ease and commodity of the monks'. It was rebuilt in the reigns of Edward I and Edward IV and the present church, late Gothic (1485–1523), fits beautifully into its small space of lawns beside the Abbey and seems to be part of it. St. Margaret's is London's most fashionable church for weddings; it is also the parish church of the Commons and until the last century the Speaker and Members attended divine service on various historic days—to commemorate the execution of Charles I and the Restoration. And, oddly, the Gunpowder Plot.

The church's greatest treasure is a *Flemish stained glass window* (1500), given to Henry VII by Katharine of Aragon's parents when she was betrothed to the young Prince Arthur. Katharine and Arthur kneel devoutly together, the Spanish princess looking like a queen in a pack of cards. But Arthur died and Henry VIII made Katharine his queen. The window apparently embarrassed him for he had it removed and packed off to an abbey in Essex.

Walter Raleigh is buried in the churchyard; he was executed in Old Palace Yard near by. Raleigh, after years of both imprisonment and hope and a final disastrous expedition for James I, was executed in 1618, victim of the king's policy of appeasing the Spanish. Raleigh died with Elizabethan panache —he was never a Jacobean. The bright window in his memory was presented by admirers from America in the last century.

England's first printer, *Caxton*, is also buried in the churchyard. He lived near the Abbey and was a favourite at the courts of both Edward IV and Richard III. The year before his death he printed a book on 'Arte and Craft How to Die'. In 1491, a few hours before his death, he was still at work on his printing.

In the ambulatory near the poor door under the tower is a mural monument to a lady—*Elizabeth Corbett*—with a poem by Pope which was much admired by Doctor Johnson. 'I have always considered,' said the doctor, 'this the most valuable of all Pope's epitaphs . . . there is scarcely one line taken from commonplaces.'

Part of the epitaph runs:

'Passion and pride were to her soul unknown
Convinced that virtue only is our own;
So unaffected, so composed a mind
So firm, yet soft, so strong, yet so refined.'

During the Civil War St. Margaret's was badly damaged, the altar destroyed, the font broken, brasses torn from the graves. The country—and St. Margaret's—recovered; during the Puritan regime the church was much attended. Long sermons had become the fashion and on one occasion two of St. Margaret's preachers gave sermons lasting seven hours. Their texts taken from the Bible had a distinctly Puritan flavour—one dealt with those men who must bear burdens and those who must oversee them. The other text from Jeremiah was 'I have appointed thee a prophet to the nations'.

In 1656 *Milton* married Katharine, his second wife, in St. Margaret's. And in 1908 *Winston Churchill* was married here.

Some fine stained glass windows, in uneven patterns of primrose and grey, are on the left of the aisle; they are the work of *John Piper*.

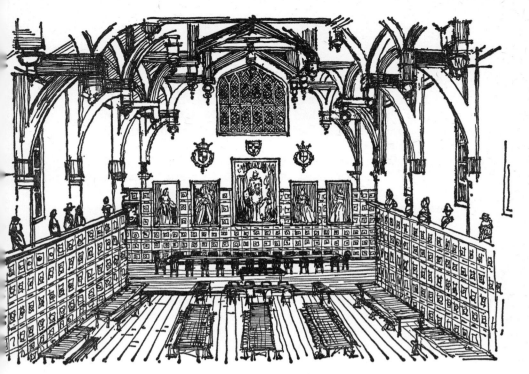

Middle Temple Hall

10 LEFT BANK
Westminster Bridge
Boadicea's Statue
Westminster Pier
Victoria Embankment
Queen Mary II's Steps
Banqueting House by Inigo Jones
Plaque to Sir Joseph Bazalgette
Victoria Embankment Gardens
York House Watergate
The Adelphi
Cleopatra's Needle
The Hospital of the Savoy—the Chapel of the Savoy
The Old Caledonia
Waterloo Bridge
Waterloo Pier
Somerset House
Roman Bath, Strand Lane
H.M.S. Discovery
City Gryphons
Submariners' Memorial
Wellington, Chrysanthemum, President
The Temple
Blackfriars Bridge

Westminster Bridge crosses the river from beside the Houses of Parliament to Lambeth. The bridge, decorated below the arches with gilded coats of arms, was built in 1854–62 by Thomas Page; but Sir Charles Barry had a hand in it, which is why it matches the decorated style of Parliament. Even the lamps on the bridge have a touch of Gothic.

For 700 years London had only one bridge—Old London Bridge. Transport across the river and up and downriver was by the thousands of boats served by the corporation of watermen, well-known for their strength, jollity and bad language. Londoners for centuries jealously opposed the building of a second bridge: London Bridge crossed at the heart of the city and that was how it must stay. When an Act of Parliament was finally passed in 1736 to build a second bridge it was fiercely opposed by the City and by the Thames watermen.

The first Westminster bridge, of Portland stone, had balustrades and fifteen arches. Between each arch was a little recess like a half-circular turret in which people could shelter. The domed turrets for some reason worked acoustically like St. Paul's Whispering Gallery—if a man whispered against the wall of one turret he could be quite clearly heard in a turret on the other side of the road. One could have a conversation with the carriages thundering on the road between.

Boswell in 1763 picked up a cheerful-looking girl, took her to Westminster Bridge and made love to her there, 'the whim of doing it there with the Thames rolling below us amused me much'. Forty years later another writer stood on the bridge with rather different emotions. Wordsworth watched a summer sunrise over the river and wrote the sonnet 'Earth hath not anything to show more fair'; he described the London he saw that morning . . .

> 'silent, bare,
> Ships, towers, domes, theatres, and temples lie
> Open unto the fields and to the sky,
> All bright and glittering in the smokeless air.'

To the left of the bridge, facing Big Ben, is the bronze statue to *Boadicea* by Thomas Thornycroft (1902), a romanticized figure upright in a chariot with her two beautiful half-naked daughters beside her. Boadicea was queen of the East Anglian Iceni tribe who united with a Kentish tribe to resist the Romans. She died in battle in A.D. 61. An early writer described her as 'huge of frame, terrifying of aspect, and with a harsh voice'.

The Roman Governor Suetonius Paulinus tried to save London during the uprising, evacuating many of the inhabitants. Those who wouldn't go with the Romans were later massacred by the tribesmen and the flourishing town of London was burned to the ground. Later there was a great battle, the Romans conquered and Boadicea took poison to escape bondage. She has become a national symbol of liberty.

From around Easter until the autumn river launches leave *Westminster Pier* on their journeys downriver to Greenwich and up as far as Hampton Court. There is also a Hovercraft service to Greenwich.

Victoria Embankment stretches from the bridge to Black-friars; it was built by Sir Joseph Bazalgette on land reclaimed from the river which until then had flowed up to the foot of Somerset House and the Temple gardens. Floods were everyday happenings before the Embankment was built—the river often rose 12 feet in three hours, and did much damage. Now the massive granite walls are sunk 14 feet below the bed of the river.

The Gothic-looking buildings on the other side of the road are New Scotland Yard, the headquarters of the Metropolitan police from 1890 until 1967; the buildings which remind one of a Scottish baronial hall were made of Dartmoor granite hewn by the convicts. Many detective novels, many plays and, in the past, TV serials featured those familiar looming buildings. They are now converted into offices for M.P's and their secretaries.

The river stretch along the Embankment here was renamed *King's Reach* in celebration of George V's Silver Jubilee. By the Embankment wall is the huge golden eagle, its wings stretched out, which commemorates the *R.A.F.* in two world wars; the monument is by Sir Reginald Blomfield and Sir W. Reid Dick (1923). A little further, on the other side of the road, is Horse Guards Avenue. In front of a block of Government offices on the left is a lawn and the remains of *Queen Mary II's Steps*. In 1691 Christopher Wren designed a terrace for the queen, to overlook the river in front of the old river wall of Whitehall Palace. The terrace projected 70 feet into the river and the curving flight of steps led from the Royal apartments to the place where the State barge was moored. Terrace and steps were rediscovered in 1939.

The Thames was the main highway of London, and eighteenth century people said 'taking the water' as we say 'taking a bus'. 'Pray did you come with oars or scullers, Mr. Handel?' asked one of his friends. And when George IV came to the throne there were still 3,000 wherries plying on the Thames, while hackney coaches numbered only 1,200 in the whole of London.

Horse Guards Avenue leads to the *Banqueting House* by Inigo Jones which faces Whitehall. Strictly speaking this is not part of Thames-side, but it is the only surviving building of the *Palace of Whitehall* which stood along the river banks here, with many stately buildings and courts, gardens, orchards and water-gates. York Place had been the London home of the Archbishops of York and was much beautified and enlarged by Cardinal Wolsey. Henry VIII envied Wolsey the mansion, as he envied him Hampton Court, and both houses had the same destiny. Henry took them when the Cardinal fell from power.

The king was granted York Place by Parliament 'because the old Palace nigh to the Monastery . . . is now, and has long been in a state of ruin and decay'. Henry forsook Westminster and moved into his new home which he renamed Whitehall.

Henry married Anne Boleyn at the Palace of Whitehall. She was, perhaps, the most alluring of all his queens; the Viscount Chateaubriand said of her, 'when she sung she would have made bears and wolves attentive'.

The king died at Whitehall Palace in 1547. From the same palace the young princess Elizabeth was taken to the Tower. But she returned to live here triumphantly when she became queen; she filled the Royal library with books in English, French, Greek and Italian, and built a new timber banqueting house where she gave 'revels and maskings, and various other mummeries'. The year that James I came to the throne, Shakespeare's *Othello* is said to have been given its first performance in the timber banqueting hall.

In later years James I chose Inigo Jones to design a grander Banqueting House. It was to be the centre of Court life and would also be a symbol of the new and glorious Stuart dynasty in much the same way that Henry VII's chapel had been a symbol of the Tudors. Inigo Jones's Banqueting House opened in 1622 and was constantly used for the Jacobean Royal masques; Jones had seen these marvellously played at the court of the Medici in Florence. They were displays of formal pageant and poetry, accompanied by music and enhanced by elaborate transformation scenes. Inigo Jones designed them to symbolize the Divine Right of the King. The performers were members of the Court—sometimes even the Queen accompanied by her ladies played a part in them. Costumes and scenery were exquisitely decorated and classical—in the transformation scenes a series of veils floated upwards, goddesses appeared in the sky.

The great hall, empty of its masquing royalty, still keeps a masterly command of airy space. Above is the ceiling painted by Rubens and said to be one of the three greatest art treasures owned by the Royal family (the others are the Raphael Cartoons in the Victoria and Albert Museum, and Mantegna's Triumphs of Caesar at Hampton Court). After his father's death Charles I invited Rubens to come to England; Rubens, the great painter of the Baroque, was at the height of his fame and the king was eager to meet a man of international reputation both for artistic genius and for intellect. It was largely due to Rubens, who had been a diplomat at the Spanish Court, that England and Spain made a peace treaty. Charles I knighted him. He also commissioned him to paint the ceilings of the Banqueting House—nine huge panels all of which would glorify James I and the sacred role of Kingship.

King James, raised heavenwards, is surrounded by cherubs holding crowns and palms. There are figures of Royal Bounty and Wise Government, there are goddesses and angels, all in the opulent glowing Rubens style.

By a grim twist of history—perhaps a deliberate Parliamentarian decision—the Banqueting House built to the glory of kingship was the place where the Stuart king died. The death warrant decreed that the king should die 'in the open streete before Whitehall'. According to contemporary writers, a passage was broken through the Banqueting House wall through which the king passed to the scaffold. Charles I walked out on a bitterly cold January morning in 1648 'with a cheerful countenance and a firm and undaunted step'. The huge crowds were completely silent. But when the axe fell they groaned. A boy who heard the sound said, 'such a groan as I never heard before, or desire I may never hear again'. On the back of the king's death warrant written in a seventeenth-century hand are the words: 'The bloody Warrant for murthering the King.'

There is a bust of the king on the staircase of the Banqueting House close to the place where he was led out to the scaffold. Outside is a plaque commemorating his death.

Cromwell moved into Whitehall Palace when he was Lord Protector and it was there that he refused the crown; the Banqueting House was used for State occasions during the Commonwealth, but with the Restoration it returned to glittering life. Great receptions were given to foreign ambassadors—

at one of these the Russian ambassador presented Charles II with fur-lined cloaks, hawks and horses. The Knights of the Garter dined in the Banqueting Hall which was hung with priceless tapestries. During Charles II's reign the ancient custom of 'touching' for the King's Evil was revived and grew tremendously popular. After a religious service, people suffering from scrofula were allowed to gather in the hall and the king touched them with both hands; this, it was believed, cured them. William III stopped this custom; he also stopped the religious ceremony on Maundy Thursday when the king washed the feet of the poor.

Whitehall Palace in Charles II's reign was brilliant with entertainments, with the beautiful women the king always had near him, with intrigue and spicey gossip. But after Charles's death—three short years later—his brother James II left Whitehall, the crown, and England. He had had the weathercock placed on the palace roof so that he could see if the wind was right for the arrival from Holland of William of Orange. Whitehall Palace did not last much longer . . . a disastrous fire in 1698 burned down almost the entire palace, including Wolsey's Tudor Chapel and a Catholic chapel designed by Wren for James II. Only the Banqueting House has survived from the vanished palace; in Victorian times it was used as a Royal chapel and, until recently, as a museum.

Beside the river, facing Northumberland Avenue on the Embankment, is a bronze plaque commemorating *Sir Joseph Bazalgette*, designer and engineer of all the Thames embankments; he has a strong Victorian face, receding hair and magnificent mutton-chop whiskers.

Beyond Charing Cross Underground station to the east are the pleasant *Victoria Embankment Gardens* on land reclaimed from the river. There are lawns and a variety of trees, flowers, statues, a fishpool and a bandstand; in sunny weather people picnic near the giant bronze to *Robert Burns* and the little sculpted camel memorial to the *Imperial Camel Corps*. Behind the gardens are the great buildings of *Shell Mex House* and the *Savoy Hotel*.

At the back of the gardens to the west is a venerable old stone arch decorated with sculpted shells and two haggard lions. This is the *York House Watergate*, the gateway from the Duke of Buckingham's garden to the flight of river steps. Boats tied up near the gate when people arrived or left the Buckingham mansion by water. In old prints the watergate stands with its feet in the river and swans and reeds round it, which shows just how far the Thames was pushed back when the Embankments were built.

York House had belonged to the Archbishop of York in Tudor times; in the reign of Charles I when George Villiers, Duke of Buckingham, was at the height of his power he rebuilt the mansion, making it very magnificent; it was surrounded with a high embattled wall and the long river terrace had the watergate in its centre.

When the Restoration came, the second Duke lived in the riverside mansion; at Court he was described as a man who 'excelled all courtiers for wit and debauchery'. Wild extravagance and huge debts forced him to sell the house and the land round it. It was agreed that his name and title should be commemorated by naming four streets built on the land that had been his garden after him. The streets were: George, Villiers, Duke and Buckingham.

Robert Adam and his brother built *The Adelphi*, a series of houses on a terrace facing the river just where the gardens now end. The terrace was on sloping land running from the Strand to the Thames and built right up to the level of the Strand, the houses supported on great arches. The Adelphi (the Greek word for 'brothers'), though bitterly criticized, became a marvellously dramatic part of the river. The houses, high above their arcades, were gracefully decorated. In front of the archways was a broad paved way similar to some in Venice, which ran a few feet above the river. Not everybody approved of the Adam venture and a verse of the time said:

> Four Scotchmen, by the name of Adam
> Who keep their coaches and their Madam,
> Quoth John, in sulky mood, to Thomas,
> Have stole the very river from us.

Although the Adelphi terrace was demolished and an uninspired 1938 block replaces it, there are traces of Adam's work in the side streets; in Robert Street a blue plaque marks the charming house where Robert Adam lived. Thomas Hood, Galsworthy and Barrie all lived at various times in the same house. The 1938 block facing the river where Adam's terrace stood is as high as the original Adelphi and there is a view of the river and a glimpse of Westminster. Below are gardens where the river used to be. Behind the Adelphi in John Adam Street is the

Royal Society of Arts, a classic Adam building of particular grace and style.

In the nineteenth century the arches under the Adam terrace became sinister places; they were used for coal wharves and as cellars and were called 'the dark arches' . . . a place used by thieves for hiding places and where vagrants came to sleep. John Timbs likened them to the catacombs in Rome.

Cleopatra's Needle is on the Embankment midway between Hungerford and Waterloo bridges. Two bronze sphinxes, scarred by bombs in the 1914–18 war, sit at its base. The obelisk was given its romantic name in the last century because, though quarried by the Pharaohs in 1500 BC, the obelisk was 'removed during the Greek dynasty to Alexandria, royal city of Cleopatra, and erected there in 12 BC, the eighteenth year of the reign of Augustus Caesar'. At the time, in fact, when Cleopatra was still the old serpent of the Nile. The obelisk is of pinkish granite 68 feet high and was presented to Britain in 1819 by the Viceroy of Egypt, Mohammed Ali. Until then, according to the inscription, it had been 'prostrate upon the sands of Alexandria for centuries'. Hyroglyphics in columns down the obelisk are prayers and records of Pharaoh's victories.

It was not until 1878 that the obelisk was placed beside the river, and many people do not know that the Victorians sealed two large earthenware jars in the pedestal, containing all kinds of things representing the then-modern times, to be preserved for posterity. There is a book on engineering, coins of the realm, china, a picture of Queen Victoria and bibles in several languages. There is also a copy of Bradshaw's Railway Guide, photographs of twelve pretty Victorian girls, some daily papers, toys, some hairpins and a case of cigars.

At this point of the riverside, a little west of the bridge and Somerset House, on ground which sloped steeply to the water was a Royal palace which later became the *Hospital of the Savoy*. Simon de Montfort built it in 1245; later it became Royal property and when John, King of France, was captured by the Black Prince at the battle of Poitiers, he was brought back to London and kept prisoner at the Savoy. John was set free but came back to visit the English Royal family and by a strange chance died at the Savoy; his body was 'honourably conveyed to St. Denis in France'.

John of Gaunt, the Black Prince's brother, was given the Savoy by his father the king; it was a palace very like a medieval French chateau with high stone walls rising straight out of the water and castellated towers. In 1372 Wat Tyler and a London mob 'for the malice they bore John of Gaunt' blew up the palace's Great Hall and destroyed other parts of it; they broke into the cellars and drank quantities of the Royal wine. They were so drunk that when a fire they had started began to burn in the cellars, many of them perished.

Henry VII beautifully restored the Savoy and turned it into a hospital for the poor. There were also government offices in the building and a printing press. As late as 1650 it was a noble place, but by the eighteenth century it was 'very great and at present a very ruinous building . . . a very spacious hall . . . the ceiling is very curiously built with wood . . . and images of angels holding before their breasts coats of arms'. In places the angel-carved roof was collapsing and open to the sky. By 1789 only a few Tudor walls and an old army prison were standing. Everything was swept away in the early 1800's 'to form the approach to Waterloo Bridge'.

All that remains of the old palace is the *Chapel of the Savoy* in Savoy Street. It has been used by royalty since Henry VII's reign, but in the way of so many of London's marvellous buildings of the past was gutted by fire (actually in the last century). The fire destroyed the roof which was covered with heraldic emblems and the arms of the Lancasters. The chapel was rebuilt after the fire and a new roof created as much as possible like the ancient one. Only the outside of the building has a trace of history.

The Old Caledonia, a floating pub which was once a passenger ship, is moored just below Waterloo Bridge. The ship was built in 1934 and carried passengers to the Isle of Arran by way of the Kyles of Bute. During the war her name was changed, she became H.M.S. Goatfell and swept mines in the North Sea, as well as taking part in the Normandy landings. She returned to work in Scotland as a passenger ship until 1969 when she was brought down to be part of the London river scene. The ship is open from 11 to 3 and from 5.30 until 11 at night and is very attractive, with restaurant and bars on and below decks. On the deck is a plaque giving the distances from the ship's present anchorage to . . . Putney 5 miles, Glasgow 395 miles, Paris 208 miles, and New York 3,342 miles.

There was a 'floating coffee house' moored in just about the same place as the Caledonia in the eighteenth century. It was called The Folly on the Thames and Pepys visited it; it was 'a whimsical piece of architecture . . . designed as a musical summer house for the entertainment of the quality'.

Waterloo Bridge crosses the Thames from Lancaster Place to the South Bank and Waterloo Station; it was designed by Sir Giles Gilbert Scott and completed in 1939, but wasn't officially opened until after the last war. A flight of steps leads from the Embankment up to the bridge from which there is a fine view of the South Bank, with the National Theatre buildings to the east. Just by the bridge on the north bank is *Waterloo Pier*, the only floating Police Station in London. It is manned by the Thames Division who also have a number of stations ashore.

The Thames has had a police force now for over 150 years. The first police force on the Thames was started in the early nineteenth century by the West India Company of Merchantmen, desperate to protect their cargoes against being looted from ships. The new river police were recruited from seamen and watermen and were strong, tough characters. They needed to be. Up and downriver were gangs who plundered the shipping on such a scale that nearly a third of all port workers were thieves or receivers, and about half of all cargoes entering London were stolen. The new police broke up the gangs, and many of the criminals were transported. In the early days the police worked in rowing and sailing boats; they first used motorboats in 1910.

Today there are 36 police duty boats patrolling the river for 24 hours a day, and 3 larger launches used by the Superintendents. The police boats have all kinds of equipment for their special river work . . . drags, lifebuoys, buoyant cushions, gear for salvage, first aid, and a new automatic resuscitator which has already saved a number of lives. The Thames Division patrols 54 miles of the river, upstream as far as Staines and downstream to Dartford Creek on the south bank, and Havering on the north. They not only police the river, they cope with ships in collisions, fires in ships, barges that have cut adrift, cargoes lost in the river, and the vital job of Flood Warning in the case of abnormally high tides.

The Regency bridge which previously spanned the river at this point and was taken down in the 1930s, was considered to be a masterpiece of 'lightness, grace and symmetry'. The Italian artist Canova said it was worth coming all the way from Rome just to admire it; a celebrated French engineer compared it to a monument worthy of the Caesars. The bridge, opened by the Prince Regent on the second anniversary of Waterloo, was owned by The Strand Bridge Company and by an act of Parliament they were allowed to change the bridge's name in honour of the great battle. There was a toll for crossing the bridge, a halfpenny for pedestrians and 2d for cabs. By 1873 it was estimated that five million people every year crossed the bridge giving the company an income of £21,000. The Board of Works later bought the bridge and the toll was abolished.

Dredged up near Waterloo Bridge was one of the greatest of Thames relics—a horned bronze helmet of pre-Roman times. Horns were not used on helmets by marauding Vikings until hundreds of years later—it's believed that this was the first use of this symbolically-shaped helmet. The Thames helmet is enamelled and embossed and must have belonged to a warrior of high rank.

Somerset House stands facing the Thames east of Waterloo Bridge, a stately eighteenth century building loved by Londoners and one of the few Georgian buildings which remain by the river. The only disadvantage to this beautiful mansion is that it has no curious history; it was never owned and lived-in by famous or infamous men and has always been a Government office. Which is probably why it is still standing.

Somerset House is on the site of a palace which belonged to the Protector Somerset. Historians think it unlikely Somerset ever lived in the palace which was begun in 1547—the year before the Protector was taken to the Tower for the first time.

Elizabeth lived occasionally at Somerset House but it wasn't a particularly favourite palace of hers. It was James I's queen Anne of Denmark who took a fancy to the place. Inigo Jones redecorated it for her and made it very beautiful; it was Anne's pleasure in this palace that made it become, by tradition, a property settled on the English queen. Henrietta Maria was given the palace and Inigo Jones (working for this second queen) designed her a chapel where she could practise her Catholic religion in the now-Protestant England. The queen had the Capuchin friars as her priests and the chapel was crowded with Catholics who had to hear Mass more or less in secret—Masses were celebrated in the chapel from six in the morning until midday every day.

In the Restoration the widowed Henrietta Maria was once again given Somerset House and returned there to live in great style. Pepys thought her rooms 'most stately and nobly furnished', and went to the chapel to watch Mass until a man came up to him and ordered him to 'go out or kneel down; so I did go out', says Pepys.

The old palace had terraced gardens facing the river, with

flights of steps at each end. The gardens were symmetrical—square flower beds, avenues and walks leading to statues of Tritons and Nereids. Beside the river was a raised terrace and a long wall.

When George III was king, the tradition of giving Somerset House to the queen ended; Charlotte was given the house 'formerly called Buckingham House'. Parliament now had the problem of what to do with the old palace; it was decided that it should be put 'to such uses as shall be found most useful to the public' and consequently pulled down. The Georgian building designed by Sir William Chambers replaced it.

The main entrance is on to the Strand; over the archways are Jove-like heads with plaited hair and beards. These represent the eight principal rivers of England, but there seems no way of knowing which river is which. The great central quadrangle, marred by ranks of parked cars, has a bronze fountain in the centre by John Bacon (1778) with a figure standing by the prow of a dolphin-decorated ship and Father Thames, seated below him, water and beard flowing.

On the high roofs are numbers of Italianate statues said to represent Justice, Truth, Valour and Moderation but—as in the case of the sculpted river heads over the archways—it is difficult to puzzle out the various virtues. They look very fine outlined against the sky.

The high balustraded terrace was built directly above the river before there was an Embankment; in the 1830s it was opened to the public and was one of the finest promenades in London, with steamers, barges and wherries passing to and fro on the then-busy river. But the stonework was so mutilated by people carving their names (one was deep in the nose of a sculpted lion) that later the terrace was locked. People who worked in Somerset House or lived locally were given keys; George Eliot worked nearby as assistant editor to the Westminster Review and she had a terrace key. Opposite Somerset House was the office of another magazine, the *Economist*, where the writer and philosopher Herbert Spencer worked. He and George Eliot became friends; on sunny days they liked to walk up and down the deserted terrace of Somerset House deep in talk, the only noises coming from the passing river steamers. It was the beginning of a love which created a great Victorian scandal and lasted a lifetime.

In the corridor of Somerset House leading from the Waterloo Bridge entrance is a display of the taxes of the past—eighteenth century lottery tickets—a Hat Tax of 1764 stamped inside every hat—a Post Horse tax; and a tax on playing cards collected 'by means of the Ace of Spades'.

Somerset House was the home of the Royal Academy from 1780 until 1856 and the annual exhibition was held here until 1837. There are many public offices in the building including the General Register of births, deaths and marriages and the Inland Revenue. The public can, if they ask, see famous wills from 1858 onwards—Charles Dickens's will, for instance. All wills previous to 1858, including Nelson's and Shakespeare's, are in the Public Record Office in Chancery Lane. The east wing of Somerset House, built in 1829, houses King's College, part of London University.

Tucked away in Strand Lane down the east side of Somerset House under a dark archway is the *Roman Bath*. This is an archeological puzzle: nobody is quite sure if it is Roman or merely Tudor. Or maybe Roman but unearthed by the Tudors. Above the bath house are two seventeenth century houses, one of which was occupied by the Watch, the men who patrolled and guarded the streets before the Police were founded. The Roman bath is 15½ feet long and built over a tributary of the Fleet river. It fills each day with 2,000 gallons of ice-cold water which overflows into a pipe running under the pavement down into the Thames.

The blue flowered tiles in the archway are eighteenth century and in the small room used by the porter are even older tiles, fifteenth century Dutch patterned with figures and windmills. The Roman Bath used to be open to the public in Victorian days—Dickens mentions it in *David Copperfield*; David goes to take cold plunges there. The bath house then was lined with marble, and decorated with marble busts to give it an antique look. It is now National Trust property; it's planned to include the Roman Bath in the new buildings of King's College.

There are four old ships moored permanently between Waterloo and Blackfriars bridges. The first, almost opposite Temple station, is the research ship H.M.S. *Discovery* built for Captain Scott when he went to the Antarctic in 1901–4. *Discovery* is built of oak and elm, a small solid ship designed with a powerful stem to ride over ice and crush it; its curiously rounded stern was to protect the rudder and screw as they worked in the broken-up ice. Icebreakers and other polar vessels today are built of steel, but *Discovery* got through the Antarctic and brought Scott and his crew safely home two years later. Many people mistakenly think that this is the ship which took Scott on his final tragic journey of 1912; that was the *Terra Nova*.

The ward room in *Discovery* shines with mahogany panelling, brass, and a highly-polished stove which used to hold an open fire. The officers' cabins, each lettered with the name of its occupant, lead off the ward room. Many of the cabins are just as they were when used for the expedition. In Captain Scott's corner cabin are mementoes of him and his crew. There are his gold uniform buttons, his snow goggles (made of wood), and sad, faded photographs of the ship in the icy polar wastes. There are china plates used on the voyage, patterned with the ship's name and a blue penguin. There are two battledores. In the ward room are Scott's skis, massive and heavy, made of solid hickory.

Discovery is used for the Navy and the Marines as a recruiting headquarters, but is also open to the public and there are interesting conducted tours.

Further along the Embankment the City of London boundary is marked on either side of the road by two cast-iron *Gryphons*. These creatures, painted silver with scarlet-veined wings, are very like the gryphon in *Alice in Wonderland* and are part of the city's coat of arms. They were made in 1849 and stood outside the old Coal Exchange until it was demolished in 1963 when they were brought here. Opposite them are the lawns and buildings of the *Temple*, described in a later paragraph.

A bas relief to the *Submariners* who died in two world wars is on the embankment wall; the sailors are grouped in the cramped interior of an old-fashioned submarine and in the deep sea round them strange underwater figures of mermen swim and sing.

The three ships, *Wellington, Chrysanthemum* and *President* are moored in a row along the Embankment west of Blackfriars Bridge. The ships are so familiar to Londoners now that they seem to grow in the river, like willows. *President* is a naval sloop belonging to the Honourable Company of Master Mariners—the other two are training ships for the R.N.V.R. *President* is also used for recruiting.

The Embankment seats at this part of the riverside have changed from the swans of Lambeth and the sphinxes of Westminster, and are decorated with kneeling camels with roped burdens on their back.

Middle Temple Lane runs from the Embankment through to the Temple to the famous 1684 gateway opening on to Fleet Street. *The Temple* is the home of two of the four Inns of Court, Inner and Middle Temple; the other two are Lincolns' and

Gray's Inn. Barristers live and practise in the Temple and some law students study here. All students, before becoming barristers, must pass their bar examinations in the Temple.

The Law has been in its riverside home for a long time, but the Temple was originally the first English house of the Knights Templar. This was an order of knights, founded in 1119, bound by monastic vows and dedicated to 'fighting the heathens'; one of their chief aims was to keep open the routes to the shrine in the Holy Land which were at that time threatened by the Muslims.

Henry I founded the original English branch of the Templars; the 'proud and at first zealous brotherhood' bought the land by the Thames and built a monastery, a church, barracks and cloisters, gardens and a river terrace for religious meditation. During the Crusades the Templars went on campaigns with the kings of England, France and Germany, but they owed allegiance only to the Pope. The Order had monasteries all over Europe and enormous garrisoned castles in the Holy Land. The Templars wore tunics over their chain mail, white as an emblem of chastity with the crimson cross of Christ on chest and back. When they were not at the wars they lived lives of self-mortification and prayer.

As warriors they were fanatics; they never retreated and if a battle wasn't won they died. In one battle alone, 200 Templars charged a host of 10,000 Saracens and very nearly defeated them. But by the beginning of the fourteenth century their day was done. The Order had grown enormously powerful, rich and arrogant. Its finest members were dead in the Crusades, it had long been the chief bank and moneylender in the East and was hated for its power and riches. In England the Templars' many enemies said they had become heretics, practised black magic, idolatry and murder. In 1312 the Order was formally abolished by the Pope, twenty-one years after the last Crusading stronghold in the Holy Land fell to the Muslims. The only building remaining of the Knights Templar's Order is their round church consecrated in 1185 at a time of great crisis, when the Holy Land was threatened by Saladin.

The nave of the church, called The Round, is built in a circular form to symbolize the church of the Holy Sepulchre in Jerusalem. Here are the tombs, not of actual Templars, but of Associates of the ancient order who went on the Crusades. The tombs were badly damaged by bombing in 1941 but are still awesomely impressive. The Crusaders, 'in cross-legged effigy devoutly stretched', wear chain mail and lie with their swords beside them. There are a number of members of the Marshall family, earls of Pembroke, many of whom died in the Crusades. The great Pembroke was William, Protector of England who was one of the leading barons who forced King John to sign Magna Carta. The Protector's son Gilbert is among the Crusaders in the Round—his effigy shows Gilbert just about to draw his sword for the cause of faith. But his sword was never used in the Holy cause for he was killed falling from his horse at a tournament on the eve of leaving for the Holy Land.

The church is noted for its choir and music, and was skilfully restored after the fire bombs of 1941. It is light and spacious after the ancient, shadowy Round. The cloisters were rebuilt by Wren, who also designed the beautiful reredos. There is a thirteenth-century effigy in the south aisle of a venerable bishop. John Selden is buried in the church vault, and Charles Lamb was christened here.

When the Templars' Order was abolished by the Pope, the land and buildings on the riverside were eventually let to professors of Common Law and their students. Many of the old retainers who had served the powerful Templars in the past became servants to the lawyers and some of the old customs and titles were still used—the judges of Common Pleas, for instance, had the title 'Knight'.

Middle Temple Hall was built in 1573 when the law was comfortably established in the Crusaders' old kingdom. The hall, the dining hall of members of the Middle Temple, is very magnificent with a double hammer-beam roof, its shiny oak pendants shaped like great upturned pieces of chess. Barristers and student members have meals in the hall. The gleaming 29 foot long table on the dais is the Bench Table for the governors of the Inn (who are called 'Benchers'). The table was made from a single oak felled in Windsor forest and floated downriver, and is believed to have been a gift from Elizabeth who dined in Middle Temple Hall. The Minutes record that by the queen's orders no members except Knights and Benchers must wear doublet or hose of light colour (except scarlet or crimson), or a Spanish cloak or rapier or 'any beard of three weeks' growing'. The Benchers added a further rule: the only gowns allowed were 'such as be of a sad colour'.

Every inch of the Middle Temple Hall walls is covered with panels of coats of arms; they decorate the walls with fascinating complexities and date from the end of the sixteenth century up

11 *H.M.S.* Discovery, *the ship which took Captain Scott to the Antarctic in 1901–4. In the foreground, one of the dolphin-wreathed Embankment lamps* (*see Chapter 10*).

12 *Launches of Thames Division patrolling the River Thames (see Chapter 10).*

13 *William the Conqueror's White Tower, of Caen stone from Normandy, was built to guard the river approach to the City (see Chapter 13).*

to the present, overflowing along the walls of the corridors. These are the coats of arms of senior members who held the position of Reader. In the past the Reader did actually read at lectures (he no longer does). But he still places his coat of arms on the wall.

The hall was used for entertainments as well as for teaching and dining; in 1601 *Twelfth Night* was performed here, and it's believed that Shakespeare was either in the cast or in the wings. In James I's reign there were Royal masques designed by Inigo Jones, similar to those at Whitehall Palace. Jones was elected a Member of the Inn; so were Raleigh and Drake. The small table in front of the Bench Table is called a 'cupboard', its Tudor name, and was made from the hatch of Drake's ship *The Golden Hind*. Sir Francis Chichester presented the Inn with the Perspex hatch of his Gypsy Moth IV.

There is a ritual about dinner in Middle Temple Hall. Just as a table has been called a cupboard for 400 years, so a horn is blown in the court outside to signal to members hunting on the south bank of the river that the meal is ready.

A walk through the courts and squares of the Temple is very pleasant and peaceful. There are unexpected walled gardens, the stately seventeenth century buildings of *King's Bench Walk*, rows of old houses, tall trees. It is marvellous to find all this in the humming centre of the city. The Temple has been the home of writers as well as lawyers. Doctor Johnson lived here for five years though 'it must be confessed' said Boswell, 'that his apartments, furniture, and morning dress were sufficiently uncouth. His brown suit of clothes looked very rusty; he had on a little old shrivelled, unpowdered red wig, which was too small for his head.'

Boswell had chambers in *Inner Temple Lane* and enjoyed living in the Temple '. . . the most agreeable in the world for a single man'. He liked closing his door, taking his key in his pocket, and coming home at any time 'without giving disturbance to any other mortal'. He often attended the Temple Church. 'Heard a very good sermon on "Set thy house in order, for thou shalt shortly die". This with the music and the good building put me in a very devout frame.'

Oliver Goldsmith lived in *Brick Court* in a house which has been rebuilt. Unlike Boswell he did disturb other mortals. He gave noisy parties. Blackstone, the legal writer and later judge, was working on his famous *Commentaries* in the Brick Court house and complained bitterly about Goldsmith's revellings.

Goldsmith's fortunes and spirits were either up or down; he was always on a see-saw of happiness or misery. At the slightest success he spent all he earned and more on satin suits, carpets and kindness. His friends loved his gaiety and his warm heart and in his lifetime he was already accepted as one of the greatest literary figures of the day. But when he died in his Temple lodgings, at only 45, his death had partly been hastened by worry over debts. He is buried in the Temple churchyard; the stone, placed there in 1860, is near where his grave is believed to be.

Charles Lamb was born in *Crown Office Row* which faces the gardens to the north. His father was a clerk and servant to a Bencher in the Inner Temple. In one of his famous essays about the Temple Lamb writes: 'I was born and passed the first seven years of my life in the Temple. Its church, its halls, its gardens, its fountain, its river I had almost said—for in those young years what was the king of rivers to me but a stream that watered our pleasant places?—these are my oldest recollections . . . a man would give something to be born in such places.'

A fountain in memory of Charles Lamb stands in the gardens facing the Embankment—it is easy to see through the railings, a graceful statue of a little boy engraved with Lamb's words: 'Lawyers were children once.'

Fountain Court, which more or less overlooks the gardens, is particularly enchanting; it has a round pool full of goldfish and old bent trees sheltering it. Lamb wrote about Fountain Court, and Dickens used it in *Martin Chuzzlewit* as the meeting-place of Tom and Ruth Pinch 'coming briskly up, with the best little laugh on her face that ever played in opposition to the fountain'. Beyond is *Garden Court* and the sloping lawns going towards the river.

Most of London's oldest buildings have suffered devastating fires; the Temple is no exception. Twelve years before the Great Fire, Elm Court and Pump Court and the Temple cloisters were destroyed by a huge fire. The Thames was frozen hard, there was no water to be had from the river, and the fire-engines were filled instead with beer from the Temple cellars. When the beer ran out the buildings were blown up with gunpowder to stop the flames from spreading.

The frozen river was not an unusual happening; the Thames often turned in winter into a field of solid ice. In the Great Frost of 1683–84, John Evelyn wrote that coaches drove from Westminster to the Temple on the river ice and hackney coaches carried passengers across from Somerset House and the Temple to Southwark. After two weeks of hard freezing, Evelyn wrote: 'The weather continuing intolerably severe, the Thames . . . was planted with boothes in formal streets . . . all sortes of trades and shops furnish'd and full of commodities, even to a printing press.' There was sledging, horse and coach races and bull-baiting on the ice. But Evelyn thought the Great Frost was 'a severe judgement on the land, the trees not only splitting as if lightning-struck, but men and cattle perishing . . . and the very seas so lock'd up with ice, that no vessels could stir out or come in'.

The Temple gardens have been here since the Crusaders used the river walk for their place of meditation. The wall ran the length of the gardens, with a watergate in its centre and a flight of steps down to the water; boats came and went to the City and Westminster. The massive blackened stone archway on the Embankment at this point was designed by Bazalgette to mark the site of the Temple Stairs; but the Thames flowed where the road is now.

Roses flourished in the Temple gardens; the old-fashioned Maiden's Blush and Old Provence, the stout thick-petalled cabbage roses. There is a tradition that the Temple's red and white roses were those used as the two emblems in the bloody Wars of the Roses; it was in the Temple gardens that the rival lords of York and Lancaster each picked a rose.

The Temple trees used to be the home of great numbers of rooks; Goldsmith called them his 'black-dressed, black-eyed chatterers'. There are still plentiful birds in the gardens and the high old trees.

The two signs of the Temple, the Lamb and Flag and the Winged Horse are carved over many of the doorways and cloisters in stone or bronze. In the eighteenth century, some wit chalked a verse in praise of lawyers on the Temple Gate:

> The clients may infer from thence
> How just is their profession;
> The lamb sets forth their innocence,
> The horse their expedition.

Somebody disagreed with that and a second verse appeared:

> ''Tis all a trick; these are all shams
> By which they mean to cheat you:
> But have a care—for *you're* the *lambs*,
> And they the *wolves* that eat you.

Nor let the thought of "no delay"
To these their courts misguide you;
'Tis you're the showy *horse*, and *they*
The *jockeys* that will ride you.'

The *Swan-Uppers* leave the Temple Stairs every year on the last Monday in July. This is a ceremony which dates back to Elizabeth's reign; six skiffs rowed by oarsmen in red, white and blue jerseys, leave the Stairs, led by the Queen's Swan Keeper in his scarlet coat and the Vintners' and Dyers' keepers wearing green and blue. They work their way upriver as far as Henley-on-Thames, taking several days on the trip. Their watery task is the 'upping' of cygnets on the river for counting and marking. The Queen's swans stay unmarked, the Dyers' swans receive one nick on the beak, the Vintners' two nicks; about a thousand swans are examined every year. The first swans in England are believed to have been sent to Richard I by the Queen of Cyprus—the beautiful birds have always stayed in the care of Royalty.

East of the Temple are the blue arches of *Blackfriars Bridge*, with stout pillars of red polished granite and bases and capitals carved with swans and herons in Portland stone. The bridge was built between 1865 and 1869 and to modern eyes is acceptable, even pleasing. Its design was violently attacked in the Victorian press. It was, they said, 'a wonder of depravity . . . the parapet is a fiddle-faddle of pretty cast-iron arcading . . . on each corner of the bridge is a huge block of masonry, a propos of nothing, a well-known evidence of desperate imbecility'.

There is an underpass for traffic here; a new riverside walk parallel to the underpass and under the bridge is quite pleasant and marina-like.

On the foreshore east of Blackfriars Bridge someone looking for river relics in the 1920s found a sealed pottery bottle; inside it was human hair, some brass pins and rusty nails, and a heart-shaped piece of felt pierced with pins. It was a seventeenth century witch bottle. Others have been discovered in Westminster and Lambeth but this was the first found in the Thames. Witch bottles were used both by witches for spells and by ordinary people to fight against the black magic. To counteract a spell, the person put a piece of his own hair, a paring of his fingernails, a symbol of his heart pierced by pins and some loose nails and pins. The bottle was filled with urine and sealed; the spell would then work against the witch herself conjuring up the black arts.

St. Benets Church, off Upper Thames Street

11 LEFT BANK
Mermaid Theatre
St. Benet's
St. Paul's Cathedral
The Samuel Pepys
Southwark Bridge
The Old Wine Shades
Fishmongers' Hall
London Bridge
The Monument
St. Magnus Martyr

The *Mermaid Theatre* beyond Blackfriars Bridge is the creation of Sir Bernard Miles who saw, long before anyone else, the possibilities of using disused wharves and docks. Puddle Dock was probably the wharf of the ancient Baynard's Castle; in 1959 Miles built his new theatre, designed by Elidir Davies, to look out over the Thames. It is an attractively lively place, with a reputation for success; when it was new both its restaurants looked directly over the water. But recently land has been reclaimed on the river frontage of the theatre, and a road runs where the Thames used to do.

The entrance to the theatre's two restaurants is down an alley to the left. The ground-floor *Tavern* is inexpensive and pleasantly full at lunchtime with people who work in the city; up the iron stairway is the more expensive and smarter Riverside restaurant, which has good food and a view of the river across to the Royal George Wharf on the South Bank.

Next to the theatre is a waste of ground, once old wharves and warehouses, which is to be a new Telecommunications building. Isolated among the dusty desert is *St. Benet's Church.* Wren built this delightful Dutch-style church in 1677; it is of warm red brick festooned with decorations of flowers and has a graceful steeple. There was a Norman church on this site; Inigo Jones and his parents were buried there. Jones left £100 for a white marble monument 'in memorie of mee'. The Great Fire destroyed the church and its monuments; there is a little plaque in the wall of Wren's church commemorating Jones. The interior of St. Benet's is very attractive, with some beautifully carved woodwork. It's hoped that, during the dusty time while the huge new buildings are being erected close by, St. Benet's will survive without damage. It was planned to demolish the little church in the 1870s but the Welsh Episcopalians took it over and saved it. The Vicar of St. Andrews-by-the-Wardrobe just up the road is at present in charge.

Very close to St. Benet's is a pinnacled white tower, all that is left of another Wren church built in 1694, *St. Mary Somerset.* The churches standing together must have looked as if they were two parts of the same building, with dissimilar towers. St. Mary's was demolished in 1872 and angels now smile down from blocked-up windows and sealed doors leading nowhere.

The Norman fortress of *Baynard's Castle* stood at this point of the river. Ralph Baynard came to England with the Conqueror and built the castle which was the headquarters of London's army for 200 years, which later became a Royal residence.

During the Wars of the Roses, the Duke of York and Richard III both lived there at some time; Shakespeare sets one of his scenes in *Richard III* in Baynard's Castle. Henry VIII transformed it into a palace; Elizabeth dined there. But the castle was burned down in the Great Fire and now exists only as a London name—there's a Baynard Castle pub in Queen Victoria Street.

On the rising slope of Queen Victoria Street, and seen from the river, are the Wren churches (rebuilt after the Fire) of *St. Andrew by the Wardrobe* and *St. Nicholas Cole Abbey* and in the same street is the handsome brick mansion of the *College of Arms* (1671). But strictly speaking none of these is a riverside building.

St. Paul's Cathedral is not by the river but has always been an integral part of the river's panorama. Centuries-old engravings show clusters of little houses and churches, with the old Gothic cathedral always dominating the river scene. 'From the times of the Saxons,' wrote Walter Thornbury in the nineteenth century, 'London's chief sanctuary of religion has stood here above the river, a landmark to the ships of all nations that have floated on the welcoming waters of the Thames.'

There have been five St. Paul's. One was destroyed by Vikings. Two Saxon churches were burnt. The fourth, which people call *Old St. Paul's*, was built in the late eleventh century in the reign of William Rufus. The cathedral, part Norman and later Gothic, was the largest in Europe except for Seville and Milan and had the highest spire ever seen. The church was very beautiful with a magnificent vaulted ceiling, a huge rose window like that of Notre Dame, and flying buttresses. Round the cathedral was a kind of miniature town—the Bishop's Palace, Deanery, Chapter House, and a Cathedral School which was the foundation of today's St. Paul's school. In the churchyard was an open-air pulpit destined to become the famous *Paul's Cross*.

Just as Westminster Abbey was the shrine of St. Edward, the old Cathedral of St. Paul's contained the bones of a miracle-working Saint . . . the Bishop Erkenwald who had preached Christianity when the country was pagan.

The Cathedral was not only the city's chief church, it was also the scene of much political and religious violence. The people gathered at Paul's Cross when Richard I was away at the Crusades and denounced their rulers as tyrants. When it seemed as if there was danger of a rebellion in Henry III's reign, all Londoners, even children of 12 years old, were

St. Paul's Cathedral

summoned to Paul's Cross to swear allegiance. In 1377 John
Wycliffe was brought to St. Paul's on a charge of heresy; he
was defended by the king's son, the powerful John of Gaunt,
who was so loathed by the people that they burst into the
Lady Chapel where the trial was going on and stopped it.
There were many church trials for heresy at the Cathedral.
Found guilty, the victims were dragged off to Smithfield to be
burned at the stake.

St. Paul's was the place for the great state ceremonies:
Katharine of Aragon's first marriage to Prince Arthur, and the
ceremony when the sword and cap of maintenance were presented to Henry VIII as a gift from the Pope. Wolsey in his
crimson Cardinal's robes celebrated Mass at the Cathedral to
give thanks for the 'eternal' peace between France, England
and Spain; the Mass was attended by Henry VIII in a tunic

'powdered with pearls'. In 1521 Wolsey sat at Paul's Cross listening to the Pope's condemnation of Luther being read aloud, and watching Luther's works publicly burned. But the Reformation was stirring and more and more men were willing to die at the stake for rebelling against the Pope's authority; in 1534 that authority was actually denied at Paul's Cross.

Much that was beautiful and irreplaceable was destroyed in Old St. Paul's when the Reformation came. The high altar and the reredos were hacked to pieces, many of the tombs damaged except for John of Gaunt's by the king's express command. Mary Tudor reinstalled the Catholic faith in the Cathedral but the citizens had become Protestants at heart. When a Catholic sermon was preached at Paul's Cross, the crowd threw a dagger at the priest.

Elizabeth came to the throne and Catholicism was banished. But the Cathedral had suffered: from damage during the Reformation and from a fire which burned down its steeple and melted the bells. The Catholics said that the fire was God's judgment.

During Elizabeth's reign, in spite of the Queen attending a great celebration service for the victory of the Armada—she arrived in a chariot with trumpets blowing—the old Cathedral had begun to die. The people ill-treated it and the Church and State did not interfere. Shops and houses were built against the walls, the long Cathedral nave was used as a street where people sold goods, carried coal or walked with their horses; servants came to be hired there, advertisements plastered the walls; it was a meeting-place for criminals. The nave was nick-named 'Paul's Walk'. One bishop described the noise there as 'that of bees, a strange hum mixed of tongues and walking feet' and another bishop wrote of 'The walk where all our British sinners swear and talk. Old hardy ruffians, bankrupts, sooth-sayers.' Nobody repaired the church. The fallen spire was never replaced. It is true that James I called in Inigo Jones to plan how the Cathedral could be rescued and refurbished, but the long and complex work had scarcely begun before the Civil War broke out.

The Parliamentary forces rode into the Cathedral and com-pleted its ruin. They sold the scaffolding, and as it was pulled down the south transept collapsed. They burned the priests' copes to extract the gold, sold the altar silver to buy artillery, used the carved woodwork for firewood. The portico was let out to hucksters, the choir became a cavalry barracks. The soldiers stationed in the church were so noisy that they were forbidden to play at ninepins from 6 a.m. to 9 p.m. The Cathedral was a wreck—a 'loathsome Golgotha' someone called it.

The Great Fire of 1666 finished it off. Londoners were filled with horror and sadness as they watched the fire destroy their city. Pepys saw 'an entire arch of fire . . . in a bow up the hill for an arch of above a mile long; it made me weep to see it . . . and a horrid noise the flames made, and the cracking of houses at their ruine'. Evelyn saw the stones of St. Paul's flying like grenades and melted lead from the Cathedral running in streams down the streets. All the ancient tombs in the Cathedral perished—the shrine of St. Erkenwald, the graves of two Saxon kings, of John of Gaunt, of Sir Philip Sidney. Pepys went by river to Paul's wharf and saw 'a miserable sight of Paul's church with all the roofs fallen and the body of the quire fallen into St. Fayths'.

On that day there was a proclamation that all churches must stay open to receive the people homeless and injured in the fire.

Resurgam

It was hoped to save something of the old cathedral; the bishop preached a sermon in a patched-up corner of the ruins. But it was soon clear that a completely new building was needed and Wren, Surveyor General of the Works for Charles II, began the designs. He wanted to build a cathedral in the shape of a Greek Cross, the arms equal in size. There is a 20 foot long oak model by Wren in St. Paul's Trophy Room which shows the way he planned the church. The commissioners chose instead the Latin cross shape, with a long central nave and side chapels.

The plan of St. Paul's is conventional but not the huge circular space, the massive piers with pillars supporting the vast arches, and the Cathedral's marvellous dome. 'I build for eternity,' Wren said.

To build the new Cathedral he gathered round him the finest craftsmen of the day: sculptors and carvers, Jean Tijou who made iron as delicate as lace, Grinling Gibbons whose wood carvings have never been equalled. During the long years of building St. Paul's, Wren was criticized by jealous and sometimes ignorant people in authority; often he sorely needed that 'sweet humanity of his disposition'. His patron Charles II died in 1685 and as the years went by new men rose to eminence in public life: not all were his friends. When in 1697 the choir of the new St. Paul's was first open for divine service, Parliament was so dissatisfied at the slow progress of the building that it decreed half of Wren's salary should be kept back until the cathedral was finished. It was not until 1711 that Wren, by personally petitioning Queen Anne, received his arrears in salary.

Forty-two years after the Great Fire the last stone was placed in position in St. Paul's in 1708. By that time the expression 'St. Paul's workman' was used as a description of slowness. Ten years afterwards the commissioners insisted on adding a stone balustrade round the dome, in spite of Wren's protests that it broke the harmony of the design. When he was overruled, Wren merely said 'Ladies think nothing well without an edging'.

Both outside and inside the vast but perfect proportions of St. Paul's inspire a sense of awe. It could be that this church is too perfect, too much of one piece. It didn't grow and change over hundreds of years. Monks never walked or worked here. No pious king pulled down most of it to create a new shrine for his patron saint, nor did another king build, in a style utterly different from the rest, a chapel for his Royal bones. Of course, nobody struck the heads off statues or stabled horses in the Lady Chapel either. When Wren created St. Paul's, the Age of Reason was beginning; the architect had become scientist and mathematician. Sir Kenneth Clarke calls the cathedral 'the chief monument to English classicism'.

Visiting St. Paul's, the first impression is of heroic scale, a vastness enclosed in golden arches. The *sanctuary gates* in the North and South aisles are extraordinary. Tijou worked for eighteen years to produce these gold and black gates, intricate, delicate, some of the most beautiful gates in the world. The *choir stalls* by Grinling Gibbons are also wonderfully rich; it doesn't seem possible that so many leaves and flowers, berries and branches could be created from the trunks of pear trees.

For eighty years of the cathedral's life there were no monuments. The first monument at St. Paul's was rightly to Christopher Wren. After that, inevitably, more and more monuments were crowded into the great cathedral. St. Paul's became in time a sort of English Pantheon: the place where great monuments were erected to the country's heroes. In the north arcade is a monument to the *Duke of Wellington* which typifies this: a huge monument decorated with lions and cannon, a frieze of Wellington's victories in battle, a statue of the Duke on horseback on the topmost pinnacle.

Under the dome and next to the transept aisle entrances are statues to *Doctor Johnson*, plumpish in Roman toga, and *Sir Joshua Reynolds*. In the south wall is one of the few monuments which somehow miraculously survived the Great Fire; it is also the strangest monument in the cathedral. *John Donne* is sculpted in his shroud, which is gathered on top of his head like a crown. He was at James I's Court, a gifted fascinating man whom the king encouraged to go into the church; when young he wrote his now-famous erotic poetry; in age his equally famous poems of religion and metaphysics. He was made Dean of St. Paul's and lived nearby in a spacious house surrounded by gardens. A preacher of extraordinary power, the best of the era, Donne drew huge crowds to his cathedral sermons. His last sermon on 'Death's Dual' was preached four weeks before his death. By his own order when he was dying he sat naked in his shroud for the portrait on which this effigy is based. The linen clings close to his body, his handsome bearded face is peaceful.

The Crypt of St. Paul's is said to be the largest in Europe; directly below the dome is the tomb of *Nelson*. His body is in a coffin made from the mast of the French flagship *L'Orient*, destroyed at the Battle of the Nile. The sarcophagus enclosing the coffin is sixteenth century; it was sculpted by Benedetto da Rovezzano and was intended for Wolsey's tomb and later for Henry VIII's. Unused, it had lain in Windsor since the time of the Tudors.

An immense coronet lies on the top of Nelson's tomb which is as massive and commanding a monument as Napoleon's. When the coffin was carried into the cathedral by a group of sailors it was covered with his flag. Just before the burial, the sailors moved forward in a single movement and tore the flag to pieces for relics. The Dean heard 'the low wail of the sailors who encircled the remains of their admiral'. Nelson's companion *Collingwood* who fought with him at Trafalgar is buried almost beside him.

The *Duke of Wellington's tomb* is also in the centre of the crypt and like Nelson's is a mighty monument which could be that of an emperor. The car used to carry his coffin at the funeral is preserved in a further room in the crypt; it is elaborately decorated with metal melted down from guns captured at Waterloo, and was made in 18 days by 100 men working in two shifts. Wellington's coffin, lying on the funeral car, was pulled through the crowded streets of London by twelve black horses.

Now the car is here in the crypt, still hung with mourning tasselled flags which are slowly turning into dust.

Wren is buried in the South choir aisle. The inscription above is thought to have been written by his son. 'Si monumentum requiris, circumspice.' 'If you seek his monument, look around.'

There are soldiers and artists, composers and doctors commemorated in the crypt of St. Paul's. Lawrence of Arabia, Turner, Florence Nightingale, Alexander Fleming. There is a calm little chapel dedicated to the *Order of the British Empire*, with grisaille paintings of the Queen, the Duke of Edinburgh and other sovereigns of this very recent Order, founded in 1917.

And in a darkish corner are a few smoke-blackened effigies which survived the holocaust of the Great Fire. They belong to ages long before the Age of Reason. Some wear chain mail, some courtly garments. Many have no legs or faces, few have names. The King of the Angles is there, and Sebba, King of the East Saxons. These charred remains, and Donne in his marble shroud in the church above, are the only proofs that Old St. Paul's ever existed.

Visitors with energy and curiosity who do not suffer from vertigo will want to walk up the 116 steps to the *Whispering Gallery*, or further to the *Stone Gallery* at the base of the dome. Or even to the ball at the top of the lantern, a total of 627 steps to the top of the cathedral from the ground floor.

The Whispering Gallery was given its name because of its acoustics—a word whispered into the wall on one side can be heard clearly right over the other side a hundred feet away. Below is a magnificent if vertiginous view of the Cathedral, with diminutive figures moving across on the chequered floor. Above is the soaring dome which Wren had planned to decorate with gilded mosaics. But the commissioners refused; it would, they said, be too costly. Sir James Thornhill was invited to decorate the dome with scenes from the life of St. Paul. The paintings are in grisaille, a form of painting in greys and browns done to imitate sculpture. Thornhill, serjeant-painter to Queen Anne and George I, painted the pictures on an unrailed scaffolding. Once, anxious to see the effect of his figures of St. Paul, he ran back too far and would in one more step have hurtled to his death. In that second a friend standing beside him on the scaffold leaned forward and smeared the still-wet face of the Apostle. Thornhill rushed forward again shouting 'What have you done!' 'Only saved your life,' was the answer.

189

There is a marvellous view from the Stone Gallery over London, with the river winding into the distance; on a fine day one can see as far as the Surrey hills. An even more dramatic and far-seeing view is from the *Golden Gallery*.

St. Paul's Churchyard is the road surrounding the cathedral; to the north is a pleasant grassy enclosed place with a few nameless gravestones, facing the old Wren *Chapter House* (much restored) and the site of *Paul's Cross*. A statue of St. Paul on a plinth in the churchyard marks the place where the huge crowds used to gather to be roused or angered by great sermons preached in an open-air pulpit. Nobody knows why the pulpit was called 'Paul's Cross' or whether there was an actual cross here. At the base of the statue is a plaque which says 'On this plot of ground stood old Paul's Cross where amid such scenes of good and evil as make up human affairs the conscience of church and nation through five centuries found public utterance—Paul's cross was first recorded in 1191 and finally removed by the order of the Long Parliament in 1645. It was re-erected in 1905 'to renew the ancient memories'.

In St. Paul's churchyard an ancient Saxon gravestone was discovered, with runic lettering along the edge of the stone and a sculptured lion and snake; the runic words say: 'Gunne let lay this stone and also Toki.'

Along Upper Thames Street citywards from St. Benets is a narrow alley leading to the riverside restaurant and pub, the *Samuel Pepys* on Brooks Wharf. The building was an old warehouse, and has kept the battered ancient door which leads into a large downstairs bar. The roof inside is timbered, the walls are hung with painted Victorian signs for sailmakers and ropemakers. London lovers sit in dark corners on high-backed settees. An open stairway leads to the first floor restaurant with huge windows overlooking the river on two sides. Traditional English food is the Samuel Pepys's speciality, Mutton with caper sauce, Whitebait, Spotted Dick with brandy butter. On the second floor is another bar, with an open terrace facing Bankside, the spires of Southwark Cathedral, the curve of Blackfriars Bridge, and a lot of the Thames.

Southwark Bridge crosses from Upper Thames Street to the old Bankside on the South Bank. The bridge by Rennie which was here first was opened in 1819 'by lamplight, as the clock of St. Paul's tolled midnight'. It was between this bridge and London Bridge that Lizzie and her father, in the opening scenes of Dickens' *Our Mutual Friend,* fished for dead bodies in the river. The present bridge opened in 1921 was by Sir Ernest George.

The Great Fire started in this part of London, and one of the few buildings which survived the blaze is the *Old Wine Shades*, west of London Bridge in Arthur Street off Upper Thames Street. It is in a little lane called St. Martin's Lane. Built as a private house in 1663 it has had no structural alterations since then. Its smoky beams and walls, glass roof, and shiny tables and settles haven't altered for hundreds of years. Dickens used to come here frequently and would recognize it still.

The men who come to the Shades and who stand in the bar having a glass of sherry or beer all wear the dark, handsome clothes and black well-polished shoes which have been traditional to city people for years. London, it seems, hasn't changed in some ways. The food is plain, and service is very swift and polite. The quality of the drink is very good.

Fishmongers' Hall faces the river west of London bridge, a stately building of the 1830s with a pillared façade. The Fishmongers are one of the richest and the oldest of the City Livery companies and have owned a building on this site since Edward III was on the throne. Sir William Walworth, the man who killed Wat Tyler and saved Richard II's life, was Prime Warden of the Fishmongers as well as happening to be London's Lord Mayor as well. The Fishmongers still have his dagger.

Despite the highest connexions and the nobility who belonged to the Company (and for that matter still do), the Fishmongers are to this day concerned with fisheries and fishing. They had a monopoly of selling fish until the fifteenth century; today their inspectors examine all the fish coming into London and the Company is concerned with freshwater salmon, shell- fish, marine biology and combating the pollution of rivers.

Three times a year the public may visit Fishmongers' Hall; one has to apply through the City of London Information Office (by St. Paul's) for tickets and dates. The hall is full of remarkable things, for the Guild's history is an integral part of London and the river.

In the entrance hall is a table said to have come from Napoleon's boudoir, a circle of pure white marble; at the head of the stairs is a wood statue of Sir William Walworth, dagger in hand.

191

One of the greatest of the Fishmongers' treasures is their pall; it was used to cover the coffins of members of the Company when lying in state, and was embroidered by nuns in 1500. There are needlework portraits of St. Peter, accompanied by peacock-winged angels; the Saint kneels before Christ who gives him the keys; on either side are a merman in armour with the tail of a fish and a fair-haired mermaid with a jewelled mirror. The faces are worked in satin, the clothes decorated with gold and silver thread.

The Fishmongers have a model of their last State Barge, decorated with fat cherubs and a statue of St. Peter; the angels and the saint were rescued from the old barge and are in the hallway.

On important occasions the Doggett's Men line the grand staircase to the first floor, wearing their scarlet coats and badges and holding their oars upright. The *Doggetts Coat and Badge Race* is a Thames curiosity . . . it takes place each year as close as possible to August 1st when Thames watermen row from London Bridge to Chelsea. Thomas Doggett, an Irish comic actor and a friend of Congreve's, founded the race in celebration of the Hanoverian accession and also as a tribute to the Thames watermen. The six competing watermen must have recently completed their apprenticeship—the race is a test of expert watermanship. Doggett decreed that the race should be rowed 'annually on the same day forever'. The winner gets a scarlet livery coat buttoned in silver, with a silver badge on the left arm showing the word 'Liberty' and the Hanoverian white horse. Doggett was a member of the Fishmongers, who have organized the race ever since he started it. There is an amusing portrait of Doggett on the first floor.

On the landing is a post-war stained glass window patterned with vividly coloured coats of arms. A secret message written with a diamond on the window was only recently discovered. Hidden away among the bright colours in miniscule writing are the words: 'Roy Merridale, aged 18, did all the work and received no credit.'

The Fishmongers' have a collection of fine pictures; there are delightful river and quayside scenes by Samuel Scott, two Romneys, and two portraits by Annigoni. The Guild is proud of commissioning Annigoni, when he was more or less unknown in England, to paint them a portrait of the Queen. He did the now world-famous painting of her in her Garter robes. He also painted Prince Philip for the Fishmongers. Annigoni has put a

14 *Dolphin and Girl fountain outside the new hotel at St. Katharine's dock built beside Tower Bridge (see Chapter 13).*

15 *Greenwich's* Cutty Sark, *the tea clipper launched in 1869, and now in dry dock near the Royal Naval College (see Chapter 14).*

pin-sized portrait of himself into both pictures; in the Queen's portrait he is a tiny figure in a boat on a river—in Prince Philip's a miniature fishmonger weighed down with a huge salmon on his back, staggering up a hillside.

The dagger which killed Wat Tyler in 1381 with a 'swashing blow', that same dagger used in the design of the City of London's flag is in the Fishmongers' Drawing Room in a glass case. It is small, sharp and deadly-looking, the handle covered with fine silver wire.

There are many other treasures in the Fishmongers' Hall: crests from gilded barges, a carved chair for the Prime Warden, wonderful eighteenth century silver candelabra. It is remarkable how many of these things are decorated with symbols of water. Everything seems carved or sculpted or painted with water signs—with shells or fishes, mermen or mermaids, Neptune, or St. Peter, the old patriarch and patron of fishermen.

London Bridge, most famous of the bridges of London, is a disappointment. It was completed in 1973 to the designs of Harold King and Charles Brown, a wide flat balustraded bridge, gracefully plain. And that is all. It stands slightly upriver from the historic first bridge that spanned London river.

There may have been a Roman bridge at this point; recent excavations have found two main Roman roads converging on the South Bank near the site of the medieval bridge—archaeologists think they may point to where a Roman bridge stood. There was certainly a wooden Saxon bridge which the Danes held during a battle until Olaf, an ally of King Ethelred, tied his ships to the bridge's piles and pulled the bridge and the enemy down into the river. Olaf was later canonized and there is a city church dedicated to him.

The first stone bridge across the river was begun in 1176 by a priest-architect called Peter de Colechurch; it took thirty-three years to build and he did not live to see it finished. Though damaged, altered, added-to and always needing repair, de Colechurch's stone bridge stood from 1208 for over 600 years. It was finally demolished in 1824.

The bridge was like a little town on the water. It had nineteen pointed stone arches and its piers were raised on platforms: on one of these a 40-foot-high chapel to St. Thomas à Becket was built, with pinnacles and a tall Gothic window. The crypt of the church was inside the pier; when the bridge was demolished, de Colechurch's tomb was found there. The street which ran from one end of the bridge to the other, like Florence's Ponte Vecchio, had houses on either side. There was a gatehouse at each end and a drawbridge in the middle. Near the drawbridge was the marvellous Nonsuch House which was brought over from Holland in Elizabeth's reign and erected with only wooden pegs to hold it together, a house four storeys high with carved and gilded balconies and four pinnacled towers. In his *Curiosities of London* in the mid-nineteenth century, John Timbs writes that 'the chronicles of this stone bridge through near six centuries and a quarter form, perhaps, the most interesting episode in the history of London. The scenes of fires and siege, insurrection and popular vengeance, of national rejoicing and of the pageant victories of man and of death, of fame or funeral—it were vain for us to attempt to recite.'

The old records and histories of the city all tell the bridge's story because so much of the city's life happened there. It was a place for state ceremonies: the citizens presented Richard II with a white horse hung with silver bells on London Bridge; the Mayor welcomed the victorious Henry V. The bridge was decorated for the King with huge effigies of a lion, a unicorn and St. George, and banners proclaimed: 'the streams of the river make glad the city of God.' There were riots and revolts too. Jack Cade and his rebels captured the bridge, but he was defeated and beheaded and his head put on a pike at the gatehouse. The barbarous custom of sticking heads on poles at the bridge's spiked gates continued for hundreds of years. In the fourteenth century the Scots patriot and hero Wallace was hanged, drawn and quartered and his head set on a pole. In Henry VIII's reign the practice became worse. Both Bishop Fisher's head, and Thomas More's, were stuck up on the bridge. Edward Hall, the Tudor historian, describes what happened when Fisher's head was put up . . .

'after . . . the space of 14 days on London Bridge . . . [the head] could not be perceived to waste or consume . . . but grew daily fresher and fresher, so that in his lifetime he never looked so well . . . the face looked as though it had beholden the people passing by, and would have spoken to them, which many took for a miracle.'

So many people crowded to see the Bishop's head that the bridge was blocked with horses, carriages and crowds, and when the head was thrown into the river at last and Thomas More's head put up to replace it, the same thing happened; the head of the saint seemed to be alive. More's daughter Margaret Roper finally bribed somebody to drop her father's head down to her in a boat under the bridge. She preserved it in a casket and it was buried with her at St. Dunstan's in Canterbury.

Except for the wide central span through which the ships passed, the tide rising and falling poured through the bridge's narrow arches in a cateract. A London sport was to 'shoot the bridge'—people in boats skimmed through the arches on the rushing tide like surf-riders, sometimes overturning and drowning. An old saying was 'London Bridge was made for wise men to go over, and fools to go under'. Many passengers left the watermen's wherries on one side of the bridge, walked over, and rejoined their boats on the other side. It was the slowing-down of the river by the narrow arches which caused the Thames to freeze sometimes, when the river was a field of ice for weeks and the great Frost Fairs were given.

The bridge must have been a curious place to live. Some of the houses and shops were joined from one side of the street to the other by little wooden bridges. People fished from their windows (the Thames was a 'fishfull river' then). Horses and carts clattered by. Holbein lived in one of the bridge houses and so did Hogarth when he was young.

The roaring waters flooding fiercely to and fro with the tides were a strong attraction to people thinking of suicide. People were often drowned by throwing themselves into the river, by murder or by accident. The bridge lasted until the mid-1700's but by then its houses were dilapidated, St. Thomas's chapel was a shabby warehouse, and the street itself had become dangerous. A contemporary writer described: 'the noise of the falling waters, the clamour of watermen, and the frequent shrieks of drowning wretches.'

It was decided to pull down the houses and to widen the bridge. A drawing of 1796 shows the bridge strangely bare and simplified without houses and gateways, with St. Magnus's spire on the north bank and the column of the Monument nearby. Rennie's stylish bridge to replace the Old London Bridge was already built by 1832 when the last remnants of so much London history was demolished. There are some fragments of the arches in the garden of St. Magnus Martyr. A model of Old London Bridge with Nonsuch House, St. Thomas à Becket's chapel and the swollen river rushing under the arches can be seen in the London Museum, soon to be housed in the Barbican.

Rennie's granite bridge was dismantled in 1968, and bought

by an American company; it was taken over to Arizona and rebuilt, stone by stone, in Lake Havasu.

The Thames by London Bridge has been the stretch of river richest in every kind of relic. Hundreds of objects, from bronze Roman lamps to Victorian clay pipes, have been found in the river mud. The most impressive, now in the British Museum, is a colossal bronze head of Hadrian fished out of the river in the 1830s. The statue is believed to have stood on a column in the forum to celebrate the Emperor's visit in AD 121.

Many, many Roman coins have been dredged from the Thames in the stretch between London Bridge and Billingsgate. The coins were in chronological layers of the river silt, thrown into the water at different dates during the long Roman occupation and may have been offerings to the river gods; people still feel irresistibly drawn to throw money into fountains.

From London Bridge, from many city streets and from the South Bank, the flaming copper urn at the top of the *Monument* can be seen. This slim Doric column was built by Wren to commemorate the Great Fire; in his mathematician's way, Wren made the column 202 feet tall and placed it 202 feet east of the place in Pudding Lane where the fire of London started. The Monument, half-way up a little rise in Fish Street hill, is very graceful; but Wren did not want the brass urn at the top, he planned a colossal brass-gilt statue of Charles II.

There is a bas-relief by Cibber at the column's base, showing the king in Roman kilt coming towards the disconsolate figure of London, her head bent and her hair loose. Behind the king the Duke of York holds a garland to crown the rising city and lifts a sword to defend her. There are goddesses in the sky above and homeless Londoners below. A Latin inscription which has an English translation describes how Charles 'son of Charles the Martyr' petitioned Parliament for rebuilding London while the ruins were still smoking. A tax was put on coal and used to rebuild the city: 'Haste is seen everywhere. London rises again.'

Defoe compared the Monument to a lighted candle, but Pope disliked it, particularly after a strong rumour was started that the Great Fire had been begun by a mad French Catholic. 'Where London's Column, pointing at the skies, Like a tall bully, lifts the head and lies' wrote Pope. Zealous Protestants living in the rebuilt 25 Pudding Lane put up an inscription about hell breaking loose as the result of the malicious hearts of barbarous priests. The inscription was taken down in Catholic James II's reign, replaced in William III's, and finally removed in 1756 because far too many people stood reading it and stopped the traffic.

When the Monument was first put up, members of the Royal Society met at the top to make astronomical observations. But it was found that the column vibrated too much and the Society moved somewhere steadier.

A notice at the Monument doorway says: 'No Lift. Just 311 Steps.' It is a long pull, but there are encouraging notices which tell how far one has climbed. 100 Steps. Half Way. There are also alcoves for visitors whose legs have begun to ache. From the top of the Monument, which is completely enclosed by an iron grill, there is a fine view of the river, Tower Bridge, the goldfish weather-vanes on the top of Billingsgate and many Wren spires. But a new block hides almost all the Tower, and St. Paul's is also jostled and partly hidden by high-rise buildings. Looking west in the often-misty distance, one can see ships at anchor . . . *Discovery* and *Chrysanthemum*, and further away still are the turrets of Westminster. Below, dwarfed in spite of its steeple, is St. Magnus Martyr.

Fish Street Hill goes down to the river past the Monument. There is a remarkable trade sign outside Number 46. The shop, which is still a ship's chandlers after 300 years, has a sign dated 1668 carved in shell-shaped wood of two boys in a boat.

South of the Monument and close to the river is *St. Magnus Martyr*, the traditional church of the fishmongers. The smell of fresh fish, pleasant and salty, hangs around the church entrance. There has been a church on this spot since William the Conqueror's reign; it stood at the entrance to Old London Bridge. Stow in 1598 described the fair parish church of St. Magnus but found most of the monuments defaced, though Henry Yvele (1400), the medieval architect of Westminster Abbey's nave, still had a monument there. St. Magnus was burned down in the Great Fire and rebuilt by Wren in 1671–78. Its spire is an elongated dome with a slither of delicate steeple. Inside, the church is dark and rich; there is a painted iron rest in which the gentlemen placed their swords during divine service, and a reredos of 'The Pelican In Her Piety'. Rare in a Wren church, it's possible to light a candle either to the Virgin Mary or to St. Magnus. People argue that the old church was dedicated to St. Magnus 100 years before this Viking saint was canonized. Can there have been another Magnus? But the Norse saint has now become the church's patron, and there is a Viking statue, wearing a horned helmet, of the saint.

Outside is an archway and a fine projecting clock, 1709, decorated with gold angels. When the houses on Old London Bridge were demolished the entrance to the bridge was under the arch of St. Magnus. Now, in a tiny courtyard with flowers and shrubs, one great stone remains from the first arch of the old bridge.

Globe Theatre, Bankside, burnt down in 1613

12 RIGHT (SOUTH) BANK
Bankside
Wren's House, Cardinal's Wharf
Bear Gardens Museum
Anchor Inn
Winchester Palace
Southwark Cathedral
George in Borough High Street
H.M.S. Belfast
Rotherhithe: Angel Inn, Mayflower Inn and
St. Mary's Church
Rotherhithe Tunnel

Bankside is as famous as Stratford, but who can find it? It lies on the south-east end of Blackfriars bridge, down a left turning off Southwark Street called Hopton Street. An oasis of little eighteenth century almshouses, founded by a Mr. Hopton in 1752, with a garden of lawns and plane trees, is on the right; then there is a dusty walk along wharves and past derelict buildings before Bankside begins.

On the right is the towering shape of the new L.E.B. Heat Station; beyond is a pretty eighteenth century house belonging to the Provost of Southwark Cathedral with a rose-emblem on the shield hanging outside the door. Next is a narrow seventeenth century house, *Cardinal's Wharf*. Spidery eighteenth century writing on a plaque says 'Here lived Sir Christopher Wren during the building of St. Paul's.' And adds that Katharine of Aragon also stayed here when she first arrived in England. Most people don't accept either story. But it would be nice to think of Wren living on Bankside, exactly opposite the growing shape of St. Paul's. Besides the great dome and towers of the cathedral there are eight Wren spires on the skyline of the north bank.

Down the side of Cardinal's Wharf is a narrow alley, *Cardinal's Cap Alley*, which passes a miniature walled garden belonging to Wren's house, with a few trees and bushes for birds to sing in.

Bankside was a quiet place of fields and marshes, with only the stately palace of the Bishops of Winchester and the abbey of St. Mary Overie built on the riverside until the 1580s. Then the London theatres suddenly sprang up and the whole place became a noisy, crowded, revelling centre of city life.

By a curious gap in the law after the monasteries were dissolved, two districts on the south bank were outside the city's jurisdiction; one was called Paris Garden, the other was near the Clink Prison which explains the curious phrase 'Liberty of the Clink'. Free of the city's laws, Bankside became a great place of pleasure. By 1613 there were four theatres, bear-baiting rings, cockpits and rings for baiting bulls. There were twenty noisy brothels, their names painted on the walls, 'The Castle', 'The Bell', and joke names referring to the Bishops of Winchester from whom the ground was leased: 'The Cardinal's Hat', 'The Cross Keys'. The whores were nicknamed 'Winchester Geese', and though their trade paid the rent to the bishops living a short distance away, the women were forbidden

Christian burial and buried in a patch of unconsecrated ground in Southwark called Cross Bones.

Shakespeare spent most of his working life on Bankside; he wrote for the players at the Swan theatre, and then for the Globe which was built in 1599. Many of the great tragedies were first performed at the Globe, including *Hamlet* and *King Lear*. In Park Street, parallel to Bankside at the end of Bear Garden Alley, is a bronze bas-relief plaque on the wall of Courage and Barclay's brewery, marking, more or less, the *site of the Globe*.

Teasingly little is known of Shakespeare's life in Southwark. Where did he live? What was his life like? When the Globe was built it was the finest theatre in London. But in 1613 it burned to the ground . . . it's said this happened during a performance of *Henry VIII* when cannon fire caught the thatch of the theatre.

Life at Bankside itself was crowded, revelling, noisy, dangerous; debtors and bankrupts, penniless actors and crowds of seamen thronged the riverside. It was a place of pleasure, poverty and crime.

Londoners coming to Bankside did not necessarily cross Old London Bridge but took wherries ferried across the river by the Thames watermen. One of these was John Taylor, who had been a seaman; 'seven times,' he wrote, 'I served Eliza queen.' He retired from the Navy with a lame leg and was a waterman for fourteen years. He began to earn money by writing verse; he was always ready with a suitable poem for a birth, a wedding or a funeral; he became a success, gave up his job on the river, bought an inn at Long Acre and printed his own poems. Ben Johnson was one of his patrons. Taylor liked to write about celebrations on the river; one of his verses describes a water pageant given by Charles I. He lived on until the Commonwealth. The river had given him two livelihoods—one as waterman, the other as Water Poet, a title he liked to give himself. 'But, noble Thames,' wrote Taylor, 'whilst I can hold a pen I will divulge thy glory unto men.' His verses, later, were looked down on—someone called him a 'literary bargee'.

Another fire, far greater than the one which burned down the Globe, was watched from Bankside when Pepys came by boat across the Thames during the Great Fire . . . 'and all over the Thames, with one's face in the wind, you were almost burned with a shower of fire drops . . . when we could endure no more upon the water, we to a little ale-house on the Bankside . . . and saw the fire grow, and as it grew darker, appeared more and more, and in corners and upon steeples, and between churches and houses, as far as we could see up the hill of the City, in a most horrid malicious bloody flame.'

Walking east along Bankside is a right turning down Bear Garden Alley leading to the *Bear Gardens Museum*. The building, an eighteenth century warehouse, is on the site of the Davies Amphitheatre, the last bull-baiting ring on Bankside. The Elizabethans relished bear-baiting and mastiffs were kept to bait the animals; Elizabeth came by barge to Bankside to see bears baited and brought the French Ambassador with her. The audiences were both courtly and plebian, thronged with seamen from the ships in the port of London. John Evelyn came to the last of the bull-baiting rings and so did Pepys, who thought it a 'rude and nasty pleasure'.

The warehouse is now part of the *Globe Playhouse Trust* and was opened in 1972 as a permanent Elizabethan theatre exhibition, with models of the Bankside theatres, those Wooden O's. The theatre models are fascinating; so is the model of a frost fair on the Thames, with Tudor houses covered in snow, the river a solid field of ice, shops and booths and a bull-baiting ring, all in the middle of the Thames. The Globe Playhouse Trust has some impressive aims: to reclaim the South Bank round Southwark, to found a world centre for Shakespeare studies, even to rebuild part of the old palace of the Winchester bishops. All kinds of lovely things are hoped for—a place for music, a riverside panorama of fine new buildings; and not a single block of high-rise flats.

The *Anchor Inn* (1775) is on the corner of Bankside facing the entrance to Clink Street; the inn stands on the site of two stews 'for the entertainment of lewd persons', the Castle On the Hoop, and the Gonne. The building was an eighteenth century coffee house; Doctor Johnson came here to be entertained by Mr. and Mrs. Thrale. The Anchor is now a restaurant and a pub and is full of historic treasures, including a 'Liberty Clink' shield of 1509 which granted a licence from the Bishops of Winchester for the use of Thames water in brewing. There are five bars, some on the ground floor, some upstairs, and also three charming panelled eighteenth century dining-rooms on the first floor overlooking the river. A little quay across Bankside and projecting into the river is used as an open-air bar in fine weather.

Clink Street, dark and gloomy, runs under Cannon Street Railway bridge, the two high black towers of which are still preserved on either side of the railway terminus entrance on the north bank. The notorious Clink Prison where the Bishops were imprisoned by Mary Tudor before they were martyred stood on this site; in 1642 the Clink was used for Royalist prisoners.

On the right in the dark narrow street next to a garage is all that's left of the thirteenth century mansion of the bishops— *Winchester Palace*. There is a lofty stone wall and the remains of a beautiful rose window only discovered in 1970. The palace was burned down in 1814. Until the Civil War the palace was a magnificent place. It was built round a series of courtyards and enclosed with high walls; there was a spacious park, gardens, fountains, and state apartments where the bishops lived. These faced the river. The flight of steps to the water was called The Bishop of Winchester's Stairs. During the Civil War the Paliamentarians took over the palace as a prison, using it as they used the Clink. The bishops' palace was returned to them in Charles II's reign but they never lived there again. As is the way with great and deserted places, it slowly fell into ruin.

Southwark Cathedral is a little west of London Bridge, slightly below street level, as the street rises at the approach to the bridge.

Originally the church was called St. Mary Overie, which Stow, in 1598, said meant 'over the Rie'—i.e. the river. A saintly lady called Mary founded a convent here; there was a ferry tradition said, in those early days and Mary inherited the profits of this ferry and bequeathed these to the convent. The church was refounded in 1106 as the priory of the Augustinian monks, called the Black Canons from the colour of their habits. The monks were dedicated to care for the poor and the sick, and founded a hospital beside the Abbey consecrated to St. Thomas. It was the first St. Thomas's Hospital.

When the abbey was dissolved at the Reformation it was re-named St. Saviour's and became the parish church of the district. St. Saviour's, like all very old churches, has been part destroyed, rebuilt, added-to, altered. It was burned down in 1206 and rebuilt in the Gothic style: the beautiful pinnacled tower with its gold pennants is thirteenth century—the highest part of the tower is Tudor. During and after the Great Fire, Hollar made many of his engravings from the vantage point at the top of the Cathedral tower.

The church's interior is spacious. On the left near the entrance are a number of *wooden bosses* which came from the fifteenth century roof of the nave; it is usually impossible to see the carvings high up in ancient roofs and these are very fascinating—boldly and coarsely carved in shiny rich wood. There is a horribly grimacing Gluttony, and a Devil eating Judas, half of whose body in a skirted coat hangs from the devil's mouth.

On the paving near the bosses is a tomb with a skeleton effigy. There is a legend that this is the effigy of an Augustinian monk who fasted for forty days in imitation of Christ.

The beautiful *altar screen* is sixteenth century, and although the rows of gilded angels and saints are more recent they suit the altar and harmonize with it.

St. Mary Overie's stood by Bankside with its bustling theatres and the church was used by actors and playwrights. Shakespeare's youngest brother *Edmund*, described in the register simply as 'a player', is buried here. He died, aged 27, in 1607. His name is carved on a slab in the floor of the choir stalls, and nearby are the names of two dramatists, *Fletcher* and *Massinger*. John Fletcher, who worked at the Globe, is believed to have collaborated with Shakespeare on *Henry VIII* and the rarely-seen *Two Noble Kinsmen*. Fletcher's best-known work written with Beaumont is the comedy *The Knight of the Burning Pestle*. Fletcher died in 1625 of the plague. Philip Massinger is buried in the same grave—he had worked with Fletcher at the Bankside theatres. Massinger wrote brilliant, heartless comedies; his many plays are seldom performed except, occasionally, *A New Way to Pay Old Debts*. He was a man always in trouble over money and died penniless. The church register called him: 'Philip Massinger, a stranger,' but the cool phrase merely means that he was not one of the parish.

On the right of the altar is the elaborate tomb of *Lancelot Andrewes*, Bishop of Winchester, who lived and died at the palace which stood next to the Cathedral. Andrewes' effigy shows him in his prelate's Garter Robes of rich dark blue. He was a man of learning and a talented preacher—Elizabeth enjoyed his sermons and made him one of her chaplains.

The massive ornamented *sixteenth century chest* behind the altar was used for storing the Parish records. The oak *effigy of a knight*, dated 1280, lies near by. The knight, with an aristocratic Norman face, may be a member of the De Warrene family who were benefactors of the old Abbey.

The effigy on the left of the altar is *Alderman Humble*, 1616, with his two well-dressed Jacobean wives and a row of their kneeling children. Opposite is the entertaining memorial to *John Trehearne*, 1618, 'Gentleman Portar' to James I. The effigies of Trehearne and his wife glare furiously at passers-by; below is an epitaph praising the Portar's many virtues.

The Harvard Chapel, on the east of the transept, was rebuilt in 1907 and commemorates the Harvard who founded the American University. The chapel is simple and colourful, with a stained glass window of angel figures, coats of arms by the American artist John Lafarge (1905) and the American flag hanging on the wall.

The decorative tomb of *Lionel Lockyer* (1672) is in the North Choir Aisle; Lockyer wears a curling full-bottomed wig and reclines gracefully asleep on one arm. He was a quack doctor, noted in Stuart times for selling pills which he claimed had substances in them extracted from the sun's rays that would cure 'a regiment of diseases'. In his long and enthusiastic epitaph are two lines:

> His virtues and his PILLS are soe well known
> That envy can't confine them under stone.

Not far from Lockyer's memorial is an enchanting Stuart plaque (1633) on the west wall, dedicated to the *Austen family*. Who were they and why were they so rural and happy? There are pretty girls with straw hats holding hay-rakes and forks, and beside them stooks of ripe golden corn.

A little of the old Norman church of St. Mary still survives in the Gothic cathedral. Through a low arch by the door of the Canon's vestry, quite 2 feet below the level of the present church, is the entrance to the monks' cloister and a stone holy-water stoup. Close to the Norman doorway in the north aisle is one of the Cathedral's most interesting tombs, the monument and tomb of *John Gower* (1408), friend of Chaucer and one of the earliest of English poets. Gower himself designed the tomb but it was repaired and repainted in 1832 by the Duke of Sutherland's family who claimed to be related to Gower. The uncompromising reds, greens and golds used in the repainting are much too coarse and destroy some of the tomb's medieval beauty. Gower's effigy is prophetlike; he has a forked auburn beard and long auburn hair. He wears a damask-patterned robe and as Stowe described it 'a chaplet of foure roses onely'. This wreath of flowers was 'in token that he in his life-daies flourished freshly in literature and science'. His head is on three of his books, one in French, one in Latin and one in English; on the wall above are delicate figures of Charity, Mercy and Pity.

This tomb was part of a chantry chapel built with the money Gower had left for his memorial. The chapel is lost and over the centuries the tomb has been moved around the cathedral a number of times but it is in good condition. 'The moral Gower', as Chaucer called him, came from the nobility; he was court poet to Richard II and also to Henry IV. Henry decorated him with the Lancastrian badge of the Silver Swan. Shakespeare took the story of *Pericles* from Gower's retold medieval legend, the *Confessio Amantis*, his masterpiece about love. Gower is a character in Shakespeare's play and acts as Chorus.

In the south aisle is the alabaster memorial to *Shakespeare*, in a decorated alcove above which are three stained glass windows showing scenes and characters from his plays . . . Lear . . . Hamlet . . . Falstaff . . . Caliban. The memorial was placed here in 1912. The graceful figure of Shakespeare is carved in a beautifully-coloured alabaster of bluish browns, creams and blacks. His hand, knee and elbow are pale and polished; one wonders if visitors affectionately touch them as they go by. Behind Shakespeare in bas-relief is the Bankside and old Southwark. The Globe's flag is flying as it did when a play was being performed.

The Borough High Street was one of the most important coach roads into London for hundreds of years. It was the entrance from Surrey, Kent and the Continent. The street was also close to the Bankside theatres and teemed with inns, of which the most famous was the Tabard where Chaucer's Canterbury-bound pilgrims collected before beginning their pilgrimage to Becket's shrine. Most of the inns from the fourteenth to the seventeenth century were built around a courtyard, with outside galleries leading to the bedrooms. The only galleried inn left in London is the *George, Borough High Street*. It is five minutes' walk from Southwark Bridge on the left through two large green gates.

The Tudor inn was partly burned down in 1760 and a second fire seven years later finished it off; but it was rebuilt to the old plan in 1777. Like the medieval inns which crowded Southwark, the George had galleries on three sides facing a central courtyard where horses and coaches waited. Only one of the George's galleries has survived but this, in the middle of modern London, is quite a miracle. The pub has a jolly, almost a country atmosphere, and is often crowded with Southwark people, though it is also much enjoyed by visitors. The restaurant, medium-priced and with good but not elaborate food, overlooks the courtyard. The bar has old-fashioned wooden benches, a fire in winter, and an old Parliament Clock; this is a relic from the days when watches and clocks were so highly taxed that people refused to own them; innkeepers kept clocks to please their customers. In the bar there are freshly-made hot pies and an excellent choice of sandwiches.

Alongside the wharves of the South Bank directly opposite Tower Pier the cruiser *Belfast* is moored; it is the only naval ship which can be visited on the Thames. *Belfast* was almost sent to the scrapyard, but was saved by a Trust begun by the Imperial War Museum. The ship is now preserved as nearly as possible in her original state, so that visitors can see a warship in working order. One can walk along the decks, visit the bridges and gun turrets. Climbing steep companionways, stooping through narrow steel doors, huddling into the turrets where the guns are kept in gleaming order, one has a keen impression of the spartan life at sea.

The *Belfast* went on Russian convoys in the last war and was in the battle which sank the *Scharnhorst*; she also supported the Normandy landings, was in the Far East, and fought in the Korean war.

There is a well-presented exhibition of maps, photographs and diagrams illustrating the role of the cruiser and the history of cruiser warfare. As different parts of the ship are made ready for visitors, these will also be opened.

Beyond Tower Bridge (covered in a later chapter) lies Bermondsey, and the now-closed Surrey Commercial Docks. Facing Wapping on the South Bank is *Rotherhithe*—once a village called Redriff, the name John Gay gave to it in the *Beggar's Opera*, and still used as a road-name. Off the Jamaica Road is the *Cherry Garden Pier*; boats needing Tower Bridge to be raised as they pass up the Thames always signal to the bridge when they reach this pier.

This part of the riverside, now open and in many places freshly rebuilt, was used as one of the darkest and most sinister settings of Dickens's *Oliver Twist*. He describes the buildings on the river banks as '[the] dirtiest and the smoke vessels on the river blackest with the dust of colliers and the smoke of close-built low-roofed houses . . . the filthiest, the strangest, the most extraordinary of the many localities that are hidden in London'. The Rotherhithe people Dickens described were 'unemployed labourers . . . ballast-heavers, coal-whippers, brazen women, ragged children, and the raff and refuse of the river', and in a ruinous warehouse here Bill Sikes fell from a roof to his death.

In Rotherhithe Street by a patch of green with the grandiose name of King's Stair Gardens is the old *Angel* pub, a pleasant eighteenth century building with an open wooden balcony directly overlooking the water. At low tide the beach of pebbles is surprisingly clean; downriver the river widens and curves, upriver is the Gothic silhouette of Tower Bridge, and barges moor beside the pub—a pleasant place for drinks and plain, good food.

Another old pub overlooking the river is in Mayflower Road, off Brunel Road. This is the *Mayflower* inn, named after the famous ship which took the pilgrims to America. Many of the ship's crew were men from Rotherhithe. The *Mayflower* is small, cramped and cosy, with models of sailing ships about, and a railed-in pier built out over the river, with a ladder leading down to the beach or a boat. It is so fresh and cheerful in Rotherhithe, sitting on this open-air terrace in fine bright weather, that it is difficult to see it with Dickens's eyes.

When Brunel was working his great project, the Rotherhithe tunnel, crowds of the navvies building the tunnel came here every day. A curious thing about the *Mayflower* is that it is the only pub in London with a licence to sell stamps . . . the licence goes back to the days when seamen, with only a few hours shore-leave, just had time to write and post a letter before taking ship again.

A street away from the *Mayflower* is *St. Mary's, Rotherhithe*; there has been a church on this spot for a thousand years. This St. Mary's was built in 1715; at the foot of the staircase leading to the west gallery is a copy of the petition made to Parliament in 1710 asking for a new church (the old one was falling down). Parliament said no, so the parishioners collected the money themselves.

Rotherhithe was a shipbuilding village and there are signs of skilled shipwrights' work in the church. The wooden frame and supports above the roof were made by a man who knew his craft well; the pillars supporting the roof are each a complete tree trunk inside a thin plaster skin.

Captain Christopher Jones, the Master of the *Mayflower*, is buried in the churchyard and so are three of the four part-owners of the ship. There is a plaque in memory of the voyage on the left of the sanctuary.

The church is beautifully cared-for, full of flowers, welcoming. The organ is magnificent, with two slender trumpeting angels at its top; it was built in 1764 by John Byfield and has been called 'the most complete ancient organ in London'. Part of the carved fruit and flowers of the reredos is by Grinling Gibbons; among the carvings are two open pea-pods, the little symbols he used to sign his work.

Facing the church is the *Charity School*, 1742–1797, with two figures of children over the doorway. In the seventeenth and eighteenth century it was often the custom to put figures like this over the doorways of the schools; the Rotherhithe boy wears a blue skirted coat, the girl a long dress and prim apron.

The churchyard next door to the school, its walls lined with old gravestones, is now a well-tended garden.

The *Rotherhithe Tunnel*, which has two lanes of traffic and a pavement for foot passengers, crosses under the Thames at Rotherhithe. It was built in 1908, and comes out on the north bank in Wapping near the King Edward Memorial Gardens.

Tower Bridge

13 LEFT BANK

Billingsgate
Custom House
St. Mary At Hill
St. Dunstan's-in-the-East
St. Olave's, Hart Street
All Hallows by the Tower
Tower Pier
Tower of London
Tower Wharf
Port of London Authority
Tower Bridge
St. Katharine's Dock: World Trade Centre and
St. Katharine-by-the-Tower
Wapping: Thames Tunnel: Town of Ramsgate: Wapping
Old Stairs: Execution Dock: Prospect of Whitby:
King Edward Memorial Park: Rotherhithe Tunnel
Bunch of Grapes, Limehouse
Royal Naval Victualling Yard, Deptford
Millwall

Billingsgate Fish Market was mentioned in Saxon times as the only wharf in London. Fish-boats brought their cargoes there. In 1699 an Act of Parliament made Billingsgate a free open market for fish for six days a week (and for mackerel on Sundays before divine service). In George II's reign a further Act stopped Billingsgate from having a monopoly.

Before the railways, travellers embarked at Billingsgate, and sailors as well as sellers of fish and fishermen collected on the wharves and quays. Even in the mid-nineteenth century coaches came clattering up to Billingsgate from Dover and Hastings.

The fish market opens at six in the mornings (in Victorian times it was four). It is enormously busy for about four hours, a place of noise and hurry, piled with the fresh catches from all the seas round Britain. The fish porters wear flat-topped hats made of wood and leather and carry about 100 lbs of fish on their heads quite comfortably. In the past their bad language, like that of the Thames watermen, was a legend; in the eighteenth century the word 'Billingsgate' came to mean a foul-mouthed person.

The market building of yellow brick with arcades facing the river was built in 1874. Above its entrance is a stone statue of Britannia with fishes on either side of her. On the market roof are gilded weather-vanes of fishes with curling tails.

Next to the fish market is a Regency building in Portland stone and brick, the *Custom House* built in 1814–17 with some alterations in 1826. The first Custom House stood here in 1385; a larger one, but still only the size of a small house, was built in Elizabeth's reign. The Great Fire destroyed that, and Wren rebuilt it as a classic stately place with porticoes and arches. When the foundations were being dug, many Roman relics were discovered. But Wren's Custom House and two further buildings were burned down. The present building seems to have stayed the course.

The Custom House is the headquarters of the board of Customs and Excise, and in the Long Room masters report their ships' arrival and cargo. A floating double-decker pier is built in front of the building: it has the ironic name of 'Harpy'. From this pier the Customs and Excise men leave in their launches on inspection tours to visit incoming vessels, check cargoes and give customs' clearance.

The quay in front of the Custom House is very long—490 feet facing the river. The poet William Cowper once planned to commit suicide here. He arrived by coach only to find that the tide was low, and 'a porter seated upon some goods there, as if on purpose to prevent me. This passage to the bottomless pit being mercifully shut against me, I returned back by coach.'

Stow called *St. Mary At Hill* 'the fair parish of St. Marie, called on the hill, because of the ascent from Billingsgate'. Lovat Lane runs straight up from the fish-market by the river and is lined with tempting signs for smoked salmon and jellied eels. Thomas à Becket is believed to have been a priest in the medieval St. Mary's which wasn't all destroyed in the Great Fire. But Wren rebuilt it in 1670, and it was partly rebuilt again in both the eighteenth and nineteenth centuries.

The interior of the church is extremely handsome; the ceiling, blue, white and gold, is decorated with palms and lilies. The roomy, comfortable old seventeenth century box pews are the only pews of their kind left in a city church. On two of these are coats of arms elaborate with dragons and coronets. The hatchments of the Duchess of Kent, Queen Victoria's mother, and of the Prince Consort, hang in the church. In the vestry outside is what is called a *Resurrection Stone* rescued from a graveyard, a very old carving of Judgement Day, showing all the coffins bursting open and the cheerful dead rising up.

An interesting passage outside the church on the south side leads under the old Rectory and into the lane. Matching the stone in the vestry is the decoration over the door, crossed bones and a skull crowned with laurel.

Two turns east on the left is *Idol Lane*, and the bombed remains of *St. Dunstan's-in-the-East*. There was a fourteenth century church here; a chronicle describes a Lord L'Estrange and his wife doing penance 'because they gave a cause of murder in this same church and polluted it'. St. Dunstan's was repaired by Wren after the Fire; when the foundations were being dug, a Purbeck marble floor was found which was worn away to a depth of several inches by the monks' sandals; there were also the monks' stone benches and some mullioned windows. Wren's church was destroyed in 1941 but its tower and lantern steeple, supported by ribs, have been preserved. A little part of the church is kept as a chapel and all the rest inside the old church walls has been turned into a delightful garden, planted and kept by the Worshipful Company of Gardeners. In fact it is three gardens, one leading into the other; there are magnolias and heathers, fig trees which bear ripe fruit, a weeping willow, clematis, flowering lavender, all within a four-minute walk of the river.

The city of London is full of churches, very few of which are on the riverside. A little distance from the Thames up Mark Lane is *St. Olave's, Hart Street* dedicated to Norway's patron saint. The Saxon church on this spot was rebuilt in the fifteenth century and escaped the Great Fire. Pepys worked in the Navy Office opposite the church and went regularly to services here—he often mentions St. Olave's in his diary, sometimes complaining of having to endure tedious long sermons. The church was seriously damaged in the 1941 bombing and only the twelfth century crypt, the tower and the 1662 vestry survived intact.

The interior of St. Olave's, in the way of many restored city churches, is too bright and light. But there are interesting memorials to be seen, including the delightful bust by John Bushnell of *Pepys's wife Elizabeth*, 'the only contemporary likeness of her in existence'. Pepys had the monument put up after her death in 1669. She has a lively face, heavy-lidded eyes and a double chin; her curled hair falls fashionably over one shoulder and she wears earrings. There is a Victorian plaque (1884) to *Pepys* by Sir Arthur Blomfield; both Pepys and his wife are buried in the vault under the chancel. On the left of the altar, the kneeling figure is said to be the *mother of Sir Philip Sidney*.

During the Plague Years of 1665, the church register in St. Olave's showed that 326 people died instead of the usual small number—many city churches had only a dozen or so burials a year. Pepys, who had stayed in London to work during the Plague, wrote: 'But Lord, what a sad time it is to see no boats upon the river, and grass grows all up and down White Hall court, and nobody but poor wretches in the streets!' When the Plague was over and he went to St. Olave's, it upset him. 'It frighted me indeed to go through the church, more than I thought it could have done, to see so many graves lie so high upon the churchyard . . . do not think to go through it again for a good while.'

The churchyard is now a cheerful place, with beds of flowers and young trees, but the entry through the old gateway is decorated with sculpted skulls and crossed bones. Dickens mentions these, and the church, in *The Uncommercial Traveller*, he calls the church 'St. Ghastly Grim'.

Within sight of the river on rising ground west of the Tower is the church of *All Hallows by the Tower*. It is on the site of a Roman villa and proudly announces its Saxon date—657. Like many city churches, it survived the Great Fire but not the 1941 bombing. The ancient side walls remain and the tower built when Cromwell was in power—the only city church tower built during the Commonwealth. Parliamentarian soldiers were transporting gunpowder down the street by the church when it exploded and destroyed the tower. Cromwell gave special permission for a new one to be built. Pepys climbed this tower to watch the Great Fire on September 5, 1666 but soon left because he was 'afeared to stay there long'.

The *Mariners Chapel* in the South Transept of the church is hung with every kind of ship's model, presented by sailors in thanksgiving for safe voyages. The sailors who thronged the riverside used to come to All Hallows to be blessed before going on a long sea voyage; a procession left the church after the blessing to accompany the sailors to their ships. When the sailors came safely home they gave All Hallows a model of the ship they had sailed in.

The *font* in the small baptistry has a carved limewood cover by Grinling Gibbons of two delightful cherubs; it is called 'Cupids stealing Grapes'.

A knowledgeable guide will take visitors round the crypt of the church. In the 1920s the church floor collapsed and a Roman tessellated pavement of AD 200 was found underneath, together with a small perfect Saxon arch of A.D. 657. Further excavations uncovered layers of ash, all that was left of London after Boadicea and her tribesmen burned it to the ground in AD 61.

The crypt is now a small museum. The Roman pavement and Saxon arch are in good condition and there is a Roman bust of Julia, found in the river mud near Tower Bridge; there are also casts of Roman tombstones found near the church, including one to a soldier of the 'Sixth Victorious Legion'. A scale model shows the temples, buildings and river of Roman London, including the vanished tributary, the Wallbrook, and the countryside and marshes which surrounded the city walls; by far the largest mass of buildings in Roman-occupied London was the barracks.

Because the church was so close to the Tower, it was used long ago as a temporary burial place for prisoners who had been executed there. Both Bishop Fisher and Thomas More were given shallow temporary graves in the churchyard. Two distinguished American names are connected with All Hallows— William Penn who founded Pennsylvania was born on Tower

Hill and baptized in this church in 1644; and J. Quincey Adams, the sixth American President, was married here in 1797.

One curious old story about the church captures the imagination. After the gunpowder explosion of 1649 when the church tower was destroyed and many people killed, a baby was found in a cradle on the upper leads of the church 'neither the child nor the cradle having the least sign of any fire'. Nobody knew who the baby was, but a man in the parish kept the child who grew up to be 'a proper maiden'.

At the bottom of Tower Hill, directly west of the Tower, is *Tower Pier*, one of the stopping-places for the river launches and hovercraft; there is also a ferry service from the pier to the *Belfast* across the river. It was from Tower Pier that Churchill's funeral flotilla left for Westminster after the State funeral service in St. Paul's. The coffin was put on board the *Havengore* and as the ship moved upriver, all the dockside cranes dipped in salute, and fighter aircraft dived overhead. Three launches went with the *Havengore* to Westminster, where the cortège landed at the Festival Pier.

The Tower of London

In 1589 Stow described the Tower as a citadel with many purposes. It was a Royal palace, a treasury for the king's jewels, an armoury; it was also a prison, the only mint in the kingdom, and a store-house for the records of Justice.

The Tower has had an army garrison since the eleventh century; today it has a Resident Governor and a staff who are all ex-Servicemen. No king has lived in the Tower for hundreds of years. Cromwell demolished a royal palace which had been built inside the Tower; other royal apartments were taken down during the reigns of James II and William and Mary. But the Tower has always been a state prison. It was used for prisoners in both world wars and spies have been executed there.

The wall of Roman London ran along the site of the Tower to Blackfriars and in Alfred's time there was a Saxon stronghold on that particular piece of ground overlooking the river. William the Conqueror decided to build a citadel in exactly the same place. It was built inside the Roman walls which still extended to the river; high above the Thames, the Tower was a fortress for protecting London and guarding the river approach to the city. It was also built to awe the people. And still does.

Over the centuries more walls and towers, houses and fortified

buildings have been added to William the Conqueror's White
Tower. The two enormous containing walls are set with many
smaller towers (the inner wall has thirteen); the whole citadel
covers eighteen acres and when it was a fortress it was guarded
by a broad moat filled with water from the river. The only river
entrance to the Tower was heavily fortified.

As a citadel the Tower was built to resist attack and many
of its walls are between 11 and 15 feet thick. It has been
besieged many times—rebels once blockaded Richard II in the
Tower and marched round the streets with the Chancellor's
head on a pike. But the Tower has never fallen.

Despite its embattled and menacing aspect, the Plantagenets
used it as a royal palace, had a banqueting hall and a chapel,
royal apartments, council chambers. The kings kept, for fun, a
menagerie of wild animals in the Tower. The outside walls were
designed for watching and defence, but many of the inner
towers had other uses: there was the Mint, the Jewel House,
and a tower which served as London river's lighthouse for
ships, the Lanthorn Tower, where a light was constantly
burning.

People today look at the Tower with mixed feelings. Skimming by in a launch one sees the venerable old walls and pinnacles of a superb piece of medieval England. The White Tower
of Caen stone is like a castle in *Les Très Riches Heures du Duc de
Berri*, and was used in an illuminated poem written by a
medieval French prince imprisoned there. In sunshine, from
the south bank or from a boat, the Tower is wonderfully imposing. On a sunny morning it has a festive air and the walks and
lawns and armouries are busy with children noisy as starlings.
The bearded Yeomen Warders in their Tudor clothes show
visitors round and describe the dramas of the past with
theatrical panache.

Yet the fortress is a bloodstained place, and when it was at
the height of its power its name struck a chill into the bravest
heart.

The White Tower is the oldest of the Tower buildings and
named after its white Normandy stone. By tradition the
English king stayed here before his coronation, setting out in
procession to ride through the city to Westminster. The last
king to do this was Charles II.

Although the sovereign sometimes lived in the White Tower,
it was also one of England's most important prisons; many
princes and queens, leaders and rebels languished in its

dungeons. Richard II signed his abdication in the Tower, and at the base of a now demolished stair the bones of what were believed to be the Little Princes were found.

The White Tower is used today for a magnificent *Royal collection of arms, armour and weapons*. Charles II began the collection when soldiers stopped wearing armour in the seventeenth century; and the collection traces the development of armour in Europe from the fifteenth century.

The armour made for Henry VIII at the Royal Workshops that he founded at Greenwich is in the *Greenwich Room*; these workshops made some of the finest armours in the world. Henry's suits bring the king into commanding reality. The huge equestrian figure in the centre of the room wears armour made for the king when Katharine of Aragon was his queen. The armour is silvered and gilded, finely engraved with scores of initials, the 'K' and the 'H' tied together in lovers' knots. The two badges, Henry's rose and Katharine's pomegranate, are engraved all over the surface of the armour.

Two of his suits of armour, one made in 1520 and the other some twenty years later, show the change from a slender young man to the massive figure that history knows as Henry—the chest and shoulders enormous. The impressive hinged codpiece became a symbol of fertility in later times . . . barren women in the seventeenth century used to stick pins into it.

There is Charles I's fine armour made for a king 5 ft. 2 ins. high, and the beautiful armour worn by Charles II as a little boy of twelve. Many of the helmets and shields are extraordinary examples of art used for war. Helmets with lions' manes sculpted on them, breastplates engraved with the scene of the Crucifixion, rapiers gilded and chased, the insides of shields painted with scenes of battle. Nothing was left undecorated.

On the second floor is the *Chapel of St. John* built in 1080, a severe, exquisite Norman chapel where the future knights of the Order of the Bath prayed all night long in vigil. Lady Jane Grey also came here to pray. And Mary Tudor was married in the chapel by proxy to Philip of Spain.

Facing the White Tower on the west of the green is the *Beauchamp Tower*, connected by a walk along the top of the wall to two other towers. A spiral staircase in the tower leads up to a large room with a window and a fireplace; this was used many times for high-ranking prisoners. Along the staircase walls and in the room are numbers of carved inscriptions made by prisoners, some in their original places, others moved from different prisons. All are numbered and catalogued.

One wonders how people under sentence of death managed to carve so well. What tools did they use? Was the stone of their prison soft? How many hours did they spend chiselling, often with considerable art, the coats of arms and prayers, symbols, messages, exhortations. And what quirk in the English character, having marched a man out to be beheaded, carefully preserved the message he left upon the wall?

Arundell, son of the Duke of Norfolk, carved: 'The more suffering for Christ in this world, so much the more glory with Christ in the world to come.' A descendant of the Duke of Clarence, left in the Tower for life, carved the hopeful message in French: 'Per passage penible, passons a port plaisant.'

One of the most intricate carvings is by John Dudley, eldest of the five Dudley brothers. He helped his father and brothers put Lady Jane Grey on the throne—Guildford Dudley was husband to the 17-year-old Lady Jane. Both Guildford and John were beheaded and so was their father. The carving shows the family arms, a bear and ragged staff, and emblems of the brothers' names: a wreath of roses (Ambrose), gillyflowers (Guildford), oak leaves (Robert) and honeysuckle (Henry). Ambrose, Robert and Henry were eventually set free and Robert became Elizabeth's beloved, the Earl of Leicester.

One word stands out on the stone walls among the inscriptions: it is simply 'IANE'. It's believed that Guildford carved the name of his young wife while he waited for his death and hers.

The open space of lawns in the centre of the Tower buildings is *Tower Green*, the place of private execution for people of royal or noble blood; others were beheaded in public on Tower Hill. Both the queens accused of infidelity and treason to Henry VIII—Anne Boleyn and Catherine Howard—died on Tower Green. So did a third queen, Lady Jane Grey. And Elizabeth's favourite, Essex. The site of the scaffold was paved over by the orders of Queen Victoria.

The chapel of *St. Peter ad Vincula* is north of the green; those who had been executed on Tower Green were buried there . . . Anne Boleyn's body 'hastily thrown into an old arrow chest'. In Stow's words, in front of the high altar are 'two dukes between two queens, to wit, the Duke of Somerset and the Duke of Northumberland, between Queen Anne and Queen Catherine, all four beheaded.'

Tower Green is cheerful now; it seems a place where school-children gather and the glossy ravens like to walk. Macaulay thought it the saddest spot on earth.

The Crown Jewels are housed in their new stronghold, the former Waterloo barracks, east of the White Tower. The jewels are not so very old—almost all the treasures of the royal family were broken up and sold during the Civil War. Charles II had some replaced and one or two very ancient jewels were recovered. In Queen Victoria's State Crown is the ruby said to have been given to the Black Prince in 1367, and worn in a circlet round his helmet by Henry V at Agincourt. There are other legendary jewels, including the giant Indian diamond called the Koh-i-noor.

There are crowns and orbs, sceptres, spurs and bracelets, vessels used at the Coronation with curious names, the Exeter Salt, the Ampulla and Spoon; the spoon was used for King John's coronation in the thirteenth century.

People enjoy being dazzled by the Crown Jewels. In an age when everybody can wear well-made fakes and see jewellery simulated cunningly in plays, films or television, there is a curious satisfaction in seeing jewels which are literally priceless. But jewels are odd things. They lie behind bars, disconnected from the graceful or imperious heads on which they've sometimes lopsidedly been placed. They are totems for the staring people.

The timber-framed house on the south side of Tower Green is the *Queen's House*, built about 1530, where Anne Boleyn spent her last days. The Gunpowder Plot conspirators were interrogated in this house and in one of the rooms overlooking the river are oak panels recording the discovery of the plot with its 'treasonous hope of overthrowing the kingdom, root and branch'. The Jacobite Lord Nithsdale escaped from this house in 1715 in women's clothes. The house is not open to the public, nor is the adjoining house where Lady Jane Grey was a prisoner.

The *Bloody Tower* had already been given its name in Tudor times—people believed the little princes were murdered there. Raleigh was a prisoner in the Bloody Tower for thirteen years. His rooms, it's said, were comfortable enough and he had two servants. He took exercise by walking along the terrace of the ramparts and during his long imprisonment he wrote his *History of the World*. Raleigh was treated as a prisoner of rank and importance and his life of captivity was not unbearable.

But for most of the huge numbers of prisoners the Tower was a place of horror and torture. The many towers are honey-combed, catacombed with cells so dark, so chill, that some of the terror of their prisoners has entered the grim walls for ever. There are cells with trap doors; cells with secret passages behind them for spies; some which filled up with rats from the river at high tide. And Little Ease, cut into the wall and so confined that a prisoner could neither stand nor lie full length. As many as a thousand prisoners at one time languished in the Tower of London.

Opposite the Bloody Tower but no longer open to the river is the *Traitors' Gate,* the river entrance used for prisoners brought from Westminster. When they landed on the steps the warder gave a receipt for their (living) bodies. The moat waters used to roar through Traitors' Gate at low tide in a great rushing flood.

When the young Princess Elizabeth was brought to the Tower by her sister's orders, all the servants and warders standing by Traitors' Gate knelt and prayed that God would preserve her. She sat down on a stone. The lieutenant came up to beg her to come out of the rain. 'Better sit here than in a worse place,' she said. She was kept a close prisoner for two months. The Tower at that time was crowded with prisoners of state, one of whom was Robert Dudley with his brothers in the Beauchamp Tower. Elizabeth had known him since she was 8; they'd played together as children and were the same age 'born on the same day and at the same hour'. It was said that their meeting when they were both imprisoned began the passionate friendship which lasted until Dudley died.

Round and about the Tower, glossy and self-confident, are the Tower ravens; they've lived here since the Tower was built and there's a legend that when they go the Tower will fall. Each bird is given a weekly allowance of food and they live in a cage in the Lantern Tower; some birds live to be as old as 40 or more.

The Tower ravens are all that is left of the royal menagerie which was in the now-demolished Lion Tower. The early Plan-tagenet kings liked to keep a private royal zoo. In 1253 Henry III had a white bear at the Tower; the bear was attached to a long chain so that it could fish and wash in the Thames. The King of France sent Henry III an elephant, the first to be seen in England since the Roman occupation. There were always lions and leopards in the royal menagerie. James I liked to

watch lions and bears baited by dogs; and in 1708 the Tower
had 11 lions, 2 leopards, some eagles, mountain cats and
a jackal. The animals were finally transferred to the zoo in
1834.

The *Tower Wharf*, also called Gun Wharf, was rebuilt after
being damaged during the last war. There has been a stone
wharf here along the Tower's river frontage from the fourteenth
century. On the wharf is a display of guns used in the Napoleonic and Crimean wars; the Honourable Artillery Company
has the special right to fire a salute from this wharf on the
anniversaries of Royal births, accessions and Coronations.

SOME OF THE TOWER'S PRISONERS AND VICTIMS

Ralph Flamard, Bishop of Durham, helped to collect money
for William Rufus for building the Tower, but was hated by
the barons for his enforcement of the law to the last penny.
On accession in 1100 of Henry I, Flamard was imprisoned in
the Tower. He was one of its first prisoners. Escaped from a
window reputedly 65 feet above ground down a rope
smuggled in a wine jar. Flamard fled safely to France.

Charles of Orleans, wounded and taken prisoner at Agincourt
1415. He was imprisoned for 25 years in the White Tower,
where in a prison overlooking the river he wrote French
and English poems. There is an illuminated poem of his
in the British Museum. Charles, finally released, returned
to France. Later became father of the future Louis XII of
France.

Henry VI. Imprisoned in the Tower when Edward IV seized
the crown. Died—some say murdered—in the Wakefield
Tower, 1471.

Duke of Clarence. Brother of Edward IV, murdered in the
Tower, 1478. The tradition persists that he was drowned in a
barrel of malmsey wine.

The Little Princes, Edward V and the Duke of York. Said to
have been murdered in 1483 by Gloucester because they were
the heirs between him and the throne. After their death he
became Richard III. Thomas More believed in the murder.
So, later, did Charles II; when two children's skeletons were
discovered in the Tower, Charles had them buried in the
Abbey with a plaque bearing their names.

Elizabeth of York whom people called 'The Good', queen to Henry VII, died in childbirth in the Tower in 1502. She was the last queen to choose the Tower as her home . . . a singular choice since the Little Princes were her brothers. She was much loved by the people.

Sir Thomas More. Loved by Henry VIII and a brilliant Chancellor, More would not take the oath that the king was Head of the Church of England, broken away from Rome; and would not accept Henry's marriage to Anne Boleyn. More was imprisoned in the Tower and beheaded for treason in 1535.

Bishop Fisher. He died for the same cause and in the same way as More in 1535. Fisher, a scholar and a saintly old man, was 80 when he was beheaded.

Anne Boleyn. Henry's passionately loved and then rejected queen. Imprisoned in the Tower in 1536, some say on trumped-up charges of infidelity when the king tired of her. She died bravely.

Catharine Howard. Henry's youthful queen . . . the fifth . . . died on the same charge of infidelity as Anne Boleyn. But the charges were true. She was beheaded in 1542 and died as courageously as Anne.

Thomas Cromwell. The man who helped Henry VIII become head of the English church and suppress the monasteries. Fell from power after he persuaded Henry to marry the plain-faced Anne of Cleves. Arrested on an absurd charge of treason and executed, 1540.

Lady Jane Grey—the nine days' queen, was brought to the Tower with her young husband Guildford Dudley in 1554; from a window she saw him taken to his execution on Tower Hill and his body brought back to the chapel. On the green they were building the scaffold for her own execution the same day.

The young Elizabeth was imprisoned in the Tower by her sister Mary for two months in 1554.

Robert Devereux, Earl of Essex. The ageing queen Elizabeth loved him. But he attempted to lead a rebellion against her. Taken prisoner at Essex House in the Strand, he was confined in the Tower. Beheaded on Tower Hill 1601.

Guy Fawkes. Together with the rest of the Gunpowder Plot conspirators, imprisoned in the Tower 1605–6. Hanged in Palace Yard.

Sir Walter Raleigh. Imprisoned in Tower by Elizabeth in 1592 (but only for eight weeks) for seducing her maid-in-waiting Bessy Throckmorton whom he afterwards married. In 1604, the year after Elizabeth died, James I sent him to the Tower —in despair Raleigh tried to stab himself. He was thirteen years in the Bloody Tower. His wife and son lived with him, and a second son was born there. He wrote his *History of the World*, carried out scientific experiments, was visited by scholars, inventors, poets and wits. Finally executed at Westminster in 1618 by James I to appease the Spanish.

Felton. The officer who murdered the hated Duke of Buckingham in Portsmouth in 1628. When brought to the Tower the people cheered him, shouting 'Lord Bless Thee.'

In James I's, Charles I's and Cromwell's time the Tower continued as a state prison. In Charles II's reign there was a frivolous imprisonment—the Duke of Richmond was in the Tower for three weeks for proposing marriage to one of the king's mistresses.

Judge Jeffreys. The Chief Justice whose reputation for cruelty is a legend, who hanged 300 and transported 800 rebels after the Monmouth Rebellion. Jeffreys was sent to the Tower after James II left England. While in the Tower he received a gift of a barrel of oysters . . . inside it was a halter. He died–– of drink— in prison in 1689.

Lord Nithsdale. Imprisoned in the Tower after the Stuart rebellion of 1715. He escaped in women's clothes brought to him by his wife. Eventually arrived in Rome in a second disguise, as footman to an Ambassador.

Roger Casement, Ireland's patriot and England's traitor, imprisoned in the Tower during the Great War. Hanged for high treason in 1916.

Rudolph Hess. Hitler's deputy. After his extraordinary peace-seeking flight to Scotland, he was imprisoned in the Tower in 1941 for a few days, before being moved to a country prison for the duration of the war. After war trials, moved to Spandau in Germany.

In *Trinity Square* behind the Tower and next to the pretty little eighteenth, century Trinity House, is the largest *statue of Father Thames* in London. It overlooks the Tower and stands at the top of the massive ugly white building which used to be the headquarters of the Port of London authority. Father Thames is naked, with hair and beard flowing, and grasping his trident with one hand points dramatically towards the sea with the other.

The *Port of London Authority*, which now has five homes in the city including one in the newly-built World Trade Centre, controls London's river—ninety-four busy miles from the estuary to the tidal waters of Teddington Lock. Beyond that the Thames Conservancy takes over. The P.L.A. is almost a Borough Council—it has numberless jobs and responsibilities; it owns and controls the enclosed docks behind both river banks and is responsible for the river running behind all the public and privately owned wharves and factories, oil installations, gasworks, power stations, sugar refineries and shipyards. The P.L.A. must look after river navigation, keep the river channels dredged, regulate river traffic. It provides public ship and barge moorings, charts tideways, removes wrecks and collects tons of Thames driftwood . . . its job is as huge as the river flooding in twice a day from the sea. Up until 1974 the P.L.A. was also in charge of that much-discussed problem of river pollution; this is now taken over by the newly-formed Thames Water Authority.

As late as the seventeenth century the river was so clear and pure that salmon swam upriver through London to spawn in the little, upstream tributaries. Noblemen who lived along the Strand bathed in the Thames constantly. The Earl of Pembroke, friend of Walpole in the eighteenth century, swam so often that Lord Chesterfield addressed a letter to him 'To the Earl of Pembroke, in the Thames, over against Whitehall'. Byron in his letters said he swam from Lambeth through Westminster and Blackfriars bridges, down to London Bridge, the length of his journey three miles. 'You see I'm in excellent training in case of a squall at sea!'

By mid-Victorian times the condition of the Thames was appalling—people called it 'The Great Stink'—and sheets soaked in disinfectant were hung up in the Houses of Parliament to counteract the terrible smell floating up from the river.

The big anti-pollution drive by the P.L.A. and the Greater London Council began in the 1950s. Gradually the quality of the Thames water began to improve—and fish, and sea and river birds started to come back. The first seafish came upstream in 1964; a year later the freshwater fish returned. From 1968 onwards there were exciting increases in bird life . . . mallard and wigeon, pintail and tufted duck, pochard and shelduck were all increasing steadily in numbers. Recently the mute swans, always Thames inhabitants, have bred more too. Waders feeding on the Thames were virtually unknown until the late 1950s; now in recent winters great flocks of lapwing and red-shank, ruff, knot and dunlin are regular winter visitors. The Thames has become one of the cleanest of the world's great industrial rivers.

The last of London bridges downstream towards the sea is *Tower Bridge*, its Gothic towers as famous as Big Ben and used, like the clock tower, as a symbol of London. The bridge built in 1894 was designed by Sir Horace Jones and Sir Wolfe Barry. There is a road across the bridge, which opens up for large ships coming through into the Upper Pool of London. The bridge used to open as much as five times a day but now, with the change of river traffic and the great ships unloading at Tibury, it is only raised a few times every week. The foot-bridge at the top between the towers was meant for pedestrians but had to be closed; the story is that people threw themselves over it. Some of the machinery which works the drawbridge is in the two towers.

Down St. Katharine's Way, east of Tower Bridge, is *St. Katharine's Dock*. A twelfth century hospital founded by Queen Matilda, wife of King Stephen, was built here in 1148. Beside it later there was a Gothic church with stalls carved with 'grotesque and fanciful monsters' and the tombs of the fifteenth century Duke and Duchess of Exeter. The church was pulled down in 1825 to make room for the docks but the stalls were saved; they are in St. Katharine's Royal Foundation in Wapping.

St. Katharine's docks were built in a year and by the 1840s, though among the smallest of the London docks, they took 1,000 ships and 10,000 lighters 'giving a vivid impression of the vast wealth of England'. In the tall, arcaded warehouses built by Telford were huge stocks of tea, wine, wool, sugar and all the other produce arriving by river from countries all over the world.

The new technique of packing goods into huge containers changed the history of London river after the last war. Loading the containers into larger and larger ships meant that most of the older upstream docks were too small; one after the other the famous old Victorian docks closed down. The East India in 1967, St. Katharines in 1968, the London Docks in 1969, and the Surrey Commercial Docks in 1970. At Tilbury today the same tonnage which passed through all these docks now goes through a single port. A vessel which used to take 14 days, working a five-day week to 'turn round' as it is called, now takes 48 hours working for 24 hours a day.

Londoners have been deeply interested in the future of St. Katharine's Dock. The new *World Trade Centre* has opened there—so this part of the riverside will be still a part of London's commerce. The Centre is described as the 'marketplace of the modern age'; as well as offices and reception rooms there is an exhibition hall which recently gave an exhibition of paintings of London river and the docks. A massive new hotel, St. Katharine's by the Tower, has been opened beside Tower Bridge.

In a city where beautiful and historic buildings are demolished weekly, St. Katharine's Dock brings a ray of light as bright as the lamp in the old Nore Lightship now moored by the new hotel. The whole conversion from decayed dockyards to Marina—the only yacht harbour in the City of London—has been done with tremendous style. It really works. The three Dock basins have been modernized and rebuilt where necessary to provide craft with 240 berths, and a kind of marine village created along the quaysides. Telford's handsome warehouses were built of yellow brick, with Italianate arches and pillars of iron and one of these, the Ivory House, once the centre of the European ivory trade, is now the centre of the village. It is topped with a clock and a bell. Why a bell? Was it sounded when ships arrived, or when the ivory sales began? Nobody seems to know. An arcade of shops with arched windows runs along the ground floor of the Ivory House, with an iron balcony above. The shops sell intriguing things needed by sailing people the world over, navigation aids and brass lamps, thick coils of rope and life jackets, sweaters and ships' clocks. There is a yacht club in the building, complete with showers for visiting sailors; service flats and flats on longer leases are built on the upper floors of the old warehouse, and at the back of the building is a new restaurant, the Beefeater By the Tower.

Five minutes from Gun Wharf by the Tower of London, St. Katharine's Dock is a fascinating place to wander. Pathways skirt the dock basins, there's a view of Tower Bridge, or a Wren spire, or that statue of Father Thames in the Old Port of London Authority building, still pointing to the sea. As well as all the variety of modern yachts and cruisers, there are two old Thames barges moored here—the Dannebrög (1901) and the Lady Daphne (1923). There's also a fine seaworn West Coast schooner, the *Emily Barratt*, which used to sail on the Newfoundland run. The ship has a figurehead of a woman in a red dress, hands folded in prayer; those prayers were answered, because the *Emily Barratt* survived the great ocean storms.

The wooden skeleton of the 1780 Hawes Brewery is in the process of being moved 150 feet north, and the building is to be restored in period just beside the docks; it should make a lively new addition to the village, as it is to be a restaurant and bar. Close by is the London School of Seamanship, and moored in the inner basin is the 400-ton steam vessel, the *St. Katharine*, now converted into a training ship for people taking the British Safety Council courses.

Happily, there are a number of late eighteenth and early nineteenth century brick houses close to the river which have been restored and are now lived in, including the Dockmaster's house which has a pretty walled garden. The dock basins are joined by three small footbridges, the outer bridge on to the Thames is a Van Goghlike swing bridge, which opens to allow craft to enter and leave the marina.

Behind the 30-feet-thick walls of the old docks are the wine vaults, arched over like the crypt of an abbey. These vaults fascinated the Victorians; one traveller described setting out to visit them as if going to visit the catacombs. Vinous fungi hung from the vaultings in woolly clouds more than a yard long and were so inflammable that the Davy safety lamp had to be used by visitors. It is now planned to turn part of the wine vaults into a shopping centre, and to cut away the roof of some of the adjoining vaults to make a sunken piazza.

St. Katharine by the Tower, with its wonderful views up and downriver, and Tower Bridge literally beside it, is the only hotel for many miles which fronts the Thames. There is a short riverside walk in front of the hotel, a fountain of a girl and a dolphin, and a huge sundial. But although the hotel is comfortable and gives good service, its style is internationally characterless and the appearance of the building is forbidding. From the upstairs bar, one looks up to the turrets of the bridge; there is a pleasant ground-floor coffee shop also facing the water.

Less than a mile downriver from St. Katharine's dock lies

Wapping. Once it was an intensely busy village surrounded by docks, a place of ship-builders, boat-builders, mast and oar and rope makers. Wapping is in an in-between stage of its development just now.

The Thames Tunnel which links Wapping with Rotherhithe was the first underwater tunnel in the world. It was begun in 1825 and meant for carriages and carts, but the ramps for wheeled vehicles were never built; for a while it was used by foot passengers; it is now a railway tunnel used by the Underground.

The tunnel was an heroic feat of early engineering; the bold and visionary Marc Brunel worked on it for years in a saga of bravery and defeat. The river broke through five times; the tunnel flooded and men were drowned; others had 'Tunnel sickness' or fainted from sewer gas. Work progressed . . . but at 2 foot 4 inches a week. Work stopped. People christened the tunnel 'The Great Bore'. Work began again and in 1827 Marc Brunel gave a banquet in the tunnel under the river to celebrate that work had started again. At last after eighteen years of 'putting a pipe into old Thames's mouth' the tunnel was opened in 1843.

On the Wapping riverside is the tall Victorian *Oliver's Wharf*, which interestingly shows what can be done with a last-century wharf, instead of knocking it down and replacing it with concrete. A few years ago thousands of chests of tea from China and India were loaded into this building, which has now been converted into very attractive flats overlooking the water. But the wharf has kept its look of belonging to the Thames.

Just east of Oliver's Wharf and right on the waterside is the new *Metropolitan Police Boatyard* on the site of the old Morocco and Eagle Sufferance Wharves. This is the yard where the Thames police craft are repaired and serviced; the work on the vessels is done under cover, and the workshops have a special lift which can hoist boats of up to 15 tons right out of the water, whatever the state of the tide. The rather ugly material used for building the boatyard is glass reinforced plastic in moulded panels, the first used for a building on the Thames . . . something of an aesthetic shock—however efficient it may be—standing among the seasoned old dock buildings that survive.

Also close to Oliver's Wharf is a pub where the fishermen used to land with their catches from Ramsgate—*The Town of Ramsgate* with a terrace overlooking the river. An alleyway beside the pub leads to *Wapping Old Stairs*, once a dark and dangerous place crowded with hard-drinking, often violent sea-men. Judge Jeffreys, James II's hated Chancellor, was captured here; he was drinking in the Red Cow tavern in disguise—Macaulay describes: 'The dress was that of a common sailor from Newcastle, and was black with coal-dust; but there was no mistaking the savage eye and mouth.' Jeffreys was taken to the Tower in a carriage followed by a mob howling for revenge. He died in the Tower, not by violence, but of drink.

Sailing along this stretch of the river one can see on the front of a warehouse the large letter 'E' which marks the site of *Execution Dock* where pirates were hanged. Stow called Wapping 'the usual place for hanging of pirates and sea-rovers, at the low water mark, and there to remain till three tides had overflowed them'. Men were hanged in chains until the beginning of the last century. One of the most notorious of all the pirates was Captain Kidd, caught and condemned in 1701. An enormous crowd gathered at Wapping on the morning of his execution. Public executions were like public holidays; loud jolly throngs came surging in to see the fun, and the shouts of ballad singers and orange sellers mixed with thousands of voices buzzing with a ghoulish interest in the coming drama. Kidd stood on the scaffold looking down at the crowd and saw one of his mistresses. 'I have lain with that bitch three times,' he said. 'And now she has come to see me hanged.'

The oldest riverside pub in London is the *Prospect of Whitby*. Wapping dockers still remember it as a tumbledown old place where watermen stayed for hours, drinking and talking. Over the years it has turned into a pilgrim-place for tourists. Anyone who is walking through Wapping and looks uncertain of the way is automatically directed to the Prospect. The pub, at the east end of Wapping Wall, was built in Tudor times but has been enlarged and smartened up and altered, even within the last ten years. Sometimes it reverberates with music from a jukebox. There's a terrace with a view of the broad river reaches, the West India Dock and the distant white tower of Limehouse Church which was a landmark for sailing ships when they came up the Thames. The pub's restaurant opens on to the terrace where one can sit, shaded by a willow, and watch the boats go by. The name of the inn was *The Devil's Tavern*; it was changed because a square rigger from Whitby, bringing stone to London, used to moor here by the river wall.

The King Edward Memorial Park borders the river off Glamis Road, a large pleasant garden with flowering trees, a bowling green and a riverside walk with plenty of seats. Opening into the gardens is the old-fashioned, decorated entrance to the *Rotherhithe Tunnel*, built in 1908. The dockers' children in the past used to enjoy that tunnel, running down its 213 steps, galloping under the river and popping up on the Rotherhithe bank to wave to friends left behind in the park.

There is a nice Wapping story about a flower discovered at Wapping. A nurseryman once saw a 'pretty West Indian flower' in a small cottage window. It had been brought home by a sailor and was unknown in England. The nurseryman took cuttings from it; it turned out to be the fuschia which became so popular that 300 cuttings, a year later, were sold at a golden guinea each.

The old dockland in this part of Thames side is full of wild flowers; there are the purple buddleias which butterflies love, with a strong sharp scent, and yellow ragwort flourishing on the waste ground and the tall brave spires of the rosebay willowherb.

In the river at Wapping a silver Head of Christ was found; it was a beautiful piece of Italian silverwork, made for holding sacred relics.

The river makes a large loop after Wapping and Shadwell, and then runs due south through *Limehouse Reach*, passing *Limehouse Pier and Dock*. The seventeenth century *Bunch of Grapes* is in Limehouse Causeway. This cosy pub has a Dickens room which opens on to a veranda looking across the water to the Surrey Commercial Docks. Dickens knew this pub well, and writes about it in *Our Mutual Friend*. He calls the pub 'The Six Jolly Fellowship Porters', and describes it as . . . 'a narrow lop-sided wooden jumble of corpulent windows . . . with a crazy wooden veranda impending over the water; indeed the whole house, inclusive of the complaining flagstaff on the roof, impended over the water, but seemed to have got into the condition of a faint-hearted diver who has paused so long on the brink that he will never go in at all'. The pub had 'red curtains matching the noses of the regular customers', and was popular for three hot mulled drinks, 'Purl, Flip, and Dog's Nose'.

Despite the cheerful sound of sizzling drinks in a bar parlour and many jokes about the landlady, the Limehouse setting of Our Mutual Friend is very dark. Dickens was fascinated by the river here . . . it was full of both mystery and horror, and the whole of Limehouse teemed with vice and poverty. The Victorian Thames of dockland plays the leading part in the book.

Just before arriving by boat at Greenwich one passes the old *Royal Naval Victualling Yards at Deptford* on the south bank. Deptford was a place of naval shipbuilding from Tudor times—Henry VIII built some of his ships here in 1513, and Elizabeth knighted Drake at Deptford after he had returned from sailing round the world. Czar Peter the Great in the eighteenth century came to stay at Deptford so that he could study the British ships before he began to plan his new Russian fleet. The old Victualling Yards were used for storing provisions, and the eighteenth century buildings were filled with bedding, salted meat, brandy, biscuits, medicine, and the famous vats of Navy rum. In 1961 the Yards were partly demolished and high-rise flats built there, but some of the Georgian buildings by the river have been preserved.

Best seen from a boat is *Millwall*, where Isambard, the younger Brunel, built his huge ship, the *Great Eastern*. There are marks along the wharf to show the ship's huge length: it was 680 feet long. Isambard Brunel was already famous for designing ocean-going steamships larger than any ever made before when he built the *Great Eastern*. His ships were designed to carry enough coal for a long outward journey at least; his *Great Western*, 236 feet long, had been the first steamship to make a regular ocean service between England and America, with the record time of fifteen days.

Like his father Sir Marc, Isambard always undertook vast and visionary projects. He began to build his ship, the *Great Eastern*, which was to be nearly three times the size of his successful Atlantic record-breaker. The new ship was finally launched in 1858 but only after appalling anxiety for Brunel and his engineers; it had to be launched broadside because of its huge size.

The *Great Eastern* proved a magnificent ship, making the voyage to Australia with only one stop for coal, carrying passengers and later troops. It was also used for laying cables at sea.

Downriver towards the sea there is still commercial traffic to be seen on the Thames, bringing and taking cargoes to the wharves lining the banks—jute, sugar, sand. And when one passes Millwall there are the large vessels of the Fred Olsen Line bringing fruit and vegetables from the Canary Isles, and ships sailing for Malta, Cyprus, Bierut, Oslo, Canada and America. Coming into the heart of London from the India and Millwall Docks are green and dried fruit, vegetables, grain, soft and hard wood, paper pulp, rubber, hemp and wine.

Greenwich

14 RIGHT (SOUTH) BANK

Greenwich
Cutty Sark
Gypsy Moth IV
Footway Tunnel to the Isle of Dogs
Trafalgar Tavern
The Yacht
Trinity Hospital Almshouses
Old Palace of Greenwich
Queen's House
Greenwich Park
Royal Naval College
National Maritime Museum

The journey by river to *Greenwich* can be done slowly on the open deck of a launch or faster in the enclosed Hovercraft. The Hovercraft journey takes about twenty-five minutes, is rather noisy and not much part of the river scene, but it gives the visitor extra time to spend at Greenwich. And the return journey can be done by launch.

The *Cutty Sark* is in dry dock only a step away from Greenwich Pier. The great clipper, launched in 1869, folded her wings and came to roost permanently at Greenwich in 1954. She was the last of the windjammers which carried tea from India and China, and grain and wool from Australia. The *Cutty Sark* was specially built for the great race home across the ocean, when the rival clippers strained every nerve and foot of sail for that extra knot of speed. In 1871 the *Cutty Sark* succeeded—she made the fastest-ever voyage from China to England: it took 107 days. The ship continued to sail back with her tea cargoes from China for seven years; then transferred to the Australia run, coming home laden with wool from 1883 to 1895.

Below the bowsprit on the V-shaped bows of the clipper is the fierce-faced wooden figurehead of a woman, her arm outstretched to urge her ship forward; she is wearing a 'cutty sark', an old name for a short chemise. The ship is now a museum; there are ships' models, charts, photographs of the clipper at sea, and the largest collection of figureheads in the world. These curious wooden people were carved to rise and dip in the great rough waves, their fixed faces and huge eyes, uniforms or dresses are painted in brilliant posterlike colours. Most of the figureheads are of Victorian heroes—Disraeli and Florence Nightingale both hung on the bow braving the oceans.

Up on the weather deck is the complex, intricate rigging of the ship's three tall masts, with ten miles of ropes which controlled 32,000 square feet of canvas sail. The *Cutty Sark* illustrates the beauty of things once made for strictly practical use.

Gipsy Moth IV, small as the *Cutty Sark* is large, is docked close by. The little yacht is 54 feet long and its interior is fitted just as it was when in 1966–7 Chichester sailed 29,630 miles round the world alone. There are the clothes he wore, his magnetic compass, his maps, the chart of Cape Horn, a bottle of champagne to celebrate his 65th birthday alone at sea. And cress growing on a tray to supply fresh daily vitamins in his diet.

In June 1967 Queen Elizabeth knighted him at the watergate of the Royal Naval College, using the same sword that Elizabeth had used on board Drake's *Golden Hind* at Deptford when he returned from sailing round the world. In 1968 it was decided to birth *Gipsy Moth IV* beside the last of the great wool clippers, whose average run he had rivalled single-handed.

The circular entrance to *Greenwich Footway Tunnel* is in Cutty Sark gardens. The tunnel was built in 1902 and much used by the workers crossing at dawn to the West India docks on the Isle of Dogs. It is the quickest way to the Isle and only takes a few minutes' walk in a chill passageway with handsome old-fashioned lifts at each end. At the time the tunnel was built, the lightermen and watermen objected strongly—they were afraid it would put them out of business.

On the other side of the river the tunnel opens on to the *Isle of Dogs*, and a little riverside garden with the best of all views of the Royal Naval College. The Isle was given its name when Charles II lived at Greenwich; all the dogs near the palace were sent off to kennels across the river so that the king's sleep would not be disturbed.

To be strictly geographical, the Trafalgar Tavern, the Yacht pub, and the Trinity Hospital almshouses all come after the Naval College, walking from west to east. But hours can be spent in the great palatial buildings of Greenwich, on Observatory Hill, in the museum and the beautiful parkland. So these are left until the last.

To the east of the College buildings is the historic *Trafalgar Tavern*, built in 1837 on the site of a riverside inn which was popular with fishermen and ferrymen, called The Old George.

Although it was built the year Victoria came to the throne, the Trafalgar is very much a Regency building, its pretty balconies overlooking the river—they were, incidentally, modelled on the galleries of an old man-of-war. The Trafalgar was a success from the moment it opened and its Whitebait Dinners were particularly celebrated. It became the height of fashion to visit the Trafalgar and eat the delicious whitebait, caught in the Thames estuary; the fish were fried crisply, served with lemon and iced champagne. Cabinet ministers came from Westminster by barge for Whitebait Dinners, the Fellows of the Royal Society held their annual visit there to eat the same popular fish. Dickens often walked ten miles from Dartford to meet friends there. 'Will you join us? Pray do. We dine at the Trafalgar. Punctually at six.' The inn appears in *Our Mutual Friend*; Bella Wilfer and John Rokesmith eat their wedding dinner at the Trafalgar and are served 'all fishes that swim in the sea'. Dickens always loved Greenwich and when in Devonshire Terrace wrote nostalgically: 'What a day for a Greenwich steamer.'

The Trafalgar closed at the beginning of the 1900s and was not opened again until 1964. Now, redecorated and stylish, it would be suited to entertain even Nelson himself. There are restaurants on the first floor overlooking the river and on the ground floor, and the famous whitebait are back on the menu.

Next door to the Trafalgar in a paved alley behind the riverfront is a pub called the *Yacht*; the building's date is uncertain but is thought to be seventeenth century. It is a homely comfortable pub, the walls covered with photographs of famous yachts and Thames maps. Up a few steps by the river front of the building is the Indoors Deck Bar; there is also an outside bar for sunny days overlooking the water. There are inexpensive salads and sandwiches, one or two hot dishes (Shepherds Pie, Sausages and Mash). The Yacht is popular and unpretentious.

The alley outside, called Crane Street, leads to a small open space of grass and flowerbeds, river railings, and the *Trinity Hospital* almshouses. These were built in 1613 with crenellated battlements, looking like a toy castle. Through the gateway there is a glimpse of a courtyard, enclosed rose gardens and a fountain. Above the almshouse is the monstrous shape, like an ogre, of the Power Station built in 1906 looming over one of the loveliest Jacobean almshouses on the river. But it is still a wonderful place for the old pensioners—there are twenty of them—to live.

London river begins and ends with a palace. Upriver among the willows and swans' nests is Hampton Court. Nearest to the sea on Greenwich Reach was the *Royal Palace of Placentia*, where now the eighteenth century Naval College stands.

It was the Good Duke Humphrey, uncle to Henry VI, who bought seventeen acres of riverside land at Greenwich near an abbey and a manor house; he built himself a great rambling palace on the river banks with a little hunting tower on the steep hill where the Royal Observatory is built. The Duke called his palace Bella Court.

When he died in 1447, Queen Margaret, Henry VI's warlike French queen, made Bella Court her own. She turned it into a 'Palace of Pleasance' and named it Placentia. Tiles were laid patterned with her royal monogram, she filled the windows with the rare luxury of glass, there were pillars sculpted with daisies which were the emblem of her name; a pier was built which made it easy to land at the palace whether the tide was high or low.

Edward IV took Placentia when he took the English crown: he made the park larger, stocking it with deer. His daughter Elizabeth of York (who later became Henry VII's good queen) was born at Placentia and grew up there. When Henry VII came to the throne, Greenwich was beautified once again, 'with the addition of a brick front to the water side'.

Henry VIII was born and baptized at Greenwich and perhaps of all the monarchs loved it most. He and Katharine of Aragon were married there in 1509; he thought Placentia a 'pleasant, perfect and princely palace'. Like the kings before him he made it larger, altered it, enjoyed hunting and hawking in the spreading park and wooded country all round Greenwich. In 1511 'his grace being young . . . rose in the morning very early to fetch May, or green bows, himself fresh and rychely appareyled, and clothed all his knyghtes, squyers and gentlemen in whyte satyn' and off they went with their bows and arrows to shoot in the woods.

The king had jousts and tournaments at Greenwich with 'ye spere of 8 fote long'. Henry was young and strong and skilled in combat. In 1515 at one of his great Christmas feasts at the palace, the first masked dance ever seen in England was given 'after the maner of Italie'. The gentlemen wore visors and cloth of gold, carried torches and asked the ladies to dance. Some of them 'because it was not a thyng commonly seen' shyly refused.

Both the royal dockyards at Deptford and at Woolwich were founded in Henry's reign. At Woolwich the 'kinges great shippe called the Harry-grace-a-Dieu' was built and launched; the new long galleons and iron cannon were built at the two dockyards It was an easy journey by river from Greenwich for Henry to supervise the building of his rapidly-growing Navy.

Henry also founded the Greenwich Armouries beside the palace, where magnificent suits of armour 'deftly joined as a lobster's shell' and inlaid with gold were made. The king built a Tilt Yard between the Palace and the Deptford-to-Woolwich road.

In the Wyngaerde drawings Placentia is an enormous palace. There were the massive towers of the watergate, the courtyards, a large banqueting hall and Royal chapel, the towered Armoury and a long line of turreted buildings with flights of steps down to the river.

When Henry stayed at Placentia the Royal standard flew

above the palace rooftops and every armed ship passing on the Thames, seeing the king in residence, fired a salute of cannon.

Princes and ambassadors came on State visits—the king received them personally at the watergate. When Charles V, joint ruler of Spain and Queen Katharine's nephew, arrived at Greenwich in 1522 he was accompanied by 2,000 courtiers and 1,000 horses.

One of the many gardens at Placentia was the Queen's Garden, made for Katharine and filled with gilly-flowers, violets, stocks and the roses which were now the emblem of national unity. Through the middle of the Queen's garden was a broad path with a four-sided stone arch over it.

In 1516 Katharine gave birth to a princess at Greenwich; the Princess Mary, afterwards Mary Tudor.

But Katharine's happy marriage was waning. In 1522 a new lady-in-waiting arrived at Placentia—it was Anne Boleyn. All through the painfully drawn-out drama of the Royal divorce, the king, Katharine and Anne Boleyn lived at Greenwich. After Anne was crowned queen, her daughter Elizabeth was born at Placentia in 1533.

Mary Tudor stayed sometimes at Greenwich but it was Elizabeth who really revived its glories—in the summer months she made it her principal court. There are many stories of Elizabeth's life at Greenwich. Raleigh is said to have thrown his cloak in the mud for her here; and when he wrote on the palace window with a diamond 'Feign would I climb, but that I fear to fall', the queen added beneath it: 'If thy heart fail thee, climb not at all.'

She had courts and councils at the palace and, like her father, received princes and ambassadors there. She knighted Francis Drake at Deptford after his voyage round the world; and signed the order to resist the Armada at Placentia. On Maundy Thursday she took part in the ceremony of washing the feet of the poor, a ceremony echoed today in the Queen's distribution of Maundy Money. Elizabeth knelt on a cushion and washed the feet of rows of poor women invited into the palace, then she gave each a little purse of money.

In 1598 the German traveller Hentzner, admitted to the presence chamber at Placentia, saw the queen. She wore a white silk dress bordered with pearls the size of beans and when she turned to either side to speak to her courtiers they fell on their knees.

When James I came to the throne he settled Placentia and

its parkland on his queen; he also commissioned Inigo Jones to build her a special house of her own—*The Queen's House*. Jones had only recently returned from Venice, and when he designed this new Royal residence he created the first Renaissance house seen in England, based on one of the villas he had so admired by Palladio.

A curious feature of this house was that it had to be built in the form of an H, spanning the public road from Deptford to Woolwich. Even a king could not annul the people's Right of Way. So the bar of the H from one side of the road to the other was a room in a bridge. Members of the Court could watch through the window the spectacle of horses and riders, rumbling coaches or carts of fruit and vegetables, going under the Royal palace.

The Queen's House was unfinished when Anne of Denmark died in 1619; perhaps the sight, even the thought, of it saddened the King for he was no longer interested in the building and work on it was stopped. But when Charles I came to the throne he ordered Inigo Jones to finish the house and gave it to his queen Henrietta Maria.

If Placentia was a palace of pleasure, the Queen's House was 'a house of delight'. Charles filled it with wonderful pictures— Titians, Raphaels, Rubens, Van Dycks. Rubens himself came to visit the queen and discussed painting some panels for her. The ceilings by Gentileschi showed . . . with an irony the Royal family were not yet conscious of . . . the arts of peace.

Although the Queen's House was Palladian and completely different in style from the old rambling Tudor palace by the waterside, it seemed to fit perfectly with the rest of the buildings. All was harmony.

But the arts of peace were ending, the Civil War broke out, and Placentia was ruined.

The palace was used for housing crowds of miserable prisoners. Some of its buildings were contemptuously sold; so were all the Royal paintings. For some reason the only building treated with respect, perhaps because of its classic simplicity, was the Queen's House. The Parliamentarians used it on three occasions as the place for a ceremonial lying-in-state. Admiral Robert Blake who died in 1657 lay in state there. Blake had commanded the Commonwealth fleet and later conquered the Spanish in brilliant naval victories. He was dear to the English of both sides as a man of patriotism and chivalry. His funeral procession went by river to Westminster Abbey.

At the Restoration, by poetic justice the Queen's House was restored to the lady for whom it was completed: Henrietta Maria came back. It was enlarged for her, enriched for her (with ceilings moulded with chains of buttercups). Charles II wanted to bring back the past glories of Greenwich and decided to build a house to match the Queen's, called the King's House. 'His Majesty,' wrote Evelyn in 1662, 'entertain'd me with his intentions of building his Palace at Greenwich and quite demolishing the old one.' The king was delighted with his plans and the *Royal Park* was laid out in a style very like Le Nôtre's park in Versailles; Charles had always admired French grandeur. Some of the trees planted in the park survive today and all are magnificent, including huge old Spanish chestnuts, oaks, limes, planes and elms. There are fallow deer in the park too, and tame squirrels and many birds.

During the Plague in 1664 people took refuge in ships in the river off Greenwich. Daniel Defoe met a waterman who told him how people were staying in the ships, their stores rowed out to them so they would escape infection. Defoe was rowed to Greenwich, climbed the hill overlooking the river and saw numbers of ships at anchor in double rows stretching as far as Rotherhithe. 'There must be several hundreds of sail,' he wrote. 'And I could not but applaud the contrivance, for ten thousand people, and more, who attended ships affairs were certainly sheltered here from the violence of the contagion, and lived very safe and easy.'

In 1675 on the steep summit of the same hill looking down to the river, the place where the Good Duke Humphrey had built his little hunting tower, the *Royal Observatory* built by Wren was established in *Flamsteed House*. The zero meridian of longitude runs through the house, and there is a mark showing the meridian in the front courtyard. The charming house, with a walled garden, is now an astronomical museum.

Henrietta Maria died, and Charles II ran out of money; although the nobly-planned King's House was begun, it was left unfinished. By the time William and Mary arrived on the English throne the days of Royal Greenwich were done. Placentia was in ruins and Wren, by William's instruction, finished it off. Mary would never live at Greenwich—it reminded her of the father she had deposed; she and William migrated to Hampton Court. They decided that when Placentia was gone, a Seamen's Hospital, similar in its aims to the hospital for soldiers at Chelsea, should be built in its place.

It was very much the queen's scheme; according to Macaulay, after Mary died William 'began to reproach himself for having neglected her wishes. No time was now lost. A plan was furnished by Wren, and soon an edifice, surpassing that asylum which the magnificent Louis had provided for his soldiers, rose on the margin of the Thames.' Greenwich was to be, said Macaulay, 'the memorial of the virtues of the good Queen Mary, of the love and sorrow of William, and of the great victory of La Hogue.'

The foundation stone was laid in 1696; the buildings took nearly thirty years and some additions were made even twenty years after that. The group of buildings are the work of the three greatest architects of English Baroque—Wren, Hawksmoor and Vanbrugh. Their work is mixed and combined, and it's not precisely known which architect is responsible for which part of Greenwich. The result has a surprising and powerful harmony.

From the beginning the buildings were much admired. 'The buildings now going on are very magnificent,' wrote Evelyn in 1705. Doctor Johnson thought them *too* magnificent for charity, and Boswell added they were too far away from the sociable hum of Fleet Street. Czar Peter the Great was deeply impressed with Greenwich but thought it more fitted for royalty than for 'worn-out seamen'. Samuel Rogers began a poem on the new Greenwich:

'Hail! noblest structure, imaged in the wave;
A nation's grateful tribute to the brave.'

The first forty-two pensioners arrived in 1705. One of them called John Worley, a pensioner of 96, is painted as the figure of Winter on the ceiling of the Painted Hall. Gradually, as there was more room for them, the number of pensioners rose—1,720 in 1763—2,710 in 1814. They were all seamen or marines who had served in the Navy and the only qualification was disability from wounds, accidents, or sickness due to naval service.

These pensioners lived in the new hospital, but there were larger numbers of out-pensioners—as many as 32,000. Pensioners were provided with a weekly allowance of food and beer, tobacco money, a suit of blue clothes, a cocked hat. Queen Mary had hoped the seamen would live 'safe moored in Greenwich'. Somehow the plan, nobly-meant, full of charity, failed. The buildings were too grand—Doctor Johnson had been right.

The pensioners weren't happy in their austere palaces; discipline was harsh and as a punishment the old men were made to wear their blue coats inside out to show the yellow lining. Local people nicknamed them 'canaries'. They were punished for drunkenness, for begging, for selling their food, for keeping pigeons. There were hard critics of Greenwich Hospital. 'Columns, colonnades and friezes ill accord with bull beef and sour beer mixed with water', wrote Captain Baillie in 1771 in a bitter attack. The pensioners complained about their food—they said it was disgusting. There were further outside attacks, saying the hospital was badly administered and even corrupt.

The numbers of pensioners began to decline in the nineteenth century—more out-pensions were given. There were fewer foreign wars. After a Commission of Inquiry in 1865 it was finally decided that the hospital should be closed.

For 150 years the old men in their flared coats and cocked hats had been more than just a part of the palatial riverside scene . . . they were the reason for it. High-flown phrases were painted and sculpted in the palace blocks, declaring the great purpose of giving old seamen this most magnificent home. The old men had walked slowly through the colonnades or sat on Observatory Hill watching the shipping through telescopes. They had lingered by the river, telling their stories of the sea and battles long ago. Now they were gone.

The Navy moved from Portsmouth to Greenwich in 1873. The Royal Naval College is now used by all three services for special training courses.

Greenwich is still stately and imposing and hasn't lost the look which someone called 'the nearest equivalent to a palace of Louis XIV'. It is a perfect place to linger on a fine day, walking along the pillared colonnades or across the quadrangles, climbing the hill to see the docks and river spread out in one of London's most marvellous views. In front of the college is a walk beside the water, and a flight of steps which has been used by every king landing at Greenwich since the Royal Hospital was built.

The Painted Hall is in King William's block. It was originally meant as the pensioners' dining hall but later was used only for important occasions, celebrating the king's birthday for instance, or his landing on English soil. Greenwich was always staunchly patriotic to the Dutch sovereign who was its founder.

Nelson's body lay in state for three days in the Painted Hall in 1806. Enormous crowds filed past to pay their respects to the most adored English hero. The coffin was taken by river to Whitehall, followed by a procession of city state barges. Every ship lowered its flag as the flotilla went by and during the procession on the water the minute guns never ceased to fire.

The Painted Hall is remarkable for the huge flamboyant ceiling which took Sir James Thornhill twenty years to complete. Thornhill probably learned much of his art from Laguerre at Chatsworth and Verrio at Hampton Court; he also designed stage sets and there is something essentially theatrical in his work. In his time he was greeted as the first great English 'history painter'.

Thornhill thought it vital that people who studied his work should 'read' it correctly, but the visitor today is unlikely to be able to read it at all. Thornhill's panorama spreads right through the hall, from the Vestibule to the Upper Hall, and covers walls and ceiling with colour, life, movement and myth. In the late seventeenth and early eighteenth centuries, people liked to mix myth and history, allegory and reality. The theme of such painting was like the theme of a symphony, with many movements and variations.

In the Lower Hall Thornhill illustrates the Triumph of Peace and Liberty—the walls of the Upper Hall are dedicated to glorifying William of Orange and George I. The ceiling shows the world acclaiming the Maritime Rulers. The messages are so complex, and the way the painter illustrates them such a mixture, that all the Painted Hall can do is dazzle and puzzle. There is Persephone running away from Pluto; a goddess representing the River Severn, and somewhere else an actual astronomer in a feathered hat whose name was Tycho Brahe. William of Orange lands at Torbay; the lady who greets him is Britannia and her friends are Reason of State and Patriotism. Thornhill himself is in front of St. Paul's (he painted the scenes of St. Paul's life inside the dome of the cathedral); Mercury is in the sky overhead. The painter stands modestly on the bottom step with the House of Hanover—George I, Queen Caroline and a bunch of princes and princesses on the top step.

In the Vestibule are two delightful lists: the money subscribed by various people painted on the walls. One Colonel (surely ambitious) presented £23,000; Queen Anne gave only £6,000 and somebody a mere £100.

In Queen Mary's Block, facing the King William Block and with a high cupola to match, is the *Chapel*. It was designed by 'Athenian' Stuart and opened in 1789 (a previous chapel, very similar, was burned down). The chapel has been little changed since the eighteenth century and is richly decorated and beautiful. The intricately patterned ceiling of plasterwork is in Adam and Wedgwood colours, the gallery carved with shells and laurel wreaths. Over the altar is a large painting by the American artist, Benjamin West. In true Greenwich style it is a story of the sea . . . St. Paul preserved from shipwreck, surrounded by seamen bringing ashore various things saved from the wreck.

The carved oak and mahogany pulpit is very handsome. Its medallions of scenes from the lives of St. Peter and St. Paul are made from the same curious substance as the lion on Westminster Bridge—Coade stone, the secret of which is lost. The chapel is used during the week by officers taking the College course, but is open to the public on Sundays.

In 1805 the Queen's House became a naval school; there was already a Royal Hospital School in one of the riverside buildings but a second school was needed. The east and west wing blocks, which harmonize pleasantly with Inigo Jones's Palladian masterpiece, were built in 1807 together with the two open colonnades, each of which is 180 feet long. Some historians say the colonnades commemorate Trafalgar, others that they were merely built as a playground for 900 schoolboys in wet weather. The naval officers lived in the Queen's House, and the wing buildings were used for dormitories, gymnasium and schoolrooms. The Navy didn't leave the Queen's House until 1933. The house stands with the busy Woolwich road between it and the riverside buildings; the long cobbled way under the house is the remains of the old Deptford to Woolwich road where the coaches and horses used to thunder when Royalty lived there.

Inigo Jones designed the *Entrance Hall* as a perfect cube. It measures 40 feet by 40 feet, a symmetrical spacious hall with an upstairs gallery from which one looks down on a dizzying black-and-white seventeenth century floor. To the left of the hall is Inigo Jones's *Tulip Staircase*, named after the pattern of the graceful wrought-iron bannisters.

The lovely symmetrical rooms of the Queen's House lead one into another, with choice pieces of furniture and a rich display of paintings. The walls of this house were once hung with Charles I's priceless collection: even now the pictures are remarkable. There are portraits of most of the famous people connected with Greenwich, each captioned with a phrase about their lives and characters. Charles I is described as 'temperate, chaste and serious'. There is a portrait of Inigo Jones, one of Queen Elizabeth in her old age, and one of black-eyed Essex whom she loved and who betrayed her. There is a brass-studded travelling trunk of the 1660s, a Mortlake tapestry of Charles II. There are scores of sea-paintings; of battles, sea-meetings, launchings, ships in storms, ships coming home to harbour. Greenwich's connexion with the sea has always been strong.

One solid relic of charity from the past is the iron-bound old *Chatham Chest*, for a fund begun after the Armada by Drake and Hawkins by which 6d a month was put into the chest from the seamen's wages to be kept for their old age. The huge sums which built up in the Chatham Chest were transferred to boost the finances of the hospital in 1814—the money was also used towards the out-pensions.

The *National Maritime Museum* founded in 1937 is housed in the buildings on either side of the Queen's House; it gives a complete and fascinating record of maritime history from the Tudors to the present day. The museum is now being modernized and some galleries may be closed, but others are newly-opened with the exhibits more spaciously arranged. There are galleries on every sort of maritime subject; eighteenth century dockyards, the Victorian Navy, Arctic Exploration, the history of boats, beginning with the coracle. There are uniforms and figureheads, ships' models and paintings. In the new Neptune Hall is the great paddle tug *Reliant* with its paddles turning.

The uniform Nelson wore at Trafalgar is here, stained and slit but with his stars and decorations. In the battles of the past, heroes dressed to kill. There is a pair of delicately darned blue and white striped stockings of Nelson's, an ivory-handled combined knife and fork and two left-hand gloves, one marked in Lady Hamilton's writing as having belonged to him.

River lovers will enjoy the *Barge House* which has many beautiful old barges. The most elaborate is William Kent's *Floating Coach* made for Frederick, Prince of Wales, George II's son. Kent used the form of a coach body with the wheels removed, and simply arranged it on a wherry. The decorations, carvings and gildings of Frederick's barge are marvellous and funny. Who today, however aristocratic, would have an enormous Garter Star on the prow of his boat? The royalty and nobility of the past were extremely fond of their signs of grandeur and liked them as large as possible. As well as the Garter star, the barge is decorated with a bunch of Prince of Wales feathers and outsized gold crowns. More lovable are the symbols not of Royal blood but of water—mermaids, whiskered dolphins, fishes and shells.

All round the walls of the barge house are last century photographs of days on the river, celebrations on the river. Such crowds and fun in wherries and barges, punts and skiffs. The flags fly and the people cheer; men wear straw hats and luscious girls hide under parasols. Truly, a river of pleasure.

GREENWICH'S ROYAL AND FAMOUS PAST

1427   The Good Duke Humphrey built Bella Court by the river.

1448   The Duke died and Queen Margaret of Anjou took the mansion, beautifying and enlarging it, and calling it Placentia, Palace of Pleasure. She and Henry VI lived there.

1461   Edward IV claimed the crown and Placentia too. He made it larger, and stocked the park with deer.

1485   Henry VII and his Queen lived in Placentia. Greenwich began its naval history . . . Henry VII started the first navy.

1491   Henry VIII born at Placentia.

1509   Henry and Katharine of Aragon married at Placentia. They lived much in the palace. Mary Tudor born there in 1516.

1533   Anne Boleyn, now Queen, travelled by river from Greenwich to London in state for her crowning. The same year, Elizabeth was born.

1552   Young Edward VI kept Christmas at Placentia.

1553   The king died at the palace.

1581   Elizabeth travelled from Placentia to Deptford to knight Francis Drake on his return from travelling round the world.

1584   Elizabeth signed Mary Queen of Scots death warrant at Placentia.

1588   Elizabeth signed the orders for resisting the Armada.

1617 James I began to build a house for his Queen, Anne of Denmark.

1635 Charles I completed it. Henrietta Maria's name carved over the central north window.

1642–52 Much of the old palace sold or misused during the Commonwealth.

1662 Charles II decided to demolish Placentia.

1664 Charles began his King's House. Pepys saw the foundation laid.

1694 William and Mary founded the Royal Hospital charter for 'the relief and support of seamen'.

1696 Wren began to demolish what was left of the old palace. The foundation stone of the new hospital buildings laid by Wren and John Evelyn.

1717 Most of the Hospital and College completed by Wren, Hawksmoor and Vanbrugh.

1778 Further colonnades finished.

1806 Nelson's body lay in state in the Painted Hall.

1865 The Royal Hospital closed. The pensioners left.

1967 H.M. the Queen knighted Sir Francis Chichester after he had sailed round the world in *Gypsy Moth IV*.

BIBLIOGRAPHY INTRODUCTION

Hampton Court. A history. Philip Lindsay.

Letters of King Henry VIII, edited by M. St. Clare Byrne.

Henry VIII by J. J. Scarisbrick.

Lives of the Queens of England, by Agnes Strickland: *Elizabeth of York, Anne Boleyn, Jane Seymour, Elizabeth, Mary Beatrice of Modena, Anne.*

Correspondence of Horace Walpole, edited by W. S. Lewis.

Memoirs of Lord Hervey, edited by Romney Sedgwick.

The First Four Georges. J. H. Plumb.

The Autobiography of Lord Clarendon.

James II, by Peter Earle.

Alexander Pope. Peter Quennell.

Prospect of Richmond. Janet Dunbar.

Queen Anne. Gila Curtis.

Life of Lady Mary Wortley Montagu. Robert Halsband.

The King's War. The King's Peace. C. V. Wedgwood.

Hogarth. Peter Quennell.

Charles II. Arthur Bryant.

The Pre-Raphaelite Tragedy. William Gaunt.

Treasure in the Thames. Ivor Noel Hume.

Chelsea. Thea Holme.

Recollections of a Westminster Antiquary. Laurence Tanner.

London. David Piper (World Cultural Guides Series).

London. The Biography of a City. Christopher Hibbert.

The Environs of London. James Thorne (1876).

Gardens of Hampton Court. Mollie Sands.

The Thames. A. P. Herbert.

A History of Hammersmith. Hammersmith Local History Group.

Royal Greenwich. Olive and Nigel Hampton.

Sweet Themmes, a chronicle in prose and verse, Irwin & Herbert.

Old and New London. E. Walford and W. Thornbury (1895).

History of England. G. M. Trevelyan.

Roman London. Ralph Merrifield.

The Romance of Thames-side Taverns. Glyn H. Morgan.

The Survey of London. John Stow (1598).

Curiosities of London. John Timbs (1864).

Boswell's London Journey.

Diaries of Samuel Pepys.

Diaries of John Evelyn.

Somerset House. L. M. Bates.

A Wanderer in London. E. V. Lucas.

INDEX

This is not a complete index. All places referred to in the text of the book are included, but people are limited only to those who are generally known and referred to in the text more than passingly.

(a) *Index of Places*

Adelphi, The, 167
Albert Bridge, 103, 118
Albert Embankment, 129
Asgill House, 56

Bankside, 200–202, 206
Banqueting House, Whitehall, 164–166
Barnes, 80
Barn Elms, 98
Battersea, 101–104
Battersea Bridge, 109
Battersea Reach, 102
Baynard's Castle, 182, 183
Bear Gardens and Museum, 202
Belfast, H.M.S., 207
Big Ben, 141
Billingsgate Fishmarket, 196, 212
Blackfriars Bridge, 180
Brentford, Ferry Lane, 66, 67
British Museum, 99, 101, 116, 196, 222
Bushey Deer Park, 30, 45

Cadogan Pier, Chelsea, 118
Cardinal's Cap Alley and Cardinal's Wharf, 200
Carlyle's House, Chelsea, 116–118
Charing Cross, 134
Chelsea, 110–123
Chelsea Bridge, 123
Chelsea Embankment, 110
Cheyne Walk, Chelsea, 108–119
Chiswick, 82–90
Chiswick Bridge, 82
Chiswick Eyot, 89
Chiswick House, 82–86
Chiswick Mall, 82, 88, 89, 91
Chiswick, Upper Mall, 90, 91
Chrysanthemum, H.M.S., 174, 197
Churches:
 All Hallows By the Tower, 214, 215
 All Saints, Fulham, 106
 All Saints, Isleworth, 62
 Chantry Chapel, Westminster Abbey, 148
 Chelsea Old Church, 113–115

Harvard Chapel, Southwark Cathedral, 205
Henry VII Chapel, Westminster Abbey, 38, 151
St. Andrew by the Wardwrobe, 183
St. Anne Church, Kew Green, 70
St. Benet, 182
St. Dunstan in the East, 213
St. Magnus the Martyr, 195, 197
St. Margaret, Westminster, 157, 159
St. Mary, Battersea, 101
St. Mary at Hill, Billingsgate, 213
St. Mary Magdalene, Mortlake, 81
St. Mary, Mortlake, 81
St. Mary, Rotherhithe, 208
St. Mary, Teddington, 31
St. Mary the Virgin, Putney, 100
St. Mary the Virgin, Twickenham, 41, 42
St. Mary Somerset, 182
St. Nicholas, Chiswick, 88, 89
St. Nicholas Cole Abbey, 183
St. Olave, Hart Street, 214
St. Paul's Cathedral, 16, 183–188, 190
St. Peter, Petersham, 53
St. Peter ad Vincula Chapel, Tower of London, 219
Savoy Chapel, 169
Southwark Cathedral, 203–206
Temple Church, 175
Westminster Abbey, 146–157
Clattern Bridge, Kingston, 50
Cleopatra's Needle, 168
College of Arms, 183
County Hall, 134
Cremorne Gardens, Chelsea, 103, 108, 109
Crosby Hall, Cheyne Walk, 112
Custom House, Billingsgate, 212
Cutty Sark, Greenwich, 234

Deptford, 232, 234, 237–239, 246
Discovery, H.M.S., 173, 197
Docks:
 East India, London, Surrey Commercial, and Tilbury, 227
 Execution, and West India, 230
 India and Millwall, 232

Docks—*cont.*
    Puddle, 182
    St. Katherine's, 226–228
    Wapping, 230, 231
Duke's Meadows, 82

Eel Pie Island, 40

Fishmongers' Hall, 191–193
Fish Street Hill, 197
Fleet, river, 173
Fulham, 99, 106–108
    Alms Houses and Bishop's Park, 107
    Palace, 107, 108
Fulham Reach, 99

Gipsy Moth IV, Greenwich, 234, 235, 247
Globe Playhouse, Bankside, 201, 202
Grand Union Canal, 67, 69
Greenwich, 23, 234–247
    Chapel, 243
    Footway Tunnel, 235
    Hospital, 242
    Painted Hall, 241, 242
    Queen's House, 239, 244, 245
    Royal Park and Observatory, 240
Guy's Hospital, 133

Ham Ferry, 44
Ham House, 44, 50–53
Ham Walks, 53
Hammersmith Bridge, 94
Hammersmith Terrace, 88, 90–93
    Brandenburgh House, 94
    Furnivall Gardens, 93
    Lower Mall, 93–95
    Pier, 93
    Westcott Lodge, 93
Hampton Court Barge Walk and Bridge, 29
Hampton Court Palace, 14–33, 44, 130
Hampton Wick, 30
Harrod's Depository, 98
Hayward Gallery, South Bank, 135
Hogarth's House, Chiswick, 87
Hogsmill River, Kingston, 50
Houses of Parliament, 138, 140–146
Hungerford Bridge, 134
Hurlingham House, 108

Isle of Dogs, Greenwich, 235
Isleworth, 62–65, 67

Jewel Tower, Westminster, 138

Kelmscott House and Press, 91, 92
Kew Bridge, 68
Kew, and Kew Green, 69, 70
Kew Gardens, 33, 64, 69 71–77
Kew Palace, 60, 70, 72, 75–77
King's Reach (Victoria Embankment), 133, 134, 163
Kingston, 29, 31–33, 50

Lambeth Bridge, 125, 126, 129
Lambeth Palace, 130
Limehouse Reach, 231
Lindsey House, Chelsea, 111
London Bridge, 15, 33, 193–196

Marble Hill, 39, 45–47
Mermaid Theatre, 182
Metropolitan Police Boatyard, 229
Millwall, 232
Monument, The, 195, 197
Mortlake Brewery, 82

National Film Theatre, 135
National Gallery, 119, 122
National Maritime Museum, Greenwich, 245
National Portrait Gallery, 46
National Theatre, 135
New Scotland Yard, 163
Nine Elms Reach, 124
Nonsuch House, 194, 195
Nonsuch Palace, 16

Old London Bridge, 162
Old St. Paul's, 38, 183–186, 189, 193, 201
Orleans House, 44, 45, 53

Parliament Square, 146
Paul's Cross, 183–185, 190
Petersham, 33, 54
    River Lane, 53
Physic Gardens, Chelsea, 119, 120
President, H.M.S. (R.N.V.R.), 174
Putney, and Putney Bridge, 99, 100
Public Houses, Hotels, Restaurants:
    Anchor Inn, Bankside, 202
    Angel Inn, Rotherhithe, 208
    Anglers' Inn, Teddington, 32
    Angus Steak House, Kingston, 50
    Barmy Arms, Twickenham, 40
    Beefeater by the Tower, 227
    Blue Anchor, Hammersmith, 93
    Bull's Head, Strand on the Green, 69
    Bunch of Grapes, Limehouse, 231
    City Barge, Strand on the Green, 69

Dove Inn, Hammersmith, 92
Duke's Head, Putney, 99
The George, Southwark, 206
King's Arms, Chelsea, 110
King's Head and Eight Bells, Chelsea, 116
London Apprentice, Isleworth, 62
Mayflower Inn, Rotherhithe, 208
The Mitre, Hampton Court, 29
Old Caledonia (ship), Waterloo Bridge, 169
Old Father Thames, Albert Embankment, 129
Old Swan, Battersea, 101
Old Wine Shades, London Bridge, 191
Prospect of Whitby, Wapping, 230
Rutland, Hammersmith, 93
St. Katharine by the Tower, 228
'Samuel Pepys', Brooks Wharf, 190
Ship Inn, Mortlake, 82
Star and Garter, Putney, 99
Steam Packet, Strand on the Green, 68
The Swan, Hampton Wick, 30
Town of Ramsgate, Wapping, 229
Trafalgar Tavern, Greenwich, 235
White Cross Inn, Richmond, 56
White Hart, Barnes, 80
White Swan, Richmond, 57
White Swan, Twickenham, 44
The Yacht, Greenwich, 235, 236

Queen Mary II's Steps, 163

Ranelagh Gardens, 122, 123
Raven's Ait, 29
Richmond, 33, 36, 56–59
Richmond Bridge, 55, 56, 59
Richmond Green, 57–59
    Maids of Honour Row, 59
    Old Palace Lane, 57
    Old Palace Yard and Trumpeters' House, 59
Richmond Palace, 56–58
Rotherhithe, 207–209, 229
    Cherry Garden Pier, 207
    Rotherhithe Tunnel, 209, 231
Royal Festival Hall, S. Bank, 134
Royal Hospital, Chelsea, 120, 121
Royal Hospital Museum, 121
Royal Hospital Old Burying Ground, 122

St. Thomas's Hospital, 132, 133, 203
    Old Operating Theatre, 133
Shell Centre, 134

Sion Row, Twickenham, 43
Somerset House, 167, 171–173
South Bank Gardens, 134
South Bank Lion, County Hall, 133
Southwark Bridge, 190
Strand Lane, Roman Bath, 173
Strand on the Green, 68–70
Strawberry Hill, Twickenham, 36–39, 65, 74
Submariners' Memorial, 174
Sudbrook House, Petersham, 44, 55
Swan Walk, Chelsea, 120
Syon House and Park, 62–67
Syon Reach, 62

Tate Gallery, 90, 110, 111, 124, 125
Teddington, 31–33
Teddington Lock, 32
Temple, The, 174–179
Temple Stairs, 180
Thames Ditton, 26, 29
Thames T.V. Studios, 33
Thames Tunnel, Wapping, 229
Tower Bridge, 207, 208, 226
Tower of London, 140, 216–224
Tower Pier, 216
Tower Wharf, 222
Trinity House, 225
Trinity Hospital Almshouses, 236
Turner's Reach, Chelsea, 110
Twickenham, 36–48
Twickenham Bridge, 62

Vauxhall Bridge, 124, 128
Vauxhall Gardens, 103, 128
Victoria Embankment Gardens, 163, 166
Victoria Tower Garden, Westminster, 138
Victoria Tower, 141

Walpole's House, Chiswick Mall, 89
Wandle, river, 101
Wandsworth Bridge and Park, 101
Wapping, 229–231
    King Edward's Memorial Park, 230
    Oliver's Wharf, 229
Waterloo Bridge, 169, 170
Waterloo Pier, 170
Wellington, H.M.S., 174
Woolwich, 237, 239
Westminster Bridge, 133, 162
Westminster, Old Palace of, 139, 140
    St. Stephen's Crypt, 146
    Westminster Hall, 144–146
Westminster Pier, 14, 163

Whitehall Palace, 129, 164–166, 177
Winchester Palace, 200, 203
Wolsey's Cottage, Hampton Wick, 30
World Trade Centre, 225, 227

York House, Twickenham, 42–44
York House Watergate, 166, 167

Zoffany House, Strand on the Green, 68

(b) *Index of People and Subjects*

à Beckett, Thomas, 148, 193, 195, 213
Adam, Robert, 38, 64, 65, 167
Adams, J. Quincey, 216
Addison, Joseph, 20, 157
Aiton, William, 71, 72
Alfred, King, 50, 216
Andrewes, Lancelot (Bishop of Winchester), 204
Anne Boleyn, 15, 24, 27, 131, 164, 219, 220, 223, 238, 246
Anne of Denmark (James I's Queen), 27, 171, 239, 247
Anne, Queen of England, 17, 19, 20, 25, 28, 43, 44, 50, 58, 70, 186, 243
Arabia, Lawrence of, 189
Argyll, 2nd Duke of, 55
Arundell, Isabel, 81
Asgill, Sir Charles, 56, 57
Augusta, Princess (wife of Frederick, Prince of Wales), 70, 71, 73

Bacon, Francis, 125
Bagot, Mary, 21
Barrie, James, 167
Barry, Charles, 140, 141, 144, 146, 162
Barry, Sir Wolfe, 226
Baynard, Ralph, 182
Bazalgette, Sir Joseph, 94, 100, 109, 129, 163, 166, 179
Bentley, Richard, 37
Berry, Agnes and Mary, 39, 54
Black Prince, 149, 167, 220
Blake, Admiral Robert, 239
Blake, William, 102, 125, 154
Blomfield, Sir Reginald, 129, 163
Boadicea, statue of, 162, 163, 215
Boat Race—Oxford and Cambridge Universities, 82, 99
Bohemia, Queen Anne of (consort of Richard II), 57
Bohemia, Elizabeth of (Winter Queen), 65
Boswell, James, 76, 128, 162, 177, 241
Bradford, Lord, 32
Brandenburgh-Anspach, Margravine of, 93
Bridgeman, Sir Orlando, 32
Brown, Capability, 67, 72

Brown, Ford Madox, 118
Brunel, Marc and Isambard, 111, 229, 232
Burlington, Earl of, 82–88, 116
Burnet, Bishop, 51
Burney, Dr. Charles, 122
Burney, Fanny, 71, 75, 122
Burns, Robert, 166
Burton, Sir Richard, 81
Buxton, Fowell, 138
Byron, Lord, 36, 55, 225

Cade, Jack, 194
Cadogan, Dr. William, 108
Canaletto, 123
Canning, George, 85
Canute, King, 139
Carey, Sir Robert, 58
Carlyle, Thomas and Jane, 112, 116–118
Caroline of Anspach (Queen of George II), 28, 44–46, 48, 71, 243
Caroline (Queen of George IV), 94
Carroll, Lewis, 119
Casement, Roger, 224
Catherine of Braganza, 28, 91
Caxton, 132, 158
Chambers, Sir William, 172
Charles I, 20, 21, 25, 27, 30, 65, 66, 107, 111, 132, 145, 146, 152, 165, 167, 201, 218, 239, 244–247
Charles II, 16, 22, 28, 29, 32, 42, 43, 51, 54, 62, 66, 89, 98, 120, 145, 157, 166, 186, 196, 217 218, 220, 235, 240, 245, 247
Charles of Orleans, 222
Charles V of Spain, 238
Charlotte (Queen of George III), 38, 52, 68, 71, 75–77, 172
Chaucer Geoffrey, 154, 205, 206
Cheyne, Lady Jane, 114, 116
Chicheley, Archbishop of Canterbury, 130
Chichester, Sir Francis, 177, 234, 247
Coade, Elinor, 133
Churchill, Sarah, 20
Churchill, Sir Winston, 144, 146, 159, 216
Chute, John, 37
Clark, Tierney, 94

252

Cleves, Anne of, 27, 223
Cleveland, Duchess, of, 89
Clive, Kitty, 36, 39, 41
Coke, Lady Mary, 54
Collingwood, Admiral, 188
Colville, Sara, 114
Compton, Bishop, 108
Constable, John, 62, 125
Cook, Captain, 68
Cooke, Henry, 120
Cowper, William, 212
Cranmer, Thomas, 131, 132
Cromwell, Mary and Frances, 88
Cromwell, Oliver, 27, 51, 68, 69, 118, 141, 150, 154, 165, 215
Cromwell, Thomas, 223
Crosby, John, 112, 113
Cross, John, 119

Darwin, Charles, 72, 126
Davies, Elidir, 182
De Colechurch, Peter, 193
Defoe, Daniel, 44, 196, 240
De Loutherbourg, Philip, 88, 90
De Montfort, Simon, 168
De Morgan, William, 107
Denbigh, Isabella Countess of, 31
De Paris, Comte, 43, 45
Dereham, Francis, 22
Devereux, Robert, Earl of Essex, 52, 66, 145, 157, 219, 223, 245
Devonshire, Georgiana Duchess of, 85
Dickens, Charles, 54, 56, 117, 129, 134, 173, 178, 190, 191, 207, 208, 214, 231, 235, 236
Disraeli, Benjamin, 59, 117, 146
Doggett Coat and Badge Race, 192
Donne, John, 188, 189
Drake, Sir Francis, 64, 177, 232, 238, 245, 246
Drayton, Michael, 154
Dryden, John, 89, 114
Dudley brothers (Ambrose, Guildford, John, Robert), 219
Dudley, Guildford, 223
Dudley, Robert, Earl of Leicester, 25, 27, 66, 221
Dysart, Charlotte and Elizabeth, Countesses of, 51, 52

Edward, Prince, 22, 26
Edward the Confessor, 38, 139, 147, 148, 151, 155
Edward I, 139, 148, 149
Edward II, 138
Edward III, 57, 138, 149, 156
Edward IV, 222, 237, 246

Edward VI, 21, 22, 23, 25, 26, 63, 139, 246
Edward VII, 25, 85, 86, 146
Eleanor of Castile, 149
Eliot, George, 119, 172
Elizabeth I, 15, 16, 21, 25, 27, 28, 52, 58, 64, 66, 69, 98, 131, 152, 157, 164, 171, 176, 183, 185, 202, 204, 221, 223, 232, 238, 245, 246
Elizabeth of York (Queen of Henry VII), 152, 223, 237
Elizabeth II, 189, 192, 234, 247
Emmett, William, 121
Epstein, 146, 154
Erkenwald, Bishop, 183, 186
Evelyn, John, 50, 66, 115, 120, 178, 179, 186, 202, 240, 241, 247

Fairbairn, Steve, 98
Fawkes, Guy, 145, 224
Fisher, Bishop, 194, 215, 223
Fitzherbert, Mrs., 48
Flamard, Ralph, Bishop of Durham, 222
Fletcher, John, 204
Forrest, G. Topham, 129
Fox, Charles James, 85
Frederick, Prince of Wales, 70, 71, 245
Frost Fairs, 178, 179, 195, 202

Gainsborough, Thomas, 70, 125
Garrick, David, 32, 41, 88
Gaskell, Mrs., 112
Gaunt, John of, 168, 169, 184–186
Gay, John, 39, 47, 53, 85, 207
Gentileschi, 239
George I, 24, 28, 59, 151, 243
George II, 14, 28, 44–47, 52, 58, 59, 71, 76, 212
George III, 26, 28, 38, 39, 52, 54, 59, 60, 64, 68, 70–76, 172
George IV, 70, 94, 144, 145, 145, 163
George V, 85, 86, 146, 151, 163
George VI, 146
George of Denmark, 19, 20
George, Sir Ernest, 191
Gibbons, Grinling, 20, 39, 121, 186, 187, 209, 215
Gibbs, James, 44, 55
Gloucester, Duke of, 20
Goldsmith, Oliver, 102, 177, 179
Gower, John, 205, 206
Gray, Thomas, 39
Great Fire of London, 186, 188, 191, 197, 201, 203, 212, 215
Greaves, Walter, 111

Grey, Lady Jane, 63, 83, 218–220, 223
Gunning (sisters), 32
Gwynn, Nell, 120

Hales, Dr. Stephen, 31, 32
Hall, Sir Benjamin, 141
Hall, Edward, 194
Handel, 28, 70, 128, 154, 163
Harold, King of England, 147
Hastings, Warren, 145
Hawksmoor, Nicholas, 241, 247
Hazlitt, William, 21, 92
Head of the River Race, 98
Henley, W. E. (poet), 80
Henrietta Maria (Queen of Charles I),
    20, 27, 43, 65, 152, 171, 239, 240,
    247
Henry I, 175, 222
Henry III, 147, 148, 151, 155, 183,
    221
Henry IV, 151, 206
Henry V, 58, 148, 150, 156, 194, 220
Henry VI, 222, 246
Henry VII, 58, 59, 140, 151–156, 158,
    169, 184, 223, 237, 246
Henry VIII, 14, 15, 18, 21–26, 30, 58,
    59, 62, 63, 113, 116, 131, 139,
    152, 155, 158, 164, 183, 184, 188,
    194, 218, 219, 223, 232, 237, 246
Hepworth, Barbara, 125
Herbert, Sir Alan, 90, 92, 124
Herbert, Lord, 46
Hervey, Lord John, 28, 45, 46, 48, 76,
    83
Hess, Rudolph, 224
Hillyard, Nicholas, 38, 125
Hogarth, Jane, 84, 87, 88
Hogarth, William, 84, 86–88, 125,
    128, 131, 195
Holst, Gustav, 80
Honourable Artillery Company, 222
Holbein, Hans, 18, 21, 38, 113, 131,
    195
Hood, Thomas, 167
Hook, Theodore, 106, 133
Horton, Lady, 55
Howard, Catherine, 22, 27, 63, 219,
    223
Howard, Charles, 46
Howe, Baroness 47
Hudson, Jeffrey, 20
Hudson's Bay Company, 54
Humphrey, Duke, 236, 240, 246
Hunt, Leigh, 87, 117
Hyde, Anne, Duchess of York, 21, 42,
    43

Hyde, Edward Lord Clarendon, 42,
    43, 51, 58

I.C.I. House, 126
Ionides, Mrs. Nellie, 44, 45

James I, 24, 27, 39, 58, 64, 111, 150,
    152, 153, 158, 164, 165, 177, 185,
    221, 224, 238, 247
James II, 16, 17, 42, 43, 52, 65, 108,
    129, 151, 166, 216
Jeffreys, Judge, 224, 230
John, King of England, 176
Jones, Captain Christopher, 208
Jones, Sir Horace, 226
Jones, Inigo, 27, 82, 84, 116, 164, 171,
    177, 182, 185, 239, 244, 245
Jones, Ivor Robert, 146
Johnson, Dr. Samuel, 41, 92, 93, 128,
    158, 177, 188, 202, 241, 242
Johnstone, James, 44
Juxon, Bishop, 107

Katharine (Queen of Henry V), 27,
    150, 156
Katharine of Aragon, 38, 58, 112, 113,
    158, 184, 200, 218, 237, 238, 246
Kent, William, 82, 84–88, 154, 245
Kidd, Captain, 230
Kingsley, Henry, 114
Kipling, Rudyard, 31
Kirby, Joshua, 70
Kit-Kat Club, 98
Kneller, Sir Godfrey, 17, 41, 47, 98,
    125
Knights Templar, Order of, 175, 176
Knott, Ralph, 134

Lafarge, John, 205
Lamb, Charles, 176, 178
Lancaster, Osbert, 103
Lasdun, Denys, 135
Lauderdale, Duke, of, 51, 52, 54, 55
Legh, Lady Margaret, 106
Lely, Sir Peter, 18, 21, 22, 51, 52, 65,
    125
Lennox and Richmond, Duke of, 152
Le Nôtre, 240
Lepell, Molly, 47, 48
Little Princes, Edward V and Duke
    of York, 153, 222, 223
Lockyer, Lionel, 205
London Corinthian Sailing Club,
    Hammersmith, 91
Lorraine, Claude, 86
Louis XIV of France, 32, 120

Luther, Martin, 185
Lutyens, Edward, 29

Macaulay, Thomas, 52, 220, 241
Maclise, Daniel, 143
Magna Carta, 142, 176
Mann, Sir Horace, 37
Mantegna, Andrea, 165
Margaret of Anjou (Queen of Henry VI), 246
Marlborough, Duke of, 20, 55, 120
Martin, Sir Leslie, 135
Mary Tudor, 21, 27, 63, 64, 131, 151, 153, 185, 203, 218, 223, 238, 246
Mary, Queen of Scots, 27, 145, 153
Mary II, Queen, 17–19, 28, 58, 240, 241, 247
Mary of Modena (Queen of James II), 129
Mary (Queen of George V), 70, 75, 85, 146
Massinger, Philip, 204
Matilda (Queen of King Stephen), 226
Matthew, Sir Robert, 135
Metropolitan Police, Thames Division, 170
Metternich, Prince Clement, 59
Michelangelo, 64
Miles, Sir Bernard, 182
Milton, John 27, 154, 159
Moore, George, 110
Moore, Henry, 124, 125, 138
Moravian Brothers, 111
Mordaunt of Avalon, Lord, 106
More, Sir Thomas, 82, 111, 113, 115, 131, 145, 194, 197, 215, 223
Morgan, William, 121
Mornington, Lady, 21
Morris, William, 90–92, 119, 153
Morton, Cardinal, 130
Mozart, 123

Napoleon III, 31
Napoleon, 54, 191
Nelson, Lord, 157, 173, 188, 242, 243, 245, 247
Nightingale, Florence, 133, 189
Nithsdale, Lord, 220, 224
Norfolk, Dukes of, 25, 145, 219
Northumberland, Earls and Dukes of, 63–67

Orleans, Duke of (Louis Philippe), 45

Page, Thomas, 162
Pankhurst, Mrs., 138
Parker, Archbishop, 132

Parr, Catherine, 21, 27, 116
Paxton, Sir Joseph, 67
Pembroke, Earls of, 176, 225
Penn, William, 54, 215
Pepys, Samuel, 22, 43, 58, 89, 93, 98, 150, 154, 157, 169, 171, 186, 201, 202, 214, 215, 247
Peter the Great, Czar of Russia, 232, 241
Philip, H.R.H. Prince, 189, 192, 193
Philip of Spain, 27, 218
Picasso, Pablo, 125
Piper, John, 103, 125, 159
Pitt, Mrs., 18
Plague, The, 214, 240
Pole, Cardinal, 131
Pope, Alexander, 19–21, 31, 37, 39, 41, 45–48, 53, 71, 82, 83, 85, 92, 98, 102, 158, 196
Port of London Authority, 225
Pugin, Augustus, 141

Radnor, Earl of, 48
Raleigh, Sir Walter, 158, 177, 220, 224, 238
Raphael, 21, 38, 165, 239
Regent, Prince, 69, 94, 170
Reid Dick, Sir W., 163
Rennie, John, 190, 195
Renoir, 124
Reynolds, Sir Joshua, 52, 70, 125, 128, 131, 188
Richard I, 141, 180, 183
Richard II, 57, 58, 144, 147, 149, 191, 194, 206, 217, 218
Richard III, 112, 183
Richmond, Frances Duchess of, 157
Robsart, Sir Terry, 37
Rodin, 125, 138
Romney, George, 131, 192
Ronald, Francis, 91
Roper, Margaret, 113, 114, 194
Rossetti, Dante Gabriel, 109, 118, 119
Roubiliac, 101, 128, 155
Rowlandson, 62
Rubens, 165, 239
Ruddle, John, 106
Rufus, William, 139, 144, 146, 183
Rupert, Prince, 54, 93
Rysbrack, 154

St. Albans, Diana de Vere Duchess of, 18
St. John, Henry, Viscount Bolingbroke, 101–103
Scott, Sir Giles Gilbert, 170

Scott, Captain, 173, 174
Scott, Sir Walter, 39, 86
Scrope, Mary, 18, 58
Seymour, Jane, 15, 21–24, 27, 113
Shakespeare, Edmund, 204
Shakespeare, William, 24, 154, 157, 164, 173, 177, 183, 201, 204, 206
Sickert, Walter, 110
Siddall, Elisabeth, 118, 119
Sidney, Sir Philip, 186
Sloane, Sir Hans, 82, 115, 116, 119, 120
Smuts, General, 146
Somerset, Protector, 63, 64, 66, 171
Spencer, Herbert, 172
Steele, Sir Richard, 20, 55
Stuart, 'Athenian', 243
Suffolk, Countess of (Henrietta Howard), 39, 45–48
Swan Uppers, 40, 180
Swift, Jonathan, 20, 46, 47, 53, 59, 71, 83

Tata, Sir Ratan J., 43
Taylor, John, 201
Tennyson, Alfred Lord, 117, 154
Thackeray, William Makepeace, 45, 54, 128
Thornbury, Walter, 183
Thornhill, Sir James, 23, 87, 189, 242, 243
Thynne, Thomas, 155
Tijou, Jean, 26, 186, 187
Timbs, John, 129, 168, 194
Tollemaches, 51
Tryon, William, 41
Turner, J. M. W., 62, 102, 109, 110, 125, 189
Tyler, Watt, 169, 191, 193

Vanburgh, Sir John, 16, 241, 247
Vancouver, Captain George, 54
Van Dyck, 131, 239
Verrio, Antonio, 16–19, 120, 242
Victoria, Queen of England, 29, 73, 86, 108, 121, 133, 220

Villiers, Barbara, 21, 89
Villiers, George, Duke of Buckingham, 152, 167

Wake, Archbishop of Canterbury, 130
Walker, Sir Emery, 90, 91
Wallace, Sir William, 194
Walpole, Horace, 16, 36–41, 46, 47, 52–54, 56, 59, 65, 74, 84, 90, 123, 128, 140
Walpole, Sir Robert, 28, 37
Walsingham, Sir Francis, 98
Walton, Izaak, 100
Walworth, Sir William, 191
Warburton, Jenny, 55
Warwick, John Dudley, Earl of, 63
Washington, George, 57
Wellington, Duke of, 21, 86, 103, 121, 129, 140, 187
Whistler, James, 101, 109–112, 115
Wilberforce, William, 102, 138
Wilkinson, Tate, 41
William the Conqueror, 139, 147, 216, 217
William III, 16–20, 26, 28, 52, 166, 216, 240, 241, 243, 247
Wilson, Richard, 62
Woffington, Margaret (Peg), 32
Wolsey, Cardinal, 14, 23–26, 30, 38, 139, 164, 184, 185, 188
Wordsworth, William, 56, 162
Wortley Montagu, Lady Mary, 41, 47, 48
Wren, Sir Christopher, 16, 17, 20, 21, 28, 30, 120, 140, 163, 182, 184, 186–190, 196, 197, 200, 212, 213, 241, 247
Wycliffe, John, 130, 184
Wynter, Sir Edward, 102

Yarmouth, Lady, 28
York, James Duke of, 42, 43
Yvele, Henry, 147, 197

Zinzendorff, Count, 111
Zoffany, John, 62, 68–70